BONEFISH FLY PATTERNS

BONEFISH ·F·L·Y· PATTERNS

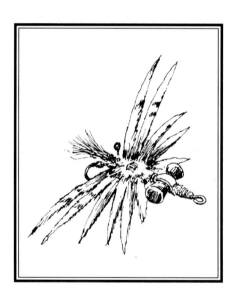

Tying, Selecting, and Fishing the Best Bonefish Flies

DICK BROWN

Illustrations by Chris Armstrong

All Photographs by Carol Wright

LYONS & BURFORD, PUBLISHERS

For those who taught me:

Jack Gartside, Dick Talleur, Bill Wilbur,

Ron Alcott, and Poul Jorgensen

Copyright © 1996 by Dick Brown
Illustrations © 1996 by Chris Armstrong
All photographs © 1996 by Carol Wright

Printed in Hong Kong

10 9 8 7 6 5 4 3 2 1

Design by Howard P. Johnson

Composition by Ling Lu, CompuDesign

Library of Congress Cataloging-in-Publication Data
Brown, Dick, 1942-
    Bonefish fly patterns : tying, selecting, and fishing the best
bonefish flies / Dick Brown.
        p.   cm.
    Includes bibliographical references and index.
    ISBN 1-55821-392-9 (cloth)
    1. Bonefishing. 2. Flies, Artificial. 3. Fly tying. 4. Fly
fishing. I. Title.
SH691.B6B75 1995
688.7'912—dc20   95-32805
                                            CIP

C O N T E N T S

ACKNOWLEDGMENTS

◆ ◆ ◆

Books about fly patterns don't happen without a lot of help from a lot of people. This one received more than its share from all quarters.

Among those who aided me in tracking down tiers near and far, I want to thank Dick Stewart, Chip Bates, Nick Wilder, Dick Talleur, John Randolph, Jim Butler, Art Scheck, Mike Michalak, Randall Kaufmann, Lefty Kreh, Bill Hunter, Ed Opler, Robert McCurdy, Bill Catherwood, and Tim Borski.

Many others gave generously of their time and energy to help me ferret out the multitude of materials, new and old, that serve as the building blocks of today's bonefish patterns. Among these, I especially want to offer my gratitude to Karl Schmuecker at Wapsi, Al Hafner at Kreinik, John Bailey at Dan Bailey's, Ken Menard at Umpqua, Bill Black at Spirit River, Doug Brewer, Scott Sanchez, Chuck Furimsky, Roman Moser, and the folks at Hedron and Hobbs. In addition, I thank Steve Kintzley at Raymond C. Rumpf & Sons, Rick Hagen at Oregon Upstream, Alan Bramley at Partridge, Paul Rowe at Bestway, Steve Lauer at Sponj-Lur, and the folks at Universal. One very special mention goes to Donna Towne at Hunter's Angling Supplies for her vigilant efforts and enduring patience chasing down odd items and helping me identify them. Another goes to Chris Ryan of Orvis, who rounded up not only materials and flies, but also (for their use in displaying the flies in the photo shoot) the largest assemblage of forceps ever brought together outside an operating room.

The photography, too, depended on lots of help from many friends. Bob O'Shaughnessy's advice and equipment were indispensable. Others worked long and hard on the processing: Diane VanDusen at Harvard Camera, Tracey Mosseau at Just Black-and-White, and the folks at Pro Black and White, Colortek, and Boris in Boston. Light Sources and E. P. Levine helped with film, backgrounds, and camera equipment. Most of all, I thank my wife, Carol Wright, who produced virtually the entire photographic portion of this book—planned it, staged it, and shot it—and then stayed on top of all the processing. I do not know how anyone could ever author such a volume while doing both the writing and the photography at the same time. And I do know with certainty—and much gratitude—I could not have completed this one without her.

There is also no way I could have done this book without Nick Lyons. Nick is that rare and unusual breed of person who comes along—if you are extraordinarily lucky—once or twice in a lifetime. His support, encouragement, and ability to open many doors made the book possible—something that he has done hundreds of times before for hundreds of other books, but that makes it no less a miracle.

In the end, I want to offer my deepest gratitude and respect to the tiers of the flies that appear in this volume. Their creations make this book what it is. It is they who gave of the fruits of their inquisitive minds and their ingenuity. It is they who are the true pioneers of this great fly-tying adventure upon which we saltwater fly-fishing anglers are all embarked.

INTRODUCTION

◆ ◆ ◆

This is a book about bonefish flies. It describes 150 of the best bonefish patterns being tied and fished in the world today.

Some of these patterns come from well-known saltwater anglers and flats guides—people you've probably read about in fishing journals or seen on cable television's angling shows, such as Lefty Kreh, Dave Whitlock, Nick Curcione, Bob Popovics, Lou Tabory, Randall Kaufmann, Steve Huff, Harry Spear, and Rick Ruoff.

Other patterns come from transplanted freshwater anglers—expert fly fishermen such as Al Caucci, John Goddard, Craig Mathews, Carl Richards, Barry and Cathy Beck, and Bill Tapply. They lead a growing cadre of highly skilled anglers who bring trout, bass, and salmon stalking strategies to the pursuit of bonefish. By stimulating the exploration of bonefish food species, these pioneers have fundamentally affected our thinking about the fly patterns that entice this shy and challenging gamefish.

Other patterns in the book come from bonefishermen whose names you won't recognize at all. These are serious, solitary angling men and women who shun the limelight and stalk the flats alone. They fish hard, they fish often, and they usually catch more fish than they

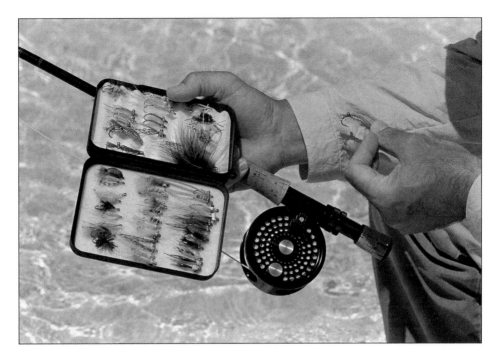

Bonefish fly design has become a hot bed of tying innovation as more and more anglers encounter the sport's rigorous demands on pattern functionality and the rich diversity of prey species.

say they do. They also create some of the sport's most inventive and effective flats flies—many of which have never been seen by anyone before.

Among these silent stalwarts of the salt you'll find: permit and bonefish fanatic Will Myers from Austin, who has created a crab pattern that lets you change its eyes (and therefore its weight) on-site; Ellen Reed, who stalks the flats of the Florida Keys daily, and whose innovative flies, with their large but quiet-landing profiles, were recommended to me by tying genius Tim Borski; Tim Merrihew, who haunts Christmas Island taking hundreds upon hundreds of fish, most of them on a single, uniquely colored pattern—the Nasty Gilbert; Andros regular Jim McVay, whose brassy Gotcha, tied from a piece of carpet he snipped from the back of a Bahamas taxicab, has become one of this decade's best producers; and Winston Moore, whose fishing log registers more than 6,000 bonefish taken and released on the world's flats over the years, most of them on the flies he submitted for this book.

A few of the book's contributors stand out not only because of their flats and fly-tying expertise, but also because of their accomplishments in other areas of life. Novelist Tom McGuane, one of America's finest writers and the author of bonefishing's first novel, *Ninety-two in the Shade,* sent his intriguing and very effective emerald green Sea Flea. World-class mountain climber, competitive surfer, and Patagonia clothing company president, Yvon Chouinard passed along the four flies that always produce for him, whether he's fishing Andros, Belize, or Christmas Island. Jim Orthwein, businessman and former owner of the Patriots football team, sent two of his workhorse flies, along with his newest, Jim's Bonefish Puff, which was responsible for his latest bonefishing world record. Jim holds four of the International Game Fish Association's six fly-rod world records for bonefish.

The flies in this book are authentic. The samples shown in the photos and in the recipes in Chapter 2 came from the flies' originators.

AN ANGLER'S AND TIER'S FLY-PATTERN HANDBOOK

If you tie your own flies, this book will show you how to construct patterns the way each fly's originator does. Color photos display samples that were tied by their originators. Fly recipes are authentic as well. They list the materials used by each pattern's creator, in the order he or she applies them; they also include the originator's tying tips. A tier of average skill should find enough information to pick the correct material and tie it onto the hook in the right sequence for each pattern in the book.

This book, however, is not just for fly tiers. Even if you buy all your flies, this book can help you. Armed with authentic specifications, you can order any pattern you want from custom tiers, specifying the correct proportions, materials, and construction methods to get the real goods.

As a practical matter, the book contains a list of sources from which you can buy finished flies—either off-the-shelf from retailers or tied-to-order from custom tiers. For those of you who *do* tie your own, this section tells you where to find tying materials.

ALSO AN ANGLER'S FISHING GUIDE

This book describes far more, however, than just *tying* bonefish flies. It also advises you how to *fish* them. A chapter on fly selection gives criteria for choosing patterns for different places and conditions, and the individual fly profiles tell you which flies fish best in different depth, wind, light, and bottom conditions. They also reveal which flies have worked well at specific destinations.

In addition, the fly profiles contain advice on what prey the flies suggest and on how the flies should be presented. They specify stripping techniques and, where appropriate, the depths and locales the flies were designed to fish.

In the end, this is a practical book of fishing flies. It should sit next to your vise or near your tackle bag. It doesn't belong in a bookcase.

—Dick Brown, 1996
 Harvard, Massachusetts

BONEFISH FLY PATTERNS

FLY CHARACTERISTICS

• • •

What Makes a Good Bonefish Fly Good ?

Just as flies for other species attract quarry by suggesting food, so bonefish flies portray the creatures eaten by *Albula vulpes.* Fly patterns for this elusive species, however, must accomplish a few other critical tasks besides just looking like dinner.

Bonefish flies must enter the water noiselessly and sink quickly and cleanly to the fish's level. They should attract the fish's attention without frightening it, and, when you strip them, they must move enticingly, without snagging on the bottom. They should also quiver—when stopped—to suggest the tense, trembling posture of startled prey. Furthermore, from a purely pragmatic point of view, they should never rust, crush, or fall apart. And, of course, they must also be easy to tie.

All that seems like a lot to ask of a fly. Yet patterns such as Charlies, MOEs, Merkins, Clousers, and Gotchas have been delivering the goods on the flats every season for decades. In capable hands, these workhorse patterns will usually take fish at any destination.

Sometimes, it seems to me that these five (plus a few other old standbys) work so well that there's no need for any new bonefish patterns at all. Indeed, it would not upset me too much to be forced to head for any bonefish flat in the world with only these five flies—but only if I had to.

If, ultimately, the test of a good bonefish fly is success, these two win hands down. Jim's Golden Eye (bottom) has taken three world records and Jim's Bonefish Puff (top) took a fourth . . . all in the able hands of their creator, Jim Orthwein.

It is the nature of our sport that we all tinker to some degree. We all try to come up with better techniques, better places to fish, and better fly patterns to fish them. Moreover, in my bonefishing, at least, the fish seem to demand this experimentation.

Over the last nine decades, as anglers have stalked this challenging species, bonefish have slowly but relentlessly grown smarter. The big fish in Florida, where anglers have stalked this species longest, are much more critical of techniques and flies than the bonefish of less pressured locales. Heavily pounded home flats at lodges in the Bahamas, Belize, and Mexico always hold a few resident bruisers that refuse anything put in front of them. Last year's flies (and techniques) may not be good enough in such places. Fish that see us and see our flies repeatedly begin to recognize a threat for what it is. Each year the ante goes up; each season, angling techniques and fly patterns must get better.

If you are a serious bonefishing angler—whether you create your own fly designs or buy your flies at a tackle shop—you will eventually grow curious about what makes good bonefish flies. You will particularly want to know how they work, and what separates the good ones from the bad.

What are the best ways to control sink rate? How do you prevent noisy landings? Can you make flies that won't snag in grass? What do the prey look like and which elements are most important in simulating them?

In the beginning, if you're like me, you'll probably focus more on what prey your fly resembles than anything else. I always seem to think I've just invented some great new shrimpy-crabby shape that's going to become the sport's next killer pattern. But in reality—at least in bonefishing reality—you'd be better off studying the way your fly functions than its prey form. Only flies that get in front of fish ever get considered—no matter how good they look. Master that and then you can move on to prey simulation.

GETTING TO THE FISH

For a bonefish fly to consistently reach fish without spooking them, it must land quietly, sink quickly to fish level, and avoid snagging when stripped. It helps, too, if you can cast it easily in wind.

Entry Impact

A friend of mine, Len Wright, characterizes one of his favorite bonefish patterns as so delicate that "it lands as quietly as a mouse peeing on a blotter." (The pattern—the very effective Len's Hackle Merkin—is literally as light as a feather.) Len's description evokes one of the most desirable traits in bonefish fly design. The less disturbance—whether noise or splashing—made by your fly when it lands, the more likely the fish will be to stick around to look it over.

Splash, as anyone who has often fished the flats knows, spooks fish badly. (A noisy landing *does* sometimes attract fish too, but you still have to know how to control splash, even if you intend to use it to your benefit.) Generally, the more experienced the fish, the smaller the impact required to disturb them. But if you have a whisper-quiet fly that lands softly, you can put it close enough to the fish—the closer the better—that they must react to it quickly.

Simply making a fly that is quiet poses no great challenge to tiers. But making a fly that is quiet *and* has a fast sink rate can truly test a fly designer's ingenuity. Since *both* soft landings and fast sink rates are so critical to flats anglers, bonefish pattern tiers have pushed to

Quiet landings avoid spooking fish. The soft folded feathers of Len's Hackle Merkin cushion its impact almost completely, making it one of the quietest crab patterns ever devised.

Before a fly can do its work it has to get down in front of the fish. The Pflueger HOY (right) sinks softly to shallow tailing fish, while the See-Bone (left) rockets to the bottom to reach deep-mudding and deep-cruising schools.

the limit the fly-design envelopes of these two discordant variables. They've invented novel blends of weight and buoyancy, achieving whisper-quiet landings and rocket-fast descents in flies such as Winston Moore's Bonefish Crab, Will Myers' Buster Crab, Ellen Reed's Honey Lamb, Lenny Moffo's Slamaroo, and Tim Merrihew's Nasty Gilbert.

Sink Rate

Of all the bonefish fly characteristics you must get right, I find that sink rate—along with its contrary sister, entry impact—accounts for more fish won or lost than anything else. Unless your fly can get down to the fish's level without spooking them, they'll never see it. It won't matter how well you aim, how far you cast, or how enticingly your pattern beckons them. They'll never know it's there and they'll never react to it. You would be better off putting your fly rod away and going bottom fishing for grouper with chopped conch.

Fly tiers have found many ways to adjust the rate at which flies descend. Some methods—such as increasing or decreasing the quantities of buoyant elements in tails, wings, and bodies—have evolved from techniques used in tying all kinds of fishing flies. Sink rate, however, is so critical in flats fishing that bonefish anglers have pioneered sinking techniques that go far beyond those of most other fly designers. Experimenting with the use of metal "eyes," for instance, bonefish fly tiers vary the size, number, and location of barbells and bead chain to achieve desired sink rates and realistic fly action. Fly makers also incorporate lead strips, wound lead wire, stacked slivers of lead, and keel hooks into their arsenal of sink rate tricks, allowing them to adjust just about any fly pattern—no matter what its shape or makeup—to fish well in any given depth of water.

In addition, tiers vary sink rate through their choice of body material. Water-sucking substances such as chenille, yarn, and Sponj-Lur sink fast when wet, while bodies made of bulky deer hair, rabbit, and dubbing mixes descend slowly and work well in tailing flies like Jeffrey Cardenas' Palmered Crab or Tim Borski's Deer Hair Critter.

Veteran flats anglers choose flies of several different sink rates to reach fish feeding at different depths. The Pflueger Hoy (left) floats softly to shallow-tailing fish; O'Keefe's bead-chain Turd Fly (middle) glides down to middle-depth cruisers; and the lead-headed See-Bone rockets deep to mudders and cruisers feeding near the bottom.

Snag-Proofing

If you fish only sand flats, weed guards will hold little value for you. But if you fish where turtle grass beds and coral heads eat your flies faster than fish do, you will need to have flies that pull through bottom structure and vegetation without hanging up.

Mono or wire weed guards shaped as spikes or loops shield hook points from catching on bottoms, grass, or coral. Stiff hackle wound in front of hook points, as seen on Jim's Golden Eye and the Pflueger HOY, also reduces hang-ups. Flared deer hair collars, favorite devices of talented tier Craig Mathews, are very effective snag-proofers in patterns such as his Pop's Bonefish Bitters and Turneffe Crab.

Many bonefish flies, such as the Crazy (or Nasty) Charlie, Lefty's Shallow H_2O Fly, and the Clouser Deep Minnow, use reversed wings to protect hook points. The grandfather of all these inverted wing guards was Pete Perinchief's Horror, a pioneering 1950s design that spawned a generation of flipped-over wing patterns—many created by the gifted hands of Chico Fernandez and Lefty Kreh to give anglers snag-proof patterns that worked just about anywhere. More recent ingenuity has resulted in integrated weedless devices such as the mono eyestalks on Les Fulcher's Bonefish Joe, which double as guards, and the deer hair stalk extending out of the body of Rick Ruoff's Backcountry Bonefish Fly.

Incidentally, I find that guides and anglers in Florida—where grass beds greet you at every turn—lead the rest of us in weed and coral guard design. If you fish such areas regularly, study the way that the flies of Rick Ruoff, Steve Huff, Tim Borski, Steve Bailey, and Harry Spear keep hook points out of harm's way. And pay close attention to the care with which Harry Spear matches weed guard diameter to hook size to make sure the mono serves as a weed guard and not a fish guard.

Weed guards help anglers avoid fish-spooking snags in coral structure and grass beds.

Castability

Punching deer hair crabs through a stiff wind teaches you the merits of aerodynamic fly design fast. You strain your arm. You lose your timing. No matter how hard you try to push that crab against the wind currents, gusts blow it off-course and you miss your target.

Aerodynamically clean designs, such as Charlies and Gotchas, cast well in wind. Even winged flies, such as the Clouser Deep Minnow or Goddard's Tropical Shrimp, have cone-shaped profiles that pierce wind. But bulky three-dimensional flies, such as many crab,

Gifted West Coast tier Terry Baird creates aerodynamic designs that cut through wind even in larger profiles.

urchin, and goby patterns, require so much force to cast that few anglers can cast them with control.

Clever designers, however, have found ingenious ways to fashion even unwieldy prey forms so that they cast well. Among these I find Craig Mathews' big Salsa and Sir Mantis Shrimps cast very well, as do the large marabou profiles in Jim Orthwein's Jim's Bonefish Puff and Doug Brewer's Standard MOE. Terry Baird is the grand master of such aerodynamic design. Look over his Stealth Crab and Shimmerskin Mantis, which cut air as easily as naked fly line yet present fish with big, meaty profiles.

LOOKING LIKE FOOD

Bonefish eat just about anything they can safely run down and ingest without fear of attack. This omnivorous appetite and the abundance of different prey forms in the bonefish's world account for the great variety of flies that deceive bonefish. This is why bonefish are such perfect targets for "attractor" patterns—flies that simply look like they should be something edible, whether or not they portray any specific creature that lives on the flats.

But some prey turn up in bonefish stomachs more often than others—maybe because these species are more abundant, maybe because they are easier to catch, or maybe because they give more nutritional bang for the bite. Among the most commonly consumed of these prey are: clams, common shrimps, snapping shrimps, and crabs.

But even more fascinating to anglers and fly tiers, some of these prey species end up inside bonefish far more often than their abundance in local habitats would lead you to expect. Enough so, at least, to encourage speculation that they have a favorite-food status on the bonefish's daily menu. Prey that fit this group include clams in the tellin and lucine families, common shrimps, and mantis shrimps.

TABLE 1.1	WHAT BONEFISH EAT THE MOST
PREY FORMS	**PREY EATEN** **(% by NUMERICAL COUNT)**
Clams *(Bivalvia)*	35.5%
Common shrimps *(Penaeidae)*	19.8
Snapping shrimps *(Alpheidae)*	13.0
Swimming crabs *(Portunidae)*	7.2
Mud & spider crabs *(Xanthidae, Majidae)*	6.9
Worms *(Polychaeta)*	6.1
Snails *(Gastropoda)*	5.0
Fish *(Gobiidae, Batrachoididae)*	4.4
Mantis shrimps *(Squillidae)*	2.1

Source: Colton and Alevizon, 1983

TABLE 1.2

PREY MOST PREFERED BY BONEFISH

PREY FORMS	PREY EATEN (%)	PREY AVAILABLE (%)	PREFERENCE RATIO
Clams (*Bivalvia*)	35.5%	6.1%	5.8
Common shrimps (*Penaeidae*)	19.8	8.7	2.2
Mantis shrimps (*Squillidae*)	2.1	1.2	1.7
Worms (*Polychaeta*)	6.1	6.5	0.9
Swimming crabs (*Portunidae*)	7.2	8.2	0.9
Snapping shrimps (*Alpheidae*)	13.0	22.0	0.6
Mud & spider crabs (*Xanthidae, Majidae*)	6.9	13.2	0.5
Fish (*Gobiidae, Batrachoididae*)	4.4	13.0	0.3
Snails (*Gastropoda*)	5.0	21.1	0.2

Source: Colton and Alevizon, 1983

Some prey on this list of favorites—mantis shrimps, juvenile swimming crabs, and gobies—appear to represent a very nutritious package to the fish, and, presumably, they are worth going to some effort to pursue.

HOW DO YOU JUDGE IF A FLY LOOKS LIKE PREY?

Many factors determine how well a fly pattern portrays prey, and fly tiers adopt many different styles in their attempts to find something that looks "real" and "appetizing." Some construct patterns that look photographically perfect. Others simulate a few key elements of the prey, emphasizing those they believe to be most seductive …perhaps a club-like claw, or an elongated antenna, or an oversized tail. Still others adopt a minimalist approach. This yields flies that seem to suggest nothing at all, like the Pop Hill Special—a spartan fly designed to let the fish fill in the blanks as to what prey is being represented.

Many anglers react to this diversity of style options with a monolithic approach. They choose flies all of one kind; they become of a "school." But a quick thumbing through of the pages of this book's fly-pattern profiles will suggest that no single style imbues bonefish fly tying (any more than any one school rules the tying of flies for any other species). I have taken fish on Carl Richards's realistic crabs and shrimps, Craig Mathews' suggestive Pop's Bonefish Bitters, and Dick Berry's minimalist Pipe Cleaner Fly. I have fished the very

Bonefish flies must suggest some form of the prey these nervous fish eat—although impressionistic interpretations often work as well as precise imitations.

suggestive McVay Gotcha until it was eaten by so many fish it fell apart. I fish Clouser Deep Minnows, Del Brown's Bonefish Fly, Jim Orthwein's Rubber Band Worms and Jim's Golden Eyes, Bill Hunter's Apricot Charlies, and Lefty's Shallow H$_2$O Flies—and find them all very effective; I wouldn't go anywhere without at least a couple of Tim Borski's devilish deceptions in my box.

I am, it seems, an eclectic in my choices of fly style. And it suits me because—simply put—I am not a bonefish. I do not know which interpretation of the bonefish's food will work day in and day out. Which will look like food on the oceanside versus deep in back-country? Or on bright days versus dark. So I do not find it contradictory to arm myself with a few of the best of each of these styles—especially since they all seem to do the job under certain conditions.

As for which styles and patterns are best, you will know how well a fly's design suggests food to your target once you test it on the flats and closely watch a fish react to it. You must see not only if he takes it, but how aggressively he takes it. Over time, your instincts for what works best will improve. You will learn much, too, from studying the physical traits of prey—especially those of favorite prey such as shrimps, crabs, mantis shrimps, gobies, toadfish—and the fly-design elements that portray them.

Bonefish prey come in many varieties. For the angler and fly tier, the most important prey attributes to simulate are: shape, color, size, appendages, and sheen.

Shape

Many shrimps display long nymph-like bodies. Others, such as snapping and mantis shrimps, have giant claws that mimic those of crayfish, or bodies that look like miniature lobsters. Crabs display oval, triangular, and trapezoidal shapes like beetles and spiders. Small eels, forage fish, and gobies look similar to the baitfish and sculpins that anglers see in other types of fishing. But some flats prey, such as burrowing clams and spine-covered urchins, have bodies like none that other anglers encounter.

Until recently, tiers mostly explored shrimp patterns, and, to a lesser degree, crabs. But as the fly profiles presented in this book show, this has changed dramatically. With the increased observation of other important prey such as mantis shrimps, seaworms, clams, gobies, and toadfish, many new types of prey are being mimicked at the vise. Mantis patterns such as Doug Schlink's Moxey Creek Shrimp and others from Bill Wilbur, Bill Catherwood, Carl Richards, and Craig Mathews, are taking fish on the flats today. Crab flies now come in many different shapes and sizes to capture the differences among the many swimming, spider, and mud species bonefish eat. Worm flies, too, show great promise: Patterns such as Ben Estes' Vernille Sparkle Worm, Michael Bednar's Intruder, Rick Ruoff's Deep Flea, and Brad Kistler's ingenious Tailbone deceive fish with their seaworm profiles.

Color

Many prey that bonefish hunt conceal themselves with camouflage, matching the surrounding sand, grass, and coral where they live. This has led many anglers to tie and select flies that match the color of flats. But I find some anglers apply this philosophy too rigidly. They believe that only light-colored prey survive on light-colored flats, and vice versa.

For several years, however, I have been pulling all sorts of non-camouflaged characters from the bottoms of flats. You need only check a good tropical saltwater identification guide, such as Peterson's or Humann's handbooks for the Atlantic and Fielding's or Ryan's for the

Many prey live on top of the flat's floor, camouflaging themselves in earth-tone colors to match sand, coral, and grass. But other food species do not blend into their surroundings and anglers will need brighter-colored and more visible flies to suggest non-camouflaged species such as sea worms, shrimps, and crabs that live in tubes or burrows, or that inhabit gay-colored hosts such as sponges and anemones.

Pacific, to see the enormous variety of non-camouflaged creatures that live on the flats. Some of these conspicuous prey survive by burrowing or hiding in abandoned shells. Some wear camouflage part of the time but at other times bear small patches of garish color, such as the orange egg sacs on certain shrimps and crabs or the dark pseudo-eyes on the armor plates of some mantises.

Other prey openly display extravagantly colored exteriors, living on gay-hued hosts such as sponges and anemones where they are, in effect, camouflaged. But when tumbled free of their hiding places during pounding storms or heavy tidal movements, they make striking targets and trigger opportunistic feeding frenzies.

Anglers armed with only drab earth-tone flies will limit themselves unnecessarily in bonefishing. Some of today's best tiers integrate color provocatively in very successful patterns that every flats angler should consider, among them the gaily splotched Bone Bug of Nick Curcione, or Bob Veverka's Foxy Lady Crab, Eddie Corrie's Paris Flat Special pattern, McVay's Gotcha, Winston Moore's Green Puff, and Lefty's Shallow H₂O Fly.

Fully camouflaged flies *do* produce well, of course. The many earth-tone colors in the flies profiled in chapter 2 reflect the popularity of this style. Some, such as Jeffrey Cardenas' Bunny Bone, Harry Spear's MOE, Tim Borski's Bristle Worm, and Randall Kaufmann's Marabou Shrimp, seem almost to disappear against a flat. But if you look closely at the creations of these clever tiers, you will see that each has built in soft, lively elements that attract fish by movement, something I have come to prefer in my camo patterns.

Reflected Color

Another way—and a unique one—that fly designers portray camouflaged prey is by tying reflective patterns such as Crazy Charlies, McVay's Gotchas, and Al Caucci's Hoochy Caucci Flies. These flies mirror—and blend with—the terrain around them.

Furthermore, their reflective bodies change to meld with new backgrounds, so when you're moving across different colored flats you don't have to change flies as often as you might with fixed-color flies. The McVay and the Caucci flies have the added advantage of lively marabou or craft hair to attract by movement.

Size

Many factors determine the best fly size for a bonefish pattern: the size of the prey at a destination; the size of the fish there; and the fish's relative sophistication, or spookiness. The overall range of a bonefish fly spans hook sizes 16 to about 1. The sweet spot where most of the action occurs is in the size 6-to-4-to-2 range. But at some locations, such as Belize, smaller flies work best because of the sizes of resident prey and because larger profiles often spook Belize's large fish in thin waters. In the Yucatan small flies work best because the fish themselves are smaller. And in Florida, where nutritious waters grow prey and fish large, sizes 4 to 1 are effective. Christmas Island's range of fish and prey sizes calls for smaller flies of sizes 6 to 10 on thinner flats, and larger sizes of 2 and 4 on reefs and in deeper water. In the Bahamas fish respond well to sizes 2 to 6, with large-fish destinations such as the Berry Islands and Bimini sometimes calling for sizes 1 and 2.

If I'm forced to fish with one size, 4 is my favorite. I find, however, that I lean toward size 2 whenever larger fish are around.

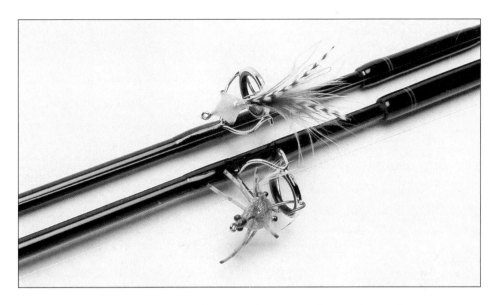

Destination—and the size of the prey that live there—often determine fly size. These two large patterns suggest the prey size found in the Florida Keys and northern Bahamas.

Appendages

The best bonefish flies recognize that appendages—legs, tails, antennae, fins, and anything else that hangs off the body and wiggles—can attract attention and trigger a bonefish into thinking it sees prey. Among shrimps, crabs, and other "decapods," the ten legs that these creatures are named for often appear as a key element in flies. Palmered hackles and collars capture their profile in flies such as Len Wright's Len's Hackle Shrimp, Ralph Woodbine's Ralph's Hackled Epoxy Bonefish Fly, and Bob Moratto's Bobby. The rubber legs in flies such as Cary Marcus' very fetching Squimp, Barry and Cathy Beck's Silly Legs Bonefish Fly, and Brewer's Lady Crab also look appealing to bonefish. Other leg materials, such as the Lumaflex in Phil Chapman's patterns and hollow Larva Lace with strands of Krystal Flash inside hold great promise too.

The claws on many good flies appear to trigger fish as well. Hackle and rubber dominate here—just as they do in leg designs—in such patterns as Capt. Crabby, Woolly Crab, and Perdi Shrimp, as well as the paired hackles in flies like Allan Finkelman's Fuzzy Hand and Rick Ruoff's Absolute Flea.

Tails attract attention because they move so rapidly to propel many prey. Shrimps, mantis shrimps, eels, worms, gobies, and juvenile fish have various telsons or caudal fins that wiggle, flap, and flip to move their owners through the water column. Flies such as Ference's Goby, Brewer's Standard MOE, Flint's Rubber Ducky, Ken Bay's Bonefish Shrimp, and Bailey's Bonefish Bunny capture this attraction. Two deserving special mention, Sullivan's Wiggle Worm and Orthwein's Jim's Rubber Band Worm, have rubber tails that drive fish crazy.

Antennae attract notice as well, because they often move even when a creature freezes. Krystal Flash can be very effective here in a fly such as Tim Merrihew's Nasty Gilbert or Ed Opler's Ed's Sassy Shrimp. Natural quills or hair make nice antennae too. Jim's Golden Eye's peccary projects an especially effective profile.

As more anglers have gained knowledge about bonefish prey, they have discovered ways to simulate the shapes, colors, and even action in their flies, to better reflect the diverse naturals that comprise this omnivorous creature's diet.

Sheen and Sparkle

One of the most attractive traits in bonefish flies is reflected light. Bonefish see most prey when they spot movement, and one of the most noticeable cues to such activity on a bright day is the sparkle emitted by a prey's hard surface as it changes position. Patterns such as Al's Glass Minnow, the Nasty Charlie, Ed's Sassy Shrimp, and the Gotcha capitalize on this very effectively. But be careful—too much shine will put fish off. It looks unnatural. It may also evoke latent fears of old enemies like barracuda.

Ultimately, the bonefish itself will teach you what works best in fly design. Watch the fish and watch its reaction—not only the act of taking or refusing, but the heat of the act. Bonefishing is a visual game, one that reveals as much about fish psychology as any.

Ease of Tying

Tying ease may seem a trivial matter compared to sink rate and prey simulation. But in the world where mangroves, reefs, and grass beds snatch hook points, and where vise-grip-jawed fish crush epoxy bodies into mauled masses, you will appreciate quickly constructed flies far more than complex ties. I like knowing I can go back to my room at night and knock off a half dozen of whatever pattern is working well in under thirty minutes. It's not just the convenience. I can take more chances casting into hazardous but likely places for bonefish along the edges of mangroves or reef lines when I'm not worried about my fly inventory.

Among the flies in this book, several shine in tying ease. The simple but effective patterns of Tim Merrihew, Yvon Chouinard, and Tom McGuane tie in a few minutes. As do Bird's Bonefish Fly, the Gotchas and the Charlies. One pattern, Gorell's Hackle Shrimp, deserves special mention in this respect. Tied of but two materials, it allows an angler to carry many different colored versions, and to tie on-site any variation needed with nothing more than a compact kit consisting of thread, a couple of boxes of hooks and metal eyes, a bag of Krystal Flash in different colors, and a few hackles.

Another pattern—and one that perhaps holds the record as the fastest and least complicated tie—comes from Bill Hunter. This gifted tier's ingenious technique for whipping up his Flats Fodder deserves every angler's attention and is described in detail in chapter 2.

Tying ease holds one other important benefit for the flats angler. You can quickly adapt flies to local circumstances. Once, on a stretch of Ambergris Flat in the Berry Islands, I found that Jim Orthwein's Jim's Rubber Band Worm attracted a lot of short strikes. I tied a shorter version, lightened the eyes by one size, and fattened the body to look more like a resident threadworm I had pulled up in my Yabby pump. The next strikes were solid and the modified Rubber Band Worm was all I fished for the rest of my stay.

Durability

Tough flies hold related benefits for anglers. Fragile patterns seldom last long on the flats, requiring you to carry a lot of them on exactly the kind of trip where you want to travel as light as possible. Of course, if a fly is easy to tie, its fragility matters less. And conversely, flies that are both durable and easy to tie—such as Lefty's Shallow H_2O Fly—are to be cherished.

Hook Corrosion

Some anglers feel carbon steel hooks give a broken-off bonefish the best chance of survival. I do not agree with this view, but I respect it. I too have strong feelings about the survival of released fish. I do not, however, like carbon hooks because they corrode—which weakens them and discolors many fly materials. I prefer crimping the barbs of stainless hooks, which makes it very easy for fish to free themselves.

PROFILES OF 150 FLIES

• • •

Recipes, Tying Notes,
Prey Suggested,
Destinations Fished,
Presentation Advice

This chapter does not contain every good bonefish pattern in the world, but it does capture most of them. Whatever destination you select, whichever habitats you stalk—from mangroves to sand flats, from grass beds to deep reefs—you should discover at least a few suitable (and proven) patterns here.

You will find, for example, flies designed for many different fishing conditions: deep water and thin, low light and bright sun, wind and flat calm. You will also see flies designed for different kinds of bonefish: big fish and small schoolies; spooky fish and aggressive eaters; resting fish and spawning fish; and tailers, cruisers, and mudders.

In addition, you will notice patterns that suggest the many different varieties of prey bonefish eat. There are snapping, grass, and mantis shrimps; spider, swimming, and mud crabs; swimming and burrowing worms; urchins; juvenile fish ... even clams.

But just as important as all these pattern variations are the many different tiers and anglers profiled in the book, the ones who created the fly designs. There are designs from full-time guides in the Florida Keys like Harry Spear, Rick Ruoff, Steve Huff, Lenny Moffo, and Jeffrey Cardenas—individuals who fish 200 to 300 days a year. Others come from residents, who live, work, and fish in places where bonefish are found: Bob Hyde and Michael

Holtzman in the Bahamas, Eddie Corrie at Christmas Island, and Tim Borski, Ellen Reed, Gordon Hill, Les Fulcher, and J. Watt Shroyer in Florida.

Many other patterns come from bonefishing's frequent travelers—those well-journeyed anglers who've caught thousands of bonefish and stalked hundreds of flats across the world: Yvon Chouinard, Winston Moore, Jim Orthwein, Bill Hunter, Lefty Kreh, Neal Rogers, Tim Merrihew, Randall Kaufmann, Al Caucci, and Craig Mathews.

Lurking among the fly patterns of all these anglers and tiers, you'll find many different kinds of flies—patterns that embrace all of fly fishing's theories—from suggestive attractors to precise imitators. There are flies from presentationists and others from "match-the-hatch" practitioners. There are even a few flies here from anglers who fish with only one fly … ever.

There are also some flies you will not find in this book. Among the missing are those *special* flies that will always remain secret—some Florida Keys patterns, for example, used exclusively in competitions, and on which the annual tournament standings of guides and anglers depend. (Although, if you look closely, a few of these have sneaked into the book too.)

Altogether, this chapter contains profiles of 150 flies. Each includes a photo of a sample tied by its originator (in about five or six cases the sample shown was tied for the originator—and to his specifications—by a carefully monitored tying house or custom tier). Each profile gives the authentic recipe of the materials needed to tie the pattern *as its creator ties it,* and each includes tying hints, location and prey information, and tips on how to fish the patterns.

Flies appear alphabetically by name. The book's index lists *alternate* names as well as primary names. So, for example, if you don't find Del Brown's famous crab pattern entered in this chapter under "Merkin," an index entry for "Merkin" will tell you to check under the proper name: "Del Brown Bonefish Fly."

ABSOLUTE FLEA

A Rick Ruoff design. Sample in photo was tied by Rick Ruoff on a size 4 34007 hook and measures horizontally 1-3/4" in length; tips are splayed 1-3/8". Fly rides hook-point up.

Hook: 34007; sizes 2, 4, 6

Thread: Monocord 3/0

Butt: White medium chenille

Tail/Claws: Two white over two cree hackles, splayed

Hackle: One large cree hackle wound as rear-position collar (angling toward hook bend) and trimmed off at bottom

Body: Tan Orvis leech yarn

Eyes/Weight: Orvis medium (1/8") nontoxic painted barbell, black on red

Weed/Coral Guard: V-shaped Ande 20-lb. mono, slight backward crimp on each fork near tip

Location Notes: The Florida Keys. Rick says this pattern is especially good for tailing fish in the backcountry of the Keys, where the fish are quite educated. It hits the water quietly and is very weedless.

Fishing Notes: Strip erratically and fairly slowly, as the splayed tail has quite a bit of breathing motion. The fly is best for tailing fish on grass bottoms, but effective in all shallow water.

Prey Notes: Grass shrimps, *Floridans gigas*.

Anecdotes: Rick says as Keys fish became more selective, he found the epoxies to be much less effective. He needed a fly that would hit the water quietly, strip weedlessly, and exhibit a lot of motion when swimming. This one does it and is part of what he calls the "Flea Series" (see also the Deep Flea, page 65).

Rick Ruoff, who has a degree in marine biology, has been guiding in the Florida Keys for twenty-four years. He is considered one of the finest anglers, guides, and fly tiers working the saltwater flats today, and is revered among his peers as a guide among guides. He was chosen to manage the initial operation at Christmas Island and to train the guides there, and has explored many potential bonefishing locations for outfitters. Rick was the first to be named Guide of the Year (1987) by *Fly Rod & Reel* magazine. Bonefish are his favorite quarry.

Agent Orange • Winston Moore

AGENT ORANGE

A Winston Moore design. Sample in photo was tied by Winston Moore on a size 4 3407 hook and measures horizontally 1-1/4" in length. Fly rides hook-point up.

Hook: 3407; sizes 4, 6

Thread: Orange Monocord 3/0

Body: Fluorescent orange chenille, medium (small for size 6)

Wing: Orange FisHair, flanked by grizzly saddle tips

Tying Notes: Use the weighted version for the Bahamas, the unweighted for most other destinations. Winston enamels the head on weighted versions so he can identify them easily when fishing.

Location Notes: Winston says this pattern has been unbelievably productive in Belize, the Yucatan, and all through the Bahamas, but he finds it ineffective in Los Roques because it spooks fish.

Fishing Notes: Winston uses very short strips for bonefish, never more than four inches. He says he often applies just enough action to move the fly—almost a twitch of the stripping fingers—generally about two inches in length.

Prey Notes: Generic shrimp suggestive of many smaller shrimps such as juvenile common shrimps (Penaeidae) and snapping shrimps (Alpheidae), as well as members of such diminutive families as Palaemonidae, Gnatophyllidae, and Hippolytidae.

Anecdotes: Renamed "Agent Bonefish" by some, but the original name persists.

Winston Moore is one of the most accomplished saltwater fly fishermen alive, and he has probably caught more bonefish than any other man on earth. His fly-fishing logs register over 6,000 bonefish and 41 permit landed and released. Winston, who is also an accomplished bluewater fly-rod angler, lives in Boise, Idaho.

AL'S GLASS MINNOW

An Al Caucci design. Sample in photo was tied by Al Caucci on a size 8 34007 hook and measures horizontally 7/8" in length. Fly rides hook-point up.

Hook: 34007; size 8

Thread: White Monocord, 3/0 or 6/0

Eyes: Crimped 100-lb. mono or extra small (3/32") bead chain

Tail: Silver Flashabou, five or six strands, 1/4" long

Body: Silver flashabou, overwrapped with clear V-Rib or narrowest Swannundaze

Wing: Craft hair, or very fine FisHair; royal blue underwing, then white overwing, layered

Tying Notes: When applying the mono eyes, crimp the middle with narrow (1/16") pliers to produce a mono barbell.

   Al says he sometimes applies a coat of clear Super-T-Acrylic Glue or a teardrop of hot glue, filling the area between the lead eyes and forward to the hook eye, for added durability and for a shellfish-like glint.

Location Notes: The Bahamas.

Fishing Notes: Al says he designed this pattern for the bonefish that often assemble around backcountry mangroves to await tidal changes. Sometimes they linger, waiting for higher tides so they can enter the mangroves. Other times they school up and await the rest of their dinner party so they can swim off to the flats together as the tide recedes. During both of these "downtimes," he has found fish flashing as they turn to feed on small minnows, which he emulates by fishing this pattern near the surface with an erratic, streamer-like stripping action.

Prey Notes: Glass minnows, *Jenkinsia lamprotaenia, Anchoa mitchelli,* or *A. cayorum.* The fly also suggests juveniles of larger gamefish species—such as the snapper *(Lutjanidae)* family—that spend their first years in the shallows.

Al Caucci is coauthor of the pivotal work *Hatches*, as well as three other books on trout food and flies, and is the father of the Comparadun. He lives in Pennsylvania and is co-owner of the Delaware River Club Fly Fishing Resort in Starlight, Pennsylvania. He is also owner of the Al Caucci Fly Fishing Schools, which teach fly fishing for trout and bonefish.

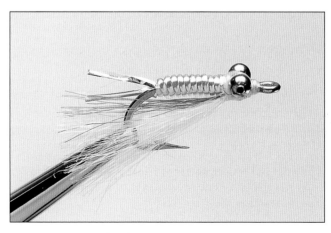

Al's Glass Minnow • Al Caucci

Apricot Charlie • Bill Hunter

APRICOT CHARLIE

A Bill Hunter design. Sample in photo was tied by Bill Hunter on a size 4 34007 hook and measures 1-3/8" in length. Fly rides hook-point up.

Hook: 34007; sizes 2, 4, 6

Thread: Orange 6/0

Eyes: Medium (1/8") brass-colored bead chain

Tail: Pearlescent orange Flashabou, or mix of pink and orange Krystal Flash

Body: Clear V-Rib over pearlescent orange Flashabou, or mix of pink and orange Krystal Flash

Wing: Pinkish-orange calf tail flanked by cree hackle tips

Tying Notes: *Author's note: You can substitute orange-dyed Mylar tubing in the tail and underbody.*

Location Notes: The Florida Keys, Andros, Abaco, the Berry Islands, North Eleuthera, Christmas Island.

Fishing Notes: Alter the eye type for the desired sink rate. Strip until the fish sees, let it drop, and watch the fish's movement to see a pick-up.

Prey Notes: Generic shrimp. Its color suggests several members of the common shrimp (Penaeidae) and mantis shrimp (Squillidae) species found in the Bahamas and the Keys.

Anecdotes: *Author's note: Of all the many Charlies this is my favorite. It has taken several hundred fish for me.*

Bill Hunter is founder and former owner of Hunter's Angling Supplies and HMH Tying Tools. He now runs an angling consultancy, writes for many fishing journals, and has fished for bonefish almost everywhere they are found.

Articulated Crab • Bill Catherwood

ARTICULATED CRAB

A Bill Catherwood design. Sample in photo was tied by Bill Catherwood on a size 4 34007 hook and measures horizontally 2-3/8" in length, and 2-3/4" in width. Fly rides hook-point down.

Hook: 34007; sizes 2, 4, with small wire "elbow" (No. 3 trolling wire) lashed to shank at hook bend, forming loop that interlocks with wire frame underbody. Hook is coated with thread and cemented sand

Wire Frame Underbody: No. 3 trolling wire, looped and splayed into a forked frame upon which crab body is tied

Thread: Tan mono 3/0

Eyes: Burnt mono, blackened

Claws: Curved pair of mottled black-and-brown feathers

Legs: Two matched (but opposing) sets of four (each) ginger variant hackles tied in at base of claws

Body: Back and belly formed with facing pair of speckled brown hen body feathers

Location Notes: The Bahamas.

Fishing Notes: Strip until the fish sees. Then let it drop and move on its own. Watch the fish's movement to see a pick-up.

Prey Notes: Generic swimming crab.

Anecdotes: This ingenious design has some of the most lifelike movements of all the crab patterns.

Bill Catherwood started chasing stripers, blues, and other salty species in the waters off Newburyport, Massachusetts, long before it was fashionable. He is best known for such pioneering inshore baitfish patterns as the Tinker Mackerel, Mullet, and Sea Pup, as well as his inventive Giant Killer billfish flies (and his lively slide shows). He has recently been exploring designs and prey for flats and other inshore fishing. See also his Magnum Mantis, page 116.

Backcountry Bonefish Fly • Rick Ruoff

BACKCOUNTRY BONEFISH FLY

A Rick Ruoff design. Sample in photo was tied by Rick Ruoff on a size 4 34007 hook and measures horizontally 1-1/2" in length. Fly rides hook-point up.

Hook: 34007; size 4

Thread: Rust Monocord 3/0

Eyes/Weight: Medium (1/8") lead barbell, with painted red-on-yellow eyes

Tail: Two pairs grizzly hackles, splayed to flank eight strands white Krystal Flash

Body: Natural tan deer body hair, spun and clipped to pear shape, leaving small shaft of standing fibers as weed or coral guard

Tying Notes: Rick says he also ties the fly in white deer hair, which works very well—especially in the Bahamas.

Location Notes: The Keys, the Bahamas.

Fishing Notes: Fish on or near the bottom; strip erratically to mimic the dart-and-stop pattern of naturals.

Prey Notes: May suggest some species of gobies (Gobiidae) and juvenile toadfish (Batrachoididae).

Rick Ruoff, see ABSOLUTE FLEA, page 19.

Bead Minnow • Bob Popovics

BEAD MINNOW

*A Bob Popovics design. Sample in photo was tied by Bob Popovics on a size 4
Tiemco 811S hook and measures horizontally 1-7/8" in length. Fly rides hook-
point up.*

Hook: Tiemco 811S; sizes 2, 4, 6

Thread: Mono

Head: Large gold bead behind hook eye

Body: Mylar tinsel wrapped roughly and crisscrossing, leaving many facets

Wing: Gold Krystal Flash, then polar bear, then tan bucktail

Collar: Matching pearlescent Estaz

Tying Notes: Jam the bead against the hook eye with thread; no glue is necessary.

Location Notes: Andros.

Fishing Notes: Use very short strips until the fish sees; let it drop; repeat; then make a
long slow-and-stop retrieve. Watch the fish's movement to see a pick-up.

Prey Notes: Glass minnows, *Jenkinsia lamprotaenia, Anchoa mitchelli*, or *A. cayorum*. The fly
may also suggest juveniles of larger gamefish species—such as the snapper (Lutjanidae) family—that spend their first years in the shallows. Thirdly, it may suggest some members of the
common shrimp (Penaeidae), snapping shrimp (Alpheidae), and mantis shrimp (Squillidae)
families.

Bob Popovics lives in New Jersey and has been creating and tying saltwater patterns for
over twenty years. He is well known for such popular striper patterns as his Surf Candy and
Pop-Lips series, and he writes for several fishing journals, gives seminars, and is founder of
the Atlantic Saltwater Fly Rodders.

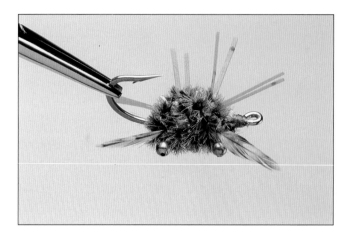

Beady Crab • Dick Brown

BEADY CRAB

Author's design. Sample in photo was tied by the author on a size 4 34007 hook and measures horizontally 1-5/8" in length. Carapace is 3/4" in diameter. Fly rides hook-point up.

Hook: 34007; sizes 2, 4, 6

Thread: Chartreuse Danville Flat Waxed Nylon 3/0

Eyes/Underbody: Two four-bead strands very small (3/32") bead chain or plastic bead, each figure-eighted to shank to form H-shaped frame

Claws: Cree hackles flared for claws, then (optional) Krystal Flash antennae

Legs: Four strands of tan, green, or beige rubber hackle or Sili Legs (color to match or contrast with body) tied to flare on top of carapace (hook-point side), then (optional) tuft of marabou

Body: Size 0 tan, green (shown), or beige Danville Speckled Crystal Sparkle chenille criss-crossed and wound around bead segments and between legs, which should be pulled so they end up on top (point side) of shank to invert fly's descent

Tying Notes: For spider crabs, omit the claws and tie in five pairs of rubber legs.
This is a faster tie than deer hair, epoxy, or yarn and wool bodied crabs. You can adjust the sink rate and angle by intermixing plastic bead chain, metal bead chain, and lead barbells. See chapter 4 on tying sequence for the underbody frame.

Location Notes: Andros, Abaco, the Berry Islands, North Eleuthera, the Keys, Yucatan, Belize.

Fishing Notes: Strip until the fish sees, let it drop, watch the fish's movement, and twitch strip to see a pick-up.

Prey Notes: Generic crab shape suggestive of many species of swimming crabs (Portunidae), mud crabs (Xanthidae), and spider crabs (Majidae), depending on size and color.

Bird's Bonefish Fly • Ralph Bird

BIRD'S BONEFISH FLY

A Ralph Bird design. Sample in photo was tied by Ralph Bird on a size 4 3407 hook and measures horizontally 1-1/8" in overall length. Fly rides hook-point up.

Hook: 3407; sizes 4, 6

Thread: Yellow mono or Flat Waxed Nylon

Eyes: Lead 1/8" (1/50 oz.) barbell eyes on top of shank or bead chain, to suit sink rate

Body: Fine yellow Poly flash or Diamond Braid or fish scale tubing wound around shank. *Author's note: Star Yellow 1/16" Kreinik Tyer's Ribbon also matches Bird's sample*

Wing: Sparse yellow Ultra Hair, only as long as hook

Tying Notes: Ralph usually uses 1/50 oz. to 1/36 oz. lead eyes (plain or nickel plated seem to work equally well). For quiet shallow water, bead-chain eyes can also be used. Use plenty of glue to hold the body together.

Location Notes: Andros, Abaco, Christmas Island.

Fishing Notes: Strip until the fish sees, let it drop, and watch the fish's movement to see a pick-up.

Prey Notes: Suggests small translucent shrimps such as Palaemonidae, Gnatophyllidae, and Hippolytidae.

Anecdotes: The fly works best on clean bottoms: sand, coral, or mud. It sinks rapidly. When moved along the bottom, it creates puffs of mud or sand, and this almost invariably results in strikes. Most bonefish take this fly deeply, so a barbless hook is essential. Even with a barbless, Ralph says he sometimes cuts the leader to minimize damage to the fish. *Author's note: I first fished this fly in Abaco's Marls when guide Donnie Lowe gave me one that Ralph had left behind, and it took fish all day, even after being mauled so badly the body material was hanging off the shank.*

Ralph Bird lives in Jackson, Wyoming.

Black Urchin • Carl Richards

Blue Crab, Juvenile • Carl Richards

BLACK URCHIN

A Carl Richards design. Sample in photo was tied by Carl Richards on a size 4 34007 hook and measures 1-3/8" in height, including antennae. Fly rides hook-point up.

Hook: 34007; sizes 4, 6

Thread: Black 3/0

Spine: Black-dyed deer hair, spun on shank and clipped from all but point side of hook

Weight: Mashed split shot glued to underside of shank (inverted) with 5-Minute Epoxy

Body or Test: Liquid latex mixed with red acrylic paint; then coat with black acrylic, leaving some red showing through

Tying Notes: Work latex into the base of the deer hair for strength.

Location Notes: Belize, the Bahamas, Yucatan.

Fishing Notes: Alter the weight type for the desired sink rate. Fish on the bottom with a very steady slow retrieve.

Prey Notes: Red rock urchins, *Echinometra lucunter*, which often inhabit the grass beds of lagoons.

Anecdotes: This pattern performed well in both the Bahamas and Belize.

Carl Richards, who along with Doug Swisher pioneered the scientific examination of trout prey, has now focused his inquisitive eye on saltwater fish and what they eat. His recently published *Prey* examines many of the species bonefish eat.

BLUE CRAB, JUVENILE

A Carl Richards design. Sample in photo was tied by Carl Richards on a size 4 34007 hook. Carapace measures 7/8" in width, and span across claw tips is 1-1/4".

Fly rides hook-point up.

Hook: Mustad 34007; sizes 2, 4, 6, 8

Thread: White Monocord 3/0

Body/Carapace: White egg-fly yarn spun Muddler fashion and clipped to desired carapace shape

Legs/Underside: Cement Rub-R-Mold leg and claw assembly under the body (liquid latex flexible mold compound from a crafts shop)

Eyes: Burnt 40-lb. to 80-lb. mono

Feelers: Cream boar bristle

Color: Sharpie waterproof or Pantone pens

Location Notes: Belize, the Berry Islands, North Eleuthera.

Fishing Notes: Alter the weight size for the desired sink rate. Fish close to the bottom with a hopping retrieve at varying speeds.

Prey Notes: Blue crabs, *Callinectes sapidus,* the juveniles of which often inhabit shorelines, inside flats, grass beds, and lagoons.

Carl Richards, see BLACK URCHIN, page 32.

Bobby • Bob Moratto

BOBBY

A Bob Moratto design. Sample in photo was tied by Bob Moratto on a size 4 34007 hook and measures horizontally 1-1/8" in length. Hackle claws measure 5/8" from base to tips. Fly rides hook-point up.

Hook: 34007; sizes 2, 4, 6

Thread: Monocord 3/0, color to match body

Eyes: Medium (1/8") bead chain

Claws: Two hackle tips (outer sides facing so they flare) tied in at base of (and on hook-eye side of) bead chain. Tips extend downward (as viewed in tying position) at an angle of about 40° and one-half shank length past bend

Body: Cream saddle hackle tip palmered over cream medium chenille

Tying Notes: The fly is also effective in brown, tan, and green; choose the color to complement the hues of the habitats you're fishing.

Location Notes: The fly has been successful in the Bahamas (Deep Water Cay, Andros, North Eleuthera, Harbour Island), Belize, Ascencion Bay, Los Roques, Mexico's Yucatan, and Christmas Island.

Fishing Notes: Alter the eye type for the desired sink rate. Strip until the fish sees, let it drop, and watch the fish's movement to see a pick-up.

Prey Notes: In different sizes and colors, suggests most of the common shrimps (Penaeidae), snapping shrimps (Alpheidae), and grass shrimps (Palaemonidae). It also suggests some mantis shrimps (Squillidae).

Bob Moratto, a realtor from northern California and a past president of Russian River Fly Fishers, took first place in the IGFA's Freshwater Fishing Contest (1978) with a thirty-pound male steelhead he caught on the Babine River in British Columbia. He's an active stalker of trout, salmon, tarpon, permit, and bonefish. His Bobby fly has now taken fish at all flats destinations.

Bone Bug • Nick Curcione

BONE BUG

A Nick Curcione design. Sample in photo was tied by Nick Curcione on a size 4 3407 hook and measures horizontally 1-7/8" in length. Fly rides hook-point up.

Hook: 3407; size 4

Thread: Fine nylon (Larva Lace)

Eyes: 1/8" lead barbell, painted black

Body: Small ball-shaped bulge tied midway on shank with bright orange chenille

Wing: Gray craft fur flanked by pair of pale green saddle hackle tips

Location Notes: This fly is a modification of a pattern called the "Beach Bug," which Nick uses for barred perch and corbina in the southern California surf. The original pattern—a bulkier design with a dark green Mylar body and wider hackle tips—managed to take some bonefish in the Caribbean but Nick later found it was much more productive when streamlined to its present configuration. In Beach Bug form, the orange chenille ball simulates the egg sac on the underside of sand crabs—a primary food source of perch and corbina. "I don't know if it represents anything in the bonefish's dietary lineup," says Nick, "but it sure got their attention." *Author's note: Several tropical crab species display orange egg clusters and other flies with "orange sac" profiles, such as the Dr. Taylor Special, Bob Veverka's Foxy Lady Crab, and Lefty Kreh's Shallow H$_2$O Fly, attract notice for the same reason.*

Fishing Notes: Nick says that because the orange chenille projects such a gaudy profile, it attracts better when presented seven or more feet from fish; closer, and it often spooks them.

Prey Notes: Suggestive of many species of swimming crabs (Portunidae) and spider crabs (Majidae).

Nick Curcione has been saltwater fly fishing for the last twenty-five years and has authored many articles on the subject as well as the important book, *The Orvis Guide to Saltwater Fly Fishing.* He's also on the Orvis Saltwater Advisory Team.

Bone-Zai Crab • Phil Chapman

BONE-ZAI CRAB

A Phil Chapman design. Sample in photo was tied by Phil Chapman on a size 4 34007 hook and measures horizontally 2-1/2" in length, including legs. The carapace measures 1-5/6" in width. Fly rides hook-point down.

Hook: 34007; sizes 4, 6

Thread: Black Flat Waxed Nylon 3/0

Weight: 1/100 oz. lead barbell

Sides: Brown rabbit tips, then three or four short strands root beer Krystal Flash

Claws: Grizzly hackle tips

Weed Guard: 15-lb. Mason

Legs: Four to six pairs Lumaflex, barred with marker

Body: Tan wool

Eyes: Melted mono enlarged by dipping in epoxy; glued in

Tying Notes: The fly can also be tied inverted.

Location Notes: The Keys.

Fishing Notes: Tailing fish. Use 1/50 oz. weight for deeper, cruising fish. Strip and pause. The fly has good leg and antenna animation when it's stopped.

Prey Notes: Generic crab shape suggestive of swimming crabs (Portunidae), mud crabs (Xanthidae), and spider crabs (Majidae).

Phil Chapman is a full-time fisheries biologist for the Florida Game and Freshwater Fish Commission, a seasonal Homosassa tarpon guide, and a member of the International Fishing Hall of Fame. He also guides and fishes for redfish and snook, and he's caught bonefish of up to twelve pounds, twelve ounces.

Bonefish Bunny • Steve Bailey/Flip Pallot

BONEFISH BUNNY

A Steve Bailey/Flip Pallot design. Sample in photo was tied by Steve Bailey on a size 4 34007 hook and measures horizontally 2-1/2" in length. With heaviest eyes, fly rides hook-point up.

Hook: 34007; size 4

Thread: Fluorescent orange Flat Waxed Nylon

Eyes: 1/50 oz. or 1/100 oz. lead, painted white or yellow

Rib: Brown Kevlar thread

Body: Orange chenille

Wing: Hot-orange-dyed rabbit strip

Hackle: Dark furnace

Weed Guard: 15-lb. to 20-lb. Mason

Tying Notes: The Bonefish Bunny is patterned after a Flip Pallot tarpon fly. Tie on and paint the eyes; double the Kevlar rib and tie it down to the rear of the body; tie in and wrap the chenille; pierce the rabbit strip, insert the hook point, and pull rabbit over the body, tying down at the head, wrap the hackle, tie in the weed guard, and epoxy the head.

Location Notes: Biscayne Bay, the Keys, the Bahamas.

Fishing Notes: Tie the fly with 1/50 oz. eyes for deepwater, mudding fish, and fish tracking stingrays; with 1/100 oz. eyes (still on size 4 hook) for tailing fish in shallow water. Use short, one- to two-inch ticks.

Prey Notes: Possibly suggests the palolo worm, or other worm species.

Steve Bailey has been an avid snook and redfish angler as well as fly tier since 1976. He caught three fish on this pattern in Biscayne Bay the first time he fished it. His other favorite fly is the Clouser Deep Minnow.

Bonefish Crab • Winston Moore

BONEFISH CRAB

A Winston Moore design. Sample in photo was tied by Winston Moore on a size 6 3407 hook and measures horizontally 1-1/8" in length; carapace measures 3/8" in diameter. Fly rides hook-point up.

Hook: 3407; sizes 2, 4, 6

Thread: Chartreuse Danville Flat Waxed Nylon 3/0

Claws/Antennae: Furnace hackle tips, creamy white marabou, then two strands Krystal Flash, all one-and-one-half shank lengths long

Body: Strands of cream wool or wool tufts from a hide, figure-eighted to shank, then brushed out, flattened, and glued with contact cement (not Super Glue) into a stiff carapace

Legs: White round rubber "hackles" tied in when wool strands are applied, before gluing

Weight: 3/32" (1/100 oz.) lead barbell; vary for hook size and water depth

Tying Notes: Winston also ties the fly in pink, brown, and tan

Location Notes: Yucatan, the Bahamas, Belize, Los Roques. Winston says this pattern has been extremely effective on Ascencion Bay permit (taking nine of eleven fish hooked on a single visit); he says bonefish like it so much they'll compete for it.

Fishing Notes: Winston uses very short strips for bonefish, never more than four inches. He says he often applies just enough action to move the fly—almost a twitch of the stripping fingers—generally about two inches in length.

Prey Notes: Generic crab suggestive of many species of swimming crabs (Portunidae), mud crabs (Xanthidae), and spider crabs (Majidae).

Winston Moore, see AGENT ORANGE, page 20.

Bonefish Explorer • Jack Gartside

BONEFISH EXPLORER

A Jack Gartside design. Sample in photo was tied by Jack Gartside on a size 4 34007 hook and measures horizontally 7/8" in length. Fly rides hook-point down.

Hook: 34007; sizes 2, 4, 6, 8

Thread: Tan or white 6/0

Tail: Pale tan marabou, then four to six strands pearl Flashabou

Body: Tan, pearl, green, or orange Mylar chenille (long)

Eyes (optional): Medium (1/8") bead chain

Location Notes: The Florida Keys, Andros, Yucatan.

Fishing Notes: Jack uses this fly as a general searching pattern when fishing drop-offs, currents, or deeper waters where bonefish are not visible. He fishes it as conditions warrant, sometimes dead-drift with slow twitches, other times very fast.

Prey Notes: Jack characterizes the Explorer as not imitative of any one prey family but suggestive of several, and he calls it a good fly to try when you don't know what else to use. He says it's "a close relative of the Woolly Bugger."

Jack Gartside is not only one of the most creative pattern designers in fly fishing today, he's also an angling pioneer who explores new saltwater territories long before the crowds do. He's recently surveyed parts of Andros seen by no other American ...or perhaps human!

Bonefish In-Furriator • Phil Chapman

BONEFISH IN-FURRIATOR

A Phil Chapman design. Sample in photo was tied by Phil Chapman on a size 4 34007 hook and measures horizontally 3-1/4" in length, including antennae. The body measures 2-1/8" in width. Fly rides hook-point down.

Hook: 34007; sizes 2, 4

Thread: Black Flat Waxed Nylon 3/0

Weight: 1/50 oz. lead barbell

Whiskers/Walking Legs: Small clump natural tan deer hair, then root beer Krystal Flash

Antennae: Two long strands brown Lumaflex

Claws: Matched pair grizzly hackles, flared outward

Eyes: Mono, melted and enlarged by dipping in epoxy

Underbody: Orange Estaz

Body: Brown rabbit, palmered

Tail: Brown Flash Chenille

Weed Guard: 15-lb. Mason

Tying Notes: The fly can also be tied inverted.

Location Notes: The Keys, the Bahamas, Los Roques.

Fishing Notes: For tailing and cruising fish. The Lumaflex antennae float and undulate in the current. This fly is good for grass as well as for sandy bottoms.

Prey Notes: Generic shrimp/crab pattern suggestive of many species of common and snapping shrimps (Penaedae and Alpheidae), mantis shrimps (Squillidae), and some swimming and spider crabs (Portunidae and Majidae), depending on color and size.

Anecdotes: The fly was adapted from Phil's Hare-Ball Crab tarpon pattern.

Phil Chapman, see BONE-ZAI CRAB, page 35.

Bonefish Joe • Les Fulcher

BONEFISH JOE

A Les Fulcher design. Sample in photo was tied by Les Fulcher on a size 4 34007 hook and measures horizontally 2-1/8" in length. The carapace measures 3/4" in width. Fly rides hook-point up.

Hook: 34007; sizes 2, 4, 6

Thread: Brown or gray Monocord 3/0

Tail: Pale pinkish-tan marabou with "collar" of pink vernille, then pair of splayed grizzly, cree, or variant hackle tips tied in front of (hook-eye side of) collar

Head/Eyes: Variegated tan/olive chenille over medium lead barbell eyes

Wing: Sparsely spun tan/brown/gray deer body hair, tied in behind eyes (letting butt ends flare) and clipped flat across shank so fly rides flat

Weed Guard: 12-lb. mono, burned at ends

Tying Notes: Vary the eyes to alter the sink rate; dress the deer hair sparsely (it is for profile, not flotation); the weed guard is cut long so the tips ride above the body and look like antennae or elevated eyestalks. Les also ties a version with orange/yellow deer hair flared on the bottom (shank side) to suggest a female's egg sac.

Location Notes: The Keys, the Bahamas, Mexico (Ascencion Bay).

Fishing Notes: Designed in the Keys to get a big "buggy" profile down fast while wading. It can be fished in short strips or retrieved like a crab (stripped and dropped). It has a large size, yet drops fairly softly for tailers. It also projects a large profile to attract cruising and mudding fish. It has taken permit, snapper, barracuda, redfish, snook, and baby tarpon, in addition to bonefish.

Prey Notes: An attractor fly with a general prey shape. From the rear it looks like a retreating crab, or a shrimp with claws and eyestalks extended. With painted eyes, and fished in long strips, it can also suggest minnows and juvenile fish either below the surface or along the bottom. The eyestalks also make it weedless. You can tie an orange chenille head to suggest a female crab with eggs during spawning. (For another spawning version, see tying notes.)

Anecdotes: Les says he named the pattern after Joe Bursel, a friend and tier, who suggested the idea.

Les Fulcher is a Sarasota County firefighter who wades the Keys flats between Long Key and Bahia Honda as often as he can. He also hangs out with Tim Borski from time to time and gets to the Bahamas once or twice a year.

Bonefish Joe Chicken Fly • George Terpenning

BONEFISH JOE CHICKEN FLY

A George Terpenning design. Sample in photo was tied by George Terpenning on a size 6 34007 hook and measures horizontally 1-3/8" in length. Fly rides hook-point up.

Hook: 34007; size 6

Thread: Tan Monocord 3/0

Eyes: Silver medium (1/8") bead chain or lead barbell

Tail: Pearl Mylar tinsel

Body: Pearl Mylar tinsel, then clear Larva Lace

Wing: Tangerine calf tail flanked by pair of brown or dark badger saddles, flared

Tying Notes: George also ties a brown version he calls "Terp's Dark" that uses dark brown thread, auburn calf tail, and chocolate Larva Lace, and substitutes pearl Krystal Flash in the tail.

Location Notes: Harbour Island, North Eleuthera, Abaco (Sandy Point).

Fishing Notes: Strip until the fish sees, let it drop, and watch the fish's movement to see a pick-up.

Prey Notes: Generic shrimp suggestive of many species of common shrimps (Penaeidae), snapping shrimps (Alpheidae), and grass shrimps (Palaemonidae).

Anecdotes: George says the name came from Harbour Island guide Joe Cleare, who had suggested that he and his fishing partner, Dr. Rodney Baine, come up with a fly with a touch of orange and some lively chicken saddle hackles in it. George says he tried to come as close as he could to the brown hackles of the local Rhode Island Red type roosters that roam the streets of the island.

George Terpenning lives along the Connecticut coastline, where he fishes for other salt-water species. He has fly fished for over forty years and tied for over twenty-five, and says he'll fish for anything that swims as long as he can use his fly rod. He's been bonefishing for over fifteen years.

Bonenanza • Michael Bednar

BONENANZA

A Michael Bednar design. Sample in photo was tied by Michael Bednar on a size 2

3407 hook and measures horizontally 2-3/8" in overall length. Fly rides hook-point up.

Hook: 3407; sizes 2, 4, 6

Thread: Prewaxed Monocord 3/0, black or white

Eyes: 1/100 oz. or 1/50 oz. nickel-plated lead

Hackle: Dun-dyed grizzly

Dubbing: Muskrat, rabbit, or other bulky material

Wing: Brown bucktail, slightly flared; then pearl Krystal Flash; then pink FisHair

Tying Notes: Cut the hackle on top, after winding it forward.

Location Notes: The Keys, the Bahamas.

Fishing Notes: Michael says he uses this one for tailers and cruisers over turtle grass beds and sandy bottoms. Let the water depth dictate the eye weight: Use the heaviest eyes for two feet plus, and go eyeless for under a foot.
For tailing, once the fish spots the fly, let it sink and wait for the fish to pick it up. Only twitch it again if the fish starts swimming away.

Prey Notes: Suggests many members of the common shrimp (Penaeidae), snapping shrimp (Alpheidae), and mantis shrimp (Squillidae) families.

Michael Bednar is a flats guide living and chasing bones on Long Key in the Florida Keys.

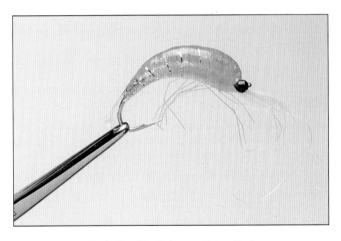

Boyle Bonefish Shrimp • Robert Boyle

BOYLE BONEFISH SHRIMP

A Robert Boyle design. Sample in photo was tied by Robert Boyle on a size 4 stainless hook bent to shape, and measures horizontally 2-1/8" in overall length. Carapace measures 5/16" in width at the shoulder. Fly rides hook-point up.

Hook: Stainless; sizes 2, 4

Thread: Transparent sewing thread

Eyes: Burnt 80-lb. mono, atop shank, just behind eye

Short Antennae: Polar bear hair

Lip Plate: Clear plastic soda straw, or section of butt end of quill from primary goose feather

Long Antennae: Hog bristle, bottom side of shank

Body: Lay strip of Larva Lace on *top* of shank; layer ever shorter strips of Larva Lace on top of shank and each other, perhaps half a dozen times, to give proper taper and lifelike "shoulders." Coat each strip with Hard As Nails or other nail polish after tying down: This both secures plastic and adds to transparency.

Tail: Clor-pane, the clear plastic sheeting used to cover office furniture. (Optional: Tie in strip of silver Mylar and pull aside to later wind over body, to delineate abdominal segments.) Tie in 1/16"-by-12" strip of Clor-pane and spiral over Larva Lace. When about 90 percent is finished, spiral optional Mylar rib for segments. You can also tie a much simplified version by omitting Mylar and Clor-pane. Just wind clear Larva lace over body to form shape; proceed to head and final coating.

Head/Face: Tie in sharply pointed piece of goose quill or Swannundaze for shrimp's rostrum or beak. (Optional: Tie in piece of black or orange Larva Lace for shrimp's digestive tract.) Wrap over with last portion of Clor-pane strip. Coat with nail polish and let dry.

Legs: Ten hog bristles set in pairs tied in with transparent thread (Optional: Use hot needle to set bends in bristles to emulate naturally cocked legs—but be very careful).

Final Finish Coats: 5-Minute Epoxy

Tying Notes: Do not spiral the Larva lace on the body. It will fill the hook gap, making the fly useless for fishing.

Location Notes: The Bahamas.

Fishing Notes: Strip the fly once or twice to get the target's attention and then watch for the fish to pick it up. The natural moves sporadically, one spurt at a time.

Prey Notes: Imitates a number of shrimp in the family Palaemonidae. This family includes hundreds of species distributed in the tropic and temperate zones of the world, often living in or near grass beds, where they swim in short spurts from blade to blade.

Anecdotes: One of the first anglers to test this fly on the flats (referring to it in a March, 1972 letter to Bob as the "Boyled Shrimp") was A. J. McClane, who managed to hook several Bahamian species of *A. vulpes* on the Boyle pattern.
This is admittedly a very complicated tie for a bonefish pattern, but it's a good-looking fly and Bob's description offers several ways to substantially simplify it. He also warns those going the whole distance to be very careful at the end. "If you amputate a leg with the hot-needle crimping process, it's a real pain in the ass to tie in a new one."

Bob Boyle, a longtime writer for *Sports Illustrated,* is one of the legends of modern realistic fly design.

Brad's Tailbone • Brad Kistler

BRAD'S TAILBONE

A Brad Kistler design. Sample in photo was tied by Brad Kistler on a size 4 hook and measures vertically 1-1/2" in height. Fly rides hook-point up.

Hook: Tiemco 800S; sizes 4, 6, 8

Thread: Yellow Monocord 3/0

Wing: Fifteen to twenty peacock herl tips

Tying Notes: Bend hook into very slight bend back. With hook inverted, tie in 1-1/2" long herl wing 3/16" behind hook eye; wind thread behind herl and build up so herl stands up "high-tie" style.

Location Notes: Ambergris Caye, Belize.

Fishing Notes: The fly has taken fish when retrieved in medium-fast strips of four to eight inches. At rest, the peacock blossoms out; then it collapses on the pull.

Prey Notes: Brad says he guesses that the Tailbone might mimic a grass shrimp or possibly small squid species. *Author's note: It could also suggest those species of fanworms that extend their feathery tentacles out of burrows or sand cases to feed. See also Rick Ruoff's Deep Flea, page 65, for a similar prey approach.*

Anecdotes: Brad came up with this novel pattern after a frustrating couple of days surrounded by non-taking tailing and waking fish in four feet of water at Belize. He says fish that refused standard tailing patterns suddenly. engulfed the Tailbone.

Brad Kistler, a young corporate sales executive, has been hooked on fishing most of his life. He got into tournament bass fishing for several years and moved exclusively to fly fishing and salt water about seven years ago.

Brain Teaser • Craig Rogers

BRAIN TEASER

A Craig Rogers design. Sample in photo was tied by Craig Rogers on a size 2 Tiemco 800S hook and measures horizontally 2" in length. Fly rides hook-point up.

Hook: Tiemco 800S; sizes 2, 4

Thread: Black Monocord 3/0

Eyes: Medium (5/32") lead barbell with black-on-yellow painted eyes

Face/Claws: Pearl Krystal Flash, flanked by flared grizzly hackle tips

Body: Black thread

Legs: Three strands clear Sili Legs figure-eighted to shank, spaced along it equally

Weed/Coral Guard: V-shaped 20-lb. mono, figure-eighted to shank

Location Notes: The Florida Keys, Yucatan.

Fishing Notes: Alter the eye type for the desired sink rate. Make quick, one- to two-inch strips.

Prey Notes: Generic shrimp suggesting many members of the common shrimp (Penaeidae), snapping shrimp (Alpheidae), and mantis shrimp (Squillidae) families. It may also portray some species of swimming and spider crabs.

Anecdotes: Using this pattern, Craig's dad Neal caught and released a fish weighing over fifteen pounds in the Florida Keys while fishing with guide Tim Hoover in October, 1994. According to a *Miami Herald* report, the fish would have qualified for the 12-pound line class world record had they not released it. The fish was thirty-two inches long and nineteen-and-one-half inches in girth.

Craig Rogers is the son of doctors Neal and Linda Rogers, who coauthored *Saltwater Fly Fishing Magic*.

Branham's Epoxy Shrimp • Joe Branham

BRANHAM'S EPOXY SHRIMP

A Joe Branham design. Sample in photo was tied by Joe Branham on a size 4 34007 hook and measures horizontally 2-5/8" in overall length. Fly rides hook-point down.

Hook: 3407, 34007, 7766; sizes 2/0, 1/0, 1, 2, 4, 6

Thread: Danville 6/0 for sizes 2 to 6; Danville 3/0 for larger sizes (color to match body)

Forelegs: Ultra hair

Mouth: Short bunch pearl Krystal Flash topped with small bunch Ultra Hair

Antennae: Two strands black Krystal Flash

Eyes: Burnt mono or sewing pins, painted black

Walking Legs: Palmered natural or dyed grizzly hackle (color to match body)

Shellback: Ultra Hair must extend past eye of hook to form tail

Weed Guard: 15-lb. to 20-lb. mono, bent into inverted V

Weight: Lead barbell eyes; 1/32" for size 4, vary for other sizes and sink rates

Overcoat: Clear liquid epoxy

Tying Notes: The fly's primary color is tan but you can vary this with prey and location; a clear-with-gray-underbody combination is another good choice. The fly can also be tied unweighted for fishing in shallow water.

Location Notes: The Florida Keys, the Bahamas (one of the top two flies at Deep Water Cay).

Fishing Notes: Alter the weight for the desired sink rate. Use strip-and-stop action until the fish sees, let it drop, and watch the fish's body language for a pick-up.

Prey Notes: This generic shape portrays many snapping (Alpheidae), common (Penaeidae), and grass (Palaemonidae) shrimps.

Joe Branham, a commercial tier from Georgia, appears frequently in the pages of *Fly Fishing in Saltwater* and other angling publications. He also appears at shows and teaches seminars in fly tying.

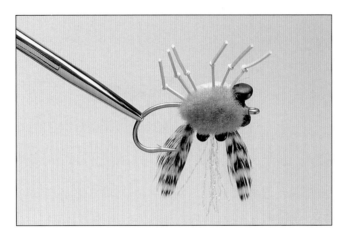

Branham's Swimming Crab • Joe Branham

BRANHAM'S SWIMMING CRAB

A Joe Branham design. Sample in photo was tied by Joe Branham on a size 4 34007 hook and measures horizontally 1" in overall length. It measures 1-3/4" tip-to-tip in width. Fly rides hook-point up.

Hook: 3407, 34007; sizes 2/0, 1/0, 1, 2, 4, 6

Thread: Flymaster 6/0 for small (sizes 2 to 6); Flymaster+ for larger sizes (color to match body)

Body: Wool on hide

Weight: Lead barbell

Eyes: Sewing pins, painted black and cut to size

Claws: Natural or dyed grizzly hackle tips

Legs: Round rubber or Sili Legs for small; rubber bands for larger sizes

Antennae: Six to eight strands Krystal Flash

Belly: Epoxy, painted white

Tying Notes: To attach the appendages, coat the bottom of the fly with contact cement; tack the claws, eyes, antennae, and legs in position on the cement; then coat each item with Super Glue to secure. Let it dry, then coat the belly with enamel-dyed epoxy.

Location Notes: The Florida Keys, the Bahamas, Belize.

Fishing Notes: Alter the weight for the desired sink rate. Use strip-and-stop action until the fish sees, let it drop, and watch the fish's body language for a pick-up.

Prey Notes: Generic crab shape good for many swimming, mud, and reef species when tied to match their colors and sizes.

Joe Branham, see BRANHAM'S EPOXY SHRIMP, page 47.

Brewer's Amber • Doug Brewer

BREWER'S AMBER

A Doug Brewer design. Sample in photo was tied by Doug Brewer on a size 4 3407 hook and measures horizontally 1-1/2" in overall length. Fly rides hook-point up.

Hook: 3407; sizes 2, 4, 6

Thread: Yellow Danville

Eyes: Medium brass bead chain

Tail: Lemon wood-duck flank

Body: Amber Swannundaze over yellow Danville Plus

Wing: Natural brown bucktail

Tying Notes: Doug Schlink of Angler Adventures (see his Moxey Creek Shrimp, page 125) says he wraps on yellow floss for an underbody and uses natural orange/tan calf tail, flanked by cree saddle tips, for the wing.

Location Notes: Bahamas. Doug Schlink says that in sizes 2 and 4, this is one of his best flies at Andros, the Berrys, and Exuma. In smaller sizes, he has also found it very good at Belize (for which it was originally developed), the Yucatan, and Los Roques.

Fishing Notes: Size 2 is good for water over eighteen inches deep; size 4, for skinnier water. The fly works well on both dark and light flats. Use strip-and-stop.

Prey Notes: The fly's amber color mimics the hue of several Bahamian species of snapping, common, and mantis shrimps—especially the golden mantis.

Anecdotes: Doug Schlink says he can't remember ever getting a refusal on this fly when he's made a good presentation. "This is a truly great bonefish pattern. Definitely in my top three," he says.

Doug Brewer is a commercial tier from Montana known for epoxy and hot-glue patterns. See his Perdi Shrimp, page 134, and his Standard MOE, page 161. He also makes the blanks used in many of Craig Mathews' innovative patterns, such as Pop's Bonefish Bitters and Hermit Crab Bitters.

Bristle Worm • Tim Borski

BRISTLE WORM

A Tim Borski design. Sample in photo was tied by Tim Borski on a size 2 34007 hook and measures horizontally 2-9/16" in overall length. Fly rides hook-point up.

Hook: 34007 or equivalent; size 2

Thread: White or tan Monocord 3/0

Eyes: Large (3/16") gold bead chain

Tail: Tan craft fur, barred with marker

Hackle: Soft long brown hackle, palmered forward

Body: Heavy dubbing of natural muskrat or other bulky material

Weed Guard: 25-lb. Mason mono

Tying Notes: Tied with bead chain, or mini lead eyes, this is a very effective fly for tailing fish. Don't be afraid to tie it heavier for mudding/cruising fish.

Location Notes: The Florida Keys.

Fishing Notes: Cast close to the fish and watch the fish for a take.

Prey Notes: A good, solid, buggy, suggestive pattern; it may suggest gobies and toadfish (Gobiidae and Batrachoididae).

Tim Borski, a resident of Islamorada in the Florida Keys, lists his occupation as artist, fly tier, and fish bum. "Each month I schedule my business obligations around the weak tides. This allows me nearly thirty-six weeks annually to gather inspiration and pull hard on strong fish." His graphic design work appears in angling books, *Saltwater Fly Fishing* magazine, and other nice places.

Bugskin Crab • Chuck Furimsky

BUGSKIN CRAB

A Chuck Furimsky design. Sample in photo was tied by Chuck Furimsky on a size 4 34007 hook and measures horizontally 1-1/2" in length. Fly rides hook-point up.

Hook: 34007; sizes 2, 4

Belly Plate: Dime-sized pancake of Sculpy II polymer craft clay

Eyes: Two 3/8" sections of black 20-lb. mono, heated to form round ball on one end

Legs/Claws: Bugskin, cut to shape

Carapace: Dime-sized pancake of Sculpy II polymer craft clay covered with layer of Bugskin

Thread: Medium brown, 4/0 (used only to tie in weight)

Weight (optional): Nontoxic black Brite Eyes (small) barbell, figure-eighted to shank between carapace and hook eye

Tying Notes: Form two pancake shapes of clay; position the hook (point up) in the bottom disk and lightly press into place the mono eyes, the Bugskin swimming legs and claws; press the second pancake into place on top, sculpting together the edges of the two disks and shaping a convex carapace on top. Bake the entire assembly in a toaster oven at 350°F for ten minutes. Remove. Glue the Bugskin carapace cover in place with waterproof cement (Barge or Weldwood DAP).
Option 1: Scratch natural markings on the belly plate before heating. Option 2: Double over the bugskin and glue it together for a stiffer effect, then cut the paddle legs and claws to shape.

Location Notes: Boca Paila, the Bahamas.

Fishing Notes: Strip the fly to show it to the fish, let it drop, and watch the fish for a pick-up.

Prey Notes: Depending on shape and color, suggestive of many species of swimming crabs (Portunidae); mud crabs (Xanthidae), and spider crabs (Majidae).

Anecdotes: A ten- to twelve-pound permit took this fly on its first sea trial at Boca Paila.

Chuck Furimsky is director of the annual International Fly Tyers Symposium and co-director of the fly-fishing Show in New Jersey and Washington, D.C. He lives near Seven Springs Mountain Resort in Champion, Pennsylvania, and spends summers in Ocean City, New Jersey, fishing and tying.

Bunny Bone • Jeffrey Cardenas

BUNNY BONE

A Jeffrey Cardenas design. Sample in photo was tied by Jeffrey Cardenas on a size 4 Partridge Sea Prince hook and measures horizontally 1-3/4" in length. Fly rides hook-point up.

Hook: Partridge Sea Prince; sizes 2, 4, 6

Thread: Black Monocord 3/0

Tail: Grizzly rabbit fur, then two long strands black Krystal Flash for antennae

Eyes: 1/50 oz. plated lead barbell

Body: Butt ends of rabbit, wrapped in a tightly pulled spiral of thread

Tying Notes: Tied in many versions with white, natural tan, and dyed rabbit fur.

Location Notes: The Florida Keys, the Bahamas, Christmas Island.

Fishing Notes: Cast close, read the fish, twitch strip as necessary ... and hang on.

Prey Notes: Suggests many members of the common shrimp (Penaeidae), snapping shrimp (Alpheidae), and grass shrimp (Palaemonidae) families.

Jeffrey Cardenas is owner of The Saltwater Angler in Key West. He guided for tarpon, permit, and bonefish in the southern Keys for many years and he was *Fly Rod & Reel's* 1989 Guide of the Year. He has also written for many fishing journals and recently completed his first book, *Marquesa: A Time and Place with Fish.*

Buster Crab • Will Myers

BUSTER CRAB

A Will Myers design. Sample in photo (colored to suggest the sargassum-swimming crab) was tied by Will Myers on a size 6 34007 hook and measures horizontally about 1-1/6" in length, and 1-13/16" tip-to-tip in width. When weighted, fly rides hook-point up.

Hook: 34007; sizes 4, 6, 8 for bonefish. Tiemco 800S; size 6 for permit

Thread: White Danville Plus 3/0

Weight Holder: rubber band

Mouth/Legs/Swimmerets: White Westrim craft fur

Eyes: 50-lb. mono with black epoxy coat

Weight: Various bead or lead eyes slipped under holder—or none

Color: Berol Artmaker or other marking pens

Carapace: Marine Goop

Body: Tie the mouth parts and swimmerets along the top of the shank; tie on the eyes; tie on fur for the legs and claws, crisscrossed on top of the shank; color. (Optional: For big crabs, tie on an egg-yarn ball for the carapace and trim to shape.) Apply Marine Goop to create (or coat) the carapace.

Tying Notes: Begin by tying on the rubber-band weight holder. Leave no thread wraps on the hook shank underneath, so that you can easily slip different weights in and out.

Location Notes: The fly has been fished successfully in Turneffe, southern Belize, and Yucatan.

Fishing Notes: This fly was designed to be adaptable to various "crab" situations. It can be tied in white, and colored or darkened on-site. You can also easily alter the weight, by changing the eyes, to adjust to different conditions. The wide profile of the legs and claws provides a nice cushion as the fly hits the water. For extremely shallow waters, craft fur also absorbs floatant.

Strip with fairly long (eighteen-inch), but slow, pulls, so as to crawl the fly across the bottom rather than hop it.

Prey Notes: With different coloration, Will's pattern suggests many crab species at different locations, among them: small sargassum crabs (Portunus sayi) at Turneffe Islands, when the sargassum weed washed in over reefs; also small blue crabs (Callinectes sapidus)—a favorite bonefish food—and many small species on the bonefish and permit flats of Mexico's Yucatan.

Anecdotes: Will says he came up with this pattern because he got tired of arriving somewhere only to find all his crab patterns were the wrong color or weight.

Will Myers, an architect who's lived in Austin, Texas, for the last twenty years, fishes for permit at least as much as for bonefish. He also stalks redfish and sea trout along the South Texas coast. Will has created some of today's most innovative patterns for flats species. When he's not fishing or tying, he devotes his energy to conservation of Texas grass flats and marsh habitat.

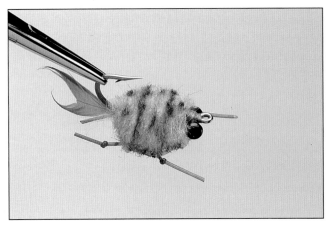

Camera's Crab • Phil Camera

CAMERA'S CRAB

A Phil Camera design. Sample in photo was tied by Phil Camera on a size 4 34007 hook and measures horizontally 1-3/8" in overall length. The carapace measures 11/16" in diameter. Fly rides hook-point up.

Hook: 34007; sizes 1, 2, 4

Thread: Larva Lace Translucent Fine

Claw: Ring-necked pheasant breast

Body: 100 percent pure wool, spun with dubbing loop

Eyes: Medium Brite Eyes

Legs: Larva Lace No. 12 with Krystal Flash inserted, then overhand-knotted

Weight: Hot glue cooled on a cold glass surface

Tying Notes: Apply hot glue lightly to the bottom of the fly with the nose of a glue gun; position the legs while the glue is still tacky; add more glue for weight and shape; then place the fly on flat, cool glass, and push on the metal eyes. Let them set and peel off.

Location Notes: Although the fly was originally tied for Ascencion Bay and Belize, its light-colored wool can be colored with markers to suggest crab species at any location.

Fishing Notes: The lead eyes sink the tail of the crab (at the hook eye), causing the carapace and claws to lift and the crab to ride straight on the bottom when stripped. Strip until the fish sees, let it drop, and watch the fish's movement to see a pick-up.

Prey Notes: Generic crab form; sand crab.

Phil Camera is author of *Fly Tying with Synthetics* and the developer of Larva Lace. He says he's a Rocky Mountain fly tier with his heart on the flats. He has fished North America, Central America, Japan, and Europe.

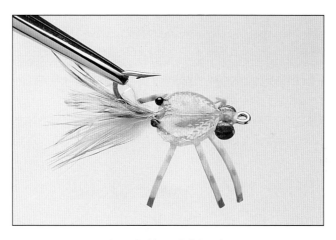

Capt. Crabby • Bob Veverka

CAPT. CRABBY

A Bob Veverka design. Sample in photo was tied by Bob Veverka on a size 2 34007 hook and measures 1-1/2" in width, claw tip to claw tip. Carapace is 1/2" in diameter. Fly rides hook-point up.

Hook: 34007; sizes 1/0, 1, 2, 4

Thread: Clear mono

Tail: Gray fox tail (or brown bucktail or tan calf tail); a few strands Flashabou; then four matching variant hackles curving outward

Body: Corsair tubing

Weight: Medium (1/8") lead barbell

Legs: Rubber bands, pulled through mesh

Eyes: Burnt mono inserted in mesh

Coating: Devcon 5-Minute Epoxy

Tying Notes: To form the carapace, puncture a two-inch length of Corsair tubing at its midpoint with the point of the hook, then push the tubing over the barb and onto the shank (the Corsair should now be pierced by and perpendicular to the shank); double the Corsair into a horseshoe shape (the bottom of the horseshoe at the hook bend; the open side of the horseshoe at the hook eye), pinching the Corsair's ends together at the hook eye; tie in the Corsair's ends behind the hook eye.

Location Notes: For bonefish, the Florida Keys, the Bahamas, Kanton Island; the fly is also fished in large sizes at all major permit locations.

Fishing Notes: Cast eight to ten feet in front of the fish. Start stripping as the fish approaches. When the fish sees it, stop, and let it sink. Watch for a take. If there's none, give the fly a short strip and watch again.

Prey Notes: Generic crab shape suggestive of many species of swimming crabs (Portunidae), mud crabs (Xanthidae), and spider crabs (Majidae).

Bob Veverka has been tying flies for both fresh- and saltwater species for twenty-five years. He is highly regarded for the extremely well-crafted Atlantic salmon patterns he ties for anglers headed for Canada, Iceland, Russia, and Norway. And his saltwater patterns are now also becoming equally well known. See also his very fetching Foxy Lady Crab pattern, page 80.

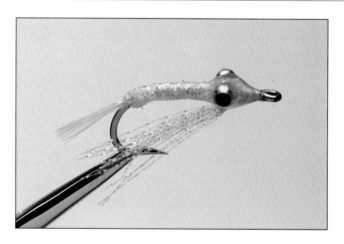

Christmas Island Flash Charlie • Ralph Woodbine

CHRISTMAS ISLAND FLASH CHARLIE

A Ralph Woodbine design. Sample in photo was tied by Ralph Woodbine on a size 6 34007 hook and measures horizontally 1-3/8" in length. Fly rides hook-point up.

Hook: 34007; sizes 2, 4, 6

Thread: White 6/0

Eyes: Medium (1/8") bead chain for size 4 or small (3/32") bead chain for size 6, painted black

Tail: Pearl Flashabou

Body: Pearl braid (on size 4) or pearl Krystal Flash (on size 6), tinted with appropriate marking pen. Coat body and eyes.

Wing: Krystal Flash, fourteen strands. Yellow and lime green are very effective. Pink, orange, and root beer are also good.

Head: Coat head with Devcon 5-Minute Epoxy

Tying Notes: Ralph ties the fly with lead barbell eyes for deep water.

Location Notes: Ralph says this is his best pattern for Christmas Island, and several other regulars have told me it's their best producer at that destination too.

Fishing Notes: Very durable. Ralph reports he has taken as many as twenty fish on a single fly. Strip until the fish sees, let it drop, and watch the fish's movement to see a pick-up.

Prey Notes: Generic shrimp suggestive of many smaller species such as Palaemonidae, Gnatophyllidae, and Hippolytidae.

Ralph Woodbine spent a month in Islamorada every year for fourteen years; he fishes Christmas Island regularly. He has also fished Ascencion Bay and, in the hands of his angling friends, his very effective flies have taken fish at just about all other locations as well. He lives in Kingston, Massachusetts.

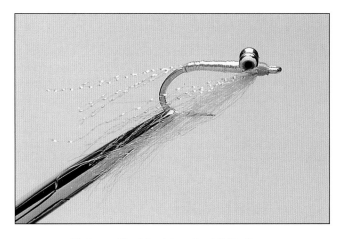

Christmas Island Special • Randall Kaufmann

CHRISTMAS ISLAND SPECIAL

A Randall Kaufmann design. Sample in photo was tied for Randall Kaufmann to his specifications by Umpqua Feather Merchants on a size 8 3407 hook and measures horizontally 1-1/4" in length. Fly rides hook-point up.

Hook: 3407; sizes 4, 6, 8

Thread: Fluorescent fire orange 6/0

Eyes: Gold-plated steel in mini for size 8, extra small for size 6, small for size 4; paint white, then fluorescent orange, then black, with epoxy over paint; Zap-A-Gap in place

Tail: Krystal Flash, No. 9 Pearl

Body: Same as tail, small diameter; apply thin coat of Zap-A-Gap

Underwing: Same as tail, sparse (trim Krystal Flash tail and underwing at angle)

Overwing: Tan craft fur, sparse (use underfur)

Tying Notes: Randall says the eyes on this pattern can be left unfinished, but he prefers to paint them. He ties the pattern in pearl, orange, yellow, and pink but all have a tan wing, which he feels is the best flats color: It is light enough to fish well on sand flats and dark enough to perform well over dark or mottled bottoms.

Location Notes: Christmas Island.

Fishing Notes: Designed for spooky, sophisticated fish on more heavily fished flats. Randall finds that the gold eyes give better visibility in deep water, and that the Krystal Flash eliminates color dilemmas. He often selects smaller sizes for large fish in thin water, or for tailing fish on hard bottoms. For fish tailing on soft bottoms, he believes larger sizes show up better in cloudy water and puff the bottom better, attracting fish with smoke signals.

Prey Notes: Depending on its color, the fly suggests many smaller shrimps such as juvenile common shrimps (Penaeidae) and snapping shrimps (Alpheidae), as well as diminutive species such as many members of the Palaemonidae, Gnatophyllidae, and Hippolytidae families.

Randall Kaufmann is founder and owner of Kaufmann's Streamborn, Inc., one of the most respected fly-fishing tackle shops in the country. He has also written several books, including *Tying Nymphs, Tying Dry Flies, Fly Patterns of Umpqua Feather Merchants,* and *Bonefishing with a Fly*. He has fished for bonefish just about everywhere they are found.

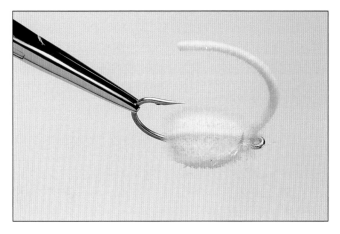

Clam Before The Storm • Craig Mathews

CLAM BEFORE THE STORM

A Craig Mathews design. Sample in photo was tied by Craig Mathews on a size 6 3407 hook and measures 1-3/4" in overall width. Fly rides hook-point down.

Hook: TMC 800S, Mustad 34007 or 3407; sizes 4, 6, 8

Thread: White Uni-Thread 6/0

Body: Keel-weight with nontoxic lead substitute fastened to bottom of hook. Tie on strip of Furry Foam in white, cream, tan, or light olive, to be pulled forward to form body

Foot/Siphon: Small vernille in worm pink or light brown, pulled over body, tied off at head, and trimmed so remaining tag end forms a foot/siphon one to one-and-one-half times body length

Location Notes: The fly has fished well on flats in Belize, Ascension Bay, and Abaco's Marls in the Bahamas.

Fishing Notes: No movement. The fly is best on mudding, tailing, or shallow *resting* fish, which are almost stationary or—as some guides refer to them—"sleeping."

Prey Notes: Mimics clams and snails on flats and in reefs; also Caribbean tellin (*Tellina caribaea*), Costate lucine (*Codakia costata*), and juvenile tiger lucines (*Codakia orbicularis*).

Anecdotes: The foot/siphon is left exaggerated in length, as this may trigger a take when "recognized" by bonefish.

Craig Mathews is founder and owner of Blue Ribbon Flies in West Yellowstone, Montana, and is regarded by many as one of the world's finest freshwater and saltwater fly-rod anglers. He is also, as his patterns show, one of the most creative fly tiers working the flats today.

Clouser Deep Minnow • Bob Clouser

CLOUSER DEEP MINNOW

Bob Clouser design. Sample in photo was tied by Bob Clouser on a size 4 34007 hook and measures horizontally 2-3/8" in length. Fly rides hook-point up.

Hook: Mustad 34007 or TMC 811S; sizes 2, 4, 6, 8

Thread: Danville Tan (No. 429) Monocord 3/0

Eyes: Metallic, sizes 4/32" or 5/32"; with acrylic lacquer, paint black pupils on red on the ends

Underwing: White calf tail or deer tail

Middle Wing: Four to six strands Krystal Flash

Overwing: Tan calf tail or deer tail

Tying Notes: The metallic eyes cause the fly to turn itself upside down so it rides with the hook point up. Bob says he ties with deer tail hair—preferably the less hollow fibers from the top two-thirds of the tail—when constructing larger sizes of Clouser Deep Minnows, say, in sizes 2 and 4. For smaller flies he substitutes calf tail, squirrel tail, or guard hairs from such animals as foxes (Arctic, gray, and red) and raccoons.

Smaller versions of the clouser Deep Minnow (sizes 4, 6, 8) can be tied Lefty Kreh style. Lefty ties the fly with all three layers of the wing on the inverted side of the hook, tying all the materials in front of the eyes.

Location Notes: This is one of very few flies known to fish well in all major destinations, including the Florida Keys, the Bahamas, Christmas Island, Los Roques, and Belize.

Fishing Notes: As a bonefish fly, Bob says the Clouser Deep Minnow excels on both shallow flats and deep edges around reefs. On bonefish it is especially effective in tan and white, chartreuse and white, and gray and white. He finds the best stripping action for bonefish is a few short strips followed by a pause. But leaving the fly lying on the bottom, and stripping as the fish come to it, can also be very effective. The fly fishes well for cruising, mudding, and (if you're careful) tailing fish. *Author's note: The fly is sometimes tied with 1/8" or 3/16" bead chain for shallow use, but many anglers feel the lead eyes work well even in skinny con-*

ditions because they kick up mud as they hit bottom after each strip, and thus look like diving shrimps.

Prey Notes: Bob says his fly represents the profile of many forms of baitfish and its forward eye position not only inverts the pattern, but gives it a darting motion usually associated with fleeing prey. In the bonefish's world, he says the tan-and-white Clouser is effective in locations where small crabs are available to bonefish. Short strips will portray the fleeing motion of the crab. *Author's note: The Clouser's highly suggestive design portrays a great variety of prey, including shrimps, juvenile fish, mantis species, crabs, and gobies, depending on its color and action.*

Anecdotes: Bob developed this fly for smallmouth bass on the Susquehanna River and it has since proven its fish-catching effectiveness worldwide. Lefty Kreh told Bob he's caught over sixty different species on the Clouser Deep Minnow using various size and color combinations.

Bob says he believes one reason this streamer fly works so well is that it has only one body. Most streamer designs have two—one on the shank and one formed by the wing. But the Clouser (like a few others: Zonkers, Soft Hackle Streamers, and Cardinelles) has only one. And—he says—most prey he has seen have only one body, too.

Bob Clouser lives in Middletown, Pennsylvania, where he owns and operates Clouser's Fly Shop and guides on the Susquehanna River. He is an outdoor writer, a photographer, and a teacher of fly-tying, casting, and fishing techniques; he also gives seminars and slide shows.

Crapoxy • Ron Leyzen

CRAPOXY

A Ron Leyzen design. Sample in photo was tied by Ron Leyzen on a size 4 3407 hook and measures horizontally 1-1/4" in length. Carapace is 1/2" in diameter.

Hook: 34007, 3407 Partridge Sea Prince, TMC 811S; sizes 2, 4, 6

Thread: Tan 6/0

Tail: Tan over brown marabou

Claws: Tan/olive hackle points

Underbody/Frame: Cream heavyweight paper

Eyes: Soft lead split shot, pinched onto underbody

Legs: Rubber legs

Outer Coating: 5-Minute or 20-Minute Epoxy mixed with ground chalk

Tying Notes: After tying in the tail and then the claws, invert the hook and glue a disk of manila-folder-type paper (with two eyes crimped onto the edge) to the top of the shank with Super Glue (cyanoacrylate). Coat the top with epoxy mixed with ground tan blackboard chalk and sparkle. Invert the hook and coat the underside of the body with clear epoxy, setting the legs in place before the epoxy hardens. Add color or mottling with felt pens, if desired, and apply a final coat of epoxy to the entire body.

Location Notes: Ambergris Caye and Placencia, Belize.

Fishing Notes: Good for cruising fish. Use smooth strips with pauses to let the fly go to the bottom. Watch the fish's movement to see a pick-up.

Prey Notes: Suggestive of many species of swimming crabs (Portunidae), mud crabs (Xanthidae), and spider crabs (Majidae). The color can be altered to suggest local species.

Ron Leyzen teaches graphic arts in Belgium and paints fishing and nature scenes in his spare time. He fishes throughout Europe for all species and has fished for bonefish in Belize, Mexico, and the Keys. He has given fly-tying demonstrations at both U.S. and European shows.

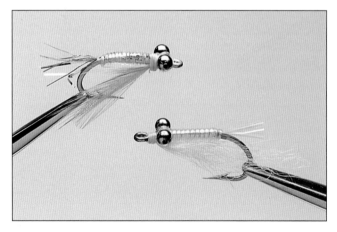

Crazy and Nasty Charlies (Nasty on left) • Bob Nauheim

CRAZY (OR NASTY) CHARLIE

> *A Bob Nauheim design. Sample in photo (the original "Nasty" version) was tied by Bob Nauheim on a size 4 34007 hook and measures horizontally about 1-3/8" in length. Fly rides hook-point up.*

Hook: 34007 or 3407; sizes 1, 2, 4, 6, 8

Thread: White Monocord 3/0, or color to match body

Eyes: 1/8" silver bead chain

Tail: Ten or twelve strands silver tinsel

Body: 15-lb. Mason or other clear mono over flat silver tinsel (underbody later changed by Bob to silver or pearl Flashabou)

Wing: Two long white saddle hackles, convex sides facing to splay tips

Tying Notes: Vary the thread color to complement or contrast with the body and/or wing. Vary the eye size and weight to alter the sink rate. The "Crazy" style of this fly, a later version popularized across the flats of the world by the Orvis Company, typically uses Flashabou for the tail, clear V-Rib or similar material over Flashabou in the body, and calf tail instead of hackle for the wing.

Location Notes: White and tan versions work everywhere. A few of the hundreds of others: chartreuse in Belize and Yucatan, apricot (see Apricot Charlie, page 22) and root beer (see Manjack Cay Charlie, page 117) in the Bahamas. This pattern has evolved with epoxy and glue-gun versions, soft body versions, and many, many, many others.

Fishing Notes: Strip the fly once or twice until the fish sees, let it drop, and watch the fish's movement to see a pick-up.

Prey Notes: Originally tied in white to suggest glass minnows, *Jenkinsia lamprotaenia*, *Anchoa mitchelli*, or *A. cayorum* at Andros. Now, however, in all its variations of color and material, the Charlie is an effective emulator of just about every species of shrimp and even some smaller crabs.

Anecdotes: By adopting the steelheaders' bead-chain weighting technique to both sink and jig the fly, this fly became the father of modern bonefish pattern design.

Bob Nauheim, owner of Fishing International (a northern California fishing travel firm), is a well-traveled and highly experienced angler who has spent much of his life pursuing fresh- and saltwater quarry. He has been instrumental in opening some of the newest and most remote bonefishing destinations.

DAVE'S (WHITLOCK) SHRIMP

A Dave Whitlock design. Sample in photo was tied by Dave Whitlock on a size 4 34011 hook and measures horizontally 3-1/4" in overall length; rubber antennae are 1-1/2" in length. Fly rides hook-point down.

Hook: 34011; sizes 2, 4, 6, 8

Thread: Tan single-strand nylon floss

Snag Guard: Clear Mason hard nylon

Nose: Squirrel body hair

Antennae: Silicon rubber strands and Krystal Flash

Back: Clear poly bag strip

Rib: Brass wire

Eyes: Black Mason nylon monofilament

Body and Tail: Rabbit hair and Antron, fifty/fifty tan-and-gold blend

Legs: Cree neck hackle

Cement: Dave's Flexament and Zap-A-Gap

Tying Notes: Dave says he ties this one in clear, gray, white, tan, gold, and olive.

Location Notes: The Florida Keys, Belize, the Bahamas, Christmas Island, Yucatan, Los Roques.

Fishing Notes: Dave retrieves this pattern to swim it erratically, or he lets it drop and crawls it off the bottom. Both methods work for tailing or cruising bonefish. He also says he's found that—with its snag guard—the Dave's Shrimp goes over most flats bottoms without picking up grass or hanging up on bottom structure.

Prey Notes: Suggests many shrimps, including members of the common shrimp (Penaeidae), snapping shrimp (Alpheidae), grass shrimp (Palaemonidae), and mantis shrimp (Squillidae) families.

Anecdotes: Dave designed this workhorse classic in 1970 for fishing the Gulf Coast of Texas and the Florida Keys, as a basic imitation of the shrimps that redfish, sea trout, tarpon, ladyfish, snappers, and bonefish eat. It has worked well on all of them.

A pioneering investigator of freshwater gamefish prey, and an innovative developer of fly patterns to suggest them, **Dave Whitlock** is one of the best known fly fishermen and fly-pattern creators in the world. These days he's as likely to be found on the sand flats as in his favorite trout and bass haunts. He is author (and illustrator) of *Dave Whitlock's Guide to Aquatic Trout Foods*, the *L.L. Bean Fly-Fishing Handbook*, and the *L.L. Bean Fly Fishing for Bass Handbook*.

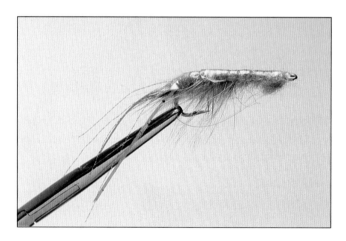

Dave's (Whitlock) Shrimp • Dave Whitlock

Deep Flea • Rick Ruoff

DEEP FLEA

A Rick Ruoff design. Sample in photo was tied by Rick Ruoff on a size 4 34007 hook and measures vertically 2" in height. Fly rides hook-point up.

Hook: 34007; size 4

Thread: White Monocord 3/0

Body: Tan Orvis leech yarn

Hackle: Two cree hackles, concave sides facing (not splayed), tied 90° to hook; then white calf tail; then white Krystal Flash

Eyes/Weight: Medium (1/8") chrome-plated lead barbell, figure-eighted to top of shank so fly inverts

Weed/Coral Guard: V-shaped 20-lb. Ande mono, with slight backward crimp on each fork near tip

Tying Notes: The fly is also tied in all-white, white with pink hackle, and white with chartreuse hackle versions.

Location Notes: Rick says he goes to this fly when fish are deep-swimming or mudding. While very effective in the Keys, he has used it everywhere.

Fishing Notes: Rick designed this fly to sink well, so it is excellent on moving, mudding fish. He also finds it very good on oceanside flats over mixed, sand-and-grass bottoms.

Prey Notes: The upright hackles imitate small sandworms, such as members of Opisthoricus family, and tube worms.

Anecdotes: Rick says he needed a simple-to-tie fly that was effective, quick sinking, and weedless. The Deep Flea is part of the series he calls the Fleas (see also the Absolute Flea).

Rick Ruoff, see ABSOLUTE FLEA, page 19.

Deepwater Bonefish Fly • Andy Burk

DEEPWATER BONEFISH FLY

An Andy Burk design. Sample in photo was tied by Andy Burk on a size 2 34007 hook and measures horizontally 1-1/2" in overall length. Fly rides hook-point up.

Hook: TMC 811S or 34007; sizes 1, 2

Thread: Orange Monocord 3/0

Eyes: Medium lead or nontoxic, painted yellow with black pupils

Tail: Bright orange marabou

Body: Root beer Krystal Flash, then brown Ultra Lace or Larva Lace

Wing: Underwing of natural tan bucktail or calf tail; then brown marabou over orange marabou; then four strands orange Krystal Flash. Finish by flanking with broad cree hackle tip on each side

Location Notes: Los Roques, the Bahamas.

Fishing Notes: Also called the "Deep H_2O," this fly was created in 1989 to fish the blue edges of flats where big bonefish often prowl. The lead eyes sink it fast and its bright, crustaceanlike colors attract readily in the low light of murky depths. Andy fishes it deep with a fairly constant short strip.

Prey Notes: Translucent yellow-gold shrimp species.

Anecdotes: The fly was designed at Los Roques for times when fish were picky, and became a solid producer when nothing else worked.

Andy Burk works at The Fly Shop in Redding, California, where—among other things—he's responsible for tying materials.

Deer Hair Critter • Tim Borski

DEER HAIR CRITTER

A Tim Borski design. Sample in photo was tied by Tim Borski on a size 2 34007 hook and measures horizontally 1-1/2" in overall length, and 1-1/2" across leg tips. Fly rides hook-point up.

Hook: 34007 or equivalent; size 2

Thread: White Monocord 3/0

Eyes: Burnt mono

Butt: Orange Crystal Chenille

Body: White spun deer hair, colored on top with permanent marker

Legs: Rubber legs, barred with marker

Weight: Mini or extra small lead eyes

Location Notes: The Florida Keys.

Fishing Notes: Tim likes to throw this fly at the last tails of the day or the first light of the morning. It lands relatively softly, animates well, and is large enough for fish to find even in low-light periods.

Prey Notes: Crab pattern suggestive of many species of swimming crabs (Portunidae) and spider crabs (Majidae).

Tim Borski, see BRISTLE WORM, page 50.

Del Brown Bonefish Fly • Del Brown

DEL BROWN BONEFISH FLY

A Del Brown design. Sample in photo was tied by Del Brown on a size 2 34007 hook and measures horizontally 1-13/16" in overall length. Carapace is 5/8" in diameter. Fly rides hook-point up.

Hook: 34007; size 2 (or size 1/0 for permit)

Thread: Chartreuse Danville Flat Waxed Nylon

Eyes: Medium chrome-plated lead

Hackle/Feelers/Claws: Five or six strands pearlescent Flashabou, body length; then three natural variant or cree neck hackles on each side of bend, splayed apart, one-and-one-half times body length

Body: Alternating strands tan and brown Sport yarn, Aunt Lydia's Rug Yarn, or other small-diameter yarn, figure-eighted tightly onto shank

Legs: Three or four strands white rubber hackle (samples Del sent had three sets of legs on the smaller size 4 version), square-knotted to shank between yarn strands; tip ends with marker

Tying Notes: Del says he uses a mono weed guard for this bonefish version of his well-known permit fly, and also uses lighter-colored yarn for light bottoms.

Location Notes: The Florida Keys, Andros, Deep Water Cay, and Honduras' Guanaja Bay Islands.

Fishing Notes: Retrieve the fly until the fish sees it and then let it dive for the bottom. Tie the fly on with a loop so it will hinge easily and dive fast.

Prey Notes: Diving action suggestive primarily of swimming crab species (Portunidae) and some spider crabs (Majidae); the design of the fly stands it on a weighted end with claws up, facing the attacker.

Anecdotes: "I caught so many bonefish on the permit size," says Brown, "that I decided to make a smaller one."

Del Brown started fishing in the San Francisco Bay area and High Sierras; he has fished the flats about fifteen years and is a highly regarded flats angler.

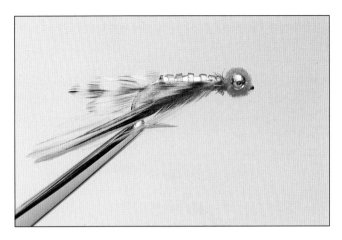

Dr. Taylor Special • Phil Taylor

DR. TAYLOR SPECIAL

A Phil Taylor design. Sample in photo was tied by Phil Taylor on a size 4 34007 hook and measures horizontally 1-15/16" in length. Fly rides hook-point up.

Hook: 34007; sizes 2, 4, 6

Thread: Orange Monocord 3/0

Eyes: Medium (1/8") bead chain or lead barbell

Wing/Tail: Pair of grizzly saddle hackles over pair of light badger saddle hackles, concave sides facing

Body: Fluorescent orange Larva lace or V-Rib, closely spiraled over flat silver Mylar tinsel

Head: Fluorescent chenille, figure-eighted around eyes

Tying Notes: Phil keeps the turns of the rib close to minimize flash from the underbody.

Location Notes: Andros, Abaco, North Eleuthera.

Fishing Notes: Especially good for deeper water and for low-light (cloudy, choppy, or muddy) conditions. Alter the eye type and size for the desired sink rate. Steady-strip until the fish sees, pause, and watch the fish's movement for a strike.

Prey Notes: Generic shrimp suggestive of many species, but the color may specifically suggest the red snapping shrimp (*Alpheus armatus*).

Anecdotes: Phil tied this fly as an attempt to marry the very effective Mini-Puff design with Joe Cleare's (of Harbour Island) great passion for saddle hackle flies for bonefish. Phil says he's still trying to run down a slow, local Dunmore Town rooster to find out if local feathers would make an even better fly! *Author's note: The venerable Mini-Puff (tied on a bare shank with a bucktail reverse wing, and a pink, orange, yellow, or tan chenille head over bead-chain* *eyes) was a very popular pattern throughout the Bahamas and I fished it many years, but Phil's Dr. Taylor Special is a far more productive pattern.*

Phil Taylor is a retired general surgeon from Columbus, Ohio. He came up with this pattern seven or eight years ago while fishing with Joe Cleare. It has since accounted for several hundred fish taken in the outer Bahamas at the hands of both Phil and several of his angling friends.

Ed's Greenie Grass Shrimp • Ed Opler

ED'S GREENIE GRASS SHRIMP

An Ed Opler design. Sample in photo was tied by Ed Opler on a size 4 34007 hook and measures horizontally 2-1/4" in length. Fly rides hook-point up.

Hook: 34007 or 3407; sizes 4, 6

Thread: Olive green Uni-Thread 6/0

Antennae: Four to six hairs gray squirrel tail mixed with ten to twelve strands green Krystal Flash

Eyes: 5/32" black plastic

Outer Body: Green and black variegated chenille overwrapped with clear V-Rib

Swimmerets/Tail: Four to six red fox squirrel tail hairs

Tail: Six to eight strands green Krystal Flash

Tying Notes: To vary the fly, you can use pearl plastic eye, and can substitute moose mane for gray squirrel tail.

Location Notes: The fly was originally tied for the super spooky bonefish that inhabit the turtle grass flats at Little Cayman Island.

Fishing Notes: Ed says this fly works very well in shallow water, or depths to three feet over grass, but fish won't give it a second look over sand or coral. He's also found it a good choice for tailing fish (over grass).

Prey Notes: Probably suggests local varieties of red snapping shrimps (*Alpheus armatus*) or common snapping shrimps *(A. heterochaelis). Author's note: Also perhaps members of the grass shrimp (Palaemonidae) family.*

Anecdotes: Ed says he tied this pattern in desperation before a trip to the Caymans, after a phone conversation with a fellow he knew who had guided there. He just used what materials were sitting on his bench, and it worked, so he left it as is. The name, he says—in spite of his earlier military experience—was never intended to mean anything negative … it's just what the fly looked like.

Ed Opler, who is president of World's Finest Chocolate in Chicago and a partner in Jack Dennis Sports in Jackson, Wyoming, is an avid saltwater and freshwater angler and has fly fished since he was seven years old. A resident of Wyoming, he has fished on Team USA 1989, 1991, 1992, and 1994. He's a former marine corps artillery officer and a graduate of Middlebury College.

Ed's Sassy Shrimp • Ed Opler

ED'S SASSY SHRIMP

An Ed Opler design. Sample in photo was tied by Ed Opler on a size 4 34007 hook and measures horizontally 1-7/8" in length. Fly rides hook-point up.

Hook: 34007 or 3407; sizes 2, 4, 6

Thread: Fluorescent orange single-strand floss

Underbody: Fluorescent orange single-strand floss

Antennae: Ten to twelve strands orange Krystal Flash over five to six red fox squirrel tail hairs

Eyes: Medium (1/8") gold bead chain

Outer Body: Three to four strands orange Krystal Flash, then clear V-Rib

Swimmerets: Four to six red fox squirrel tail hairs

Tail: Six to eight strands orange Krystal Flash

Tying Notes: After the floss underbody, attach the antennae and eyes at a 45° angle along the bend; taper the body with floss, rib with Krystal Flash, and overwrap with V-Rib; tie in the swimmerets and tail, then trim them to natural shape.

Location Notes: The Bahamas, Yucatan, and Belize. The fly was originally tied to imitate a tidal creek shrimp found at Andros Island when the McVay Gotcha failed in that location.

Fishing Notes: Ed says he's fished the fly in depths from six inches to four feet. He retrieves it in three short, quick strips, then stops to let it settle. He waits a second or two and repeats this pattern over and over. He's used the fly successfully for both tailing and cruising fish. For very shallow water he ties a version with plastic eyes (pearl or black). Also, he says, when pink seems to be the color of the moment you can tie one with fluorescent pink floss, silver eyes, gray squirrel hairs, and pink Krystal Flash.

Prey Notes: Probably suggests local varieties of red snapping shrimps (*Alpheus armatus*) or common snapping shrimps (*A. heterochaelis*).

Anecdotes: Ed says that besides attracting bonefish, the fly can attract permit: Three of four permit he's caught have attacked it like "heat-seeking missiles." Two were in the Yucatan, and one in Bimini. If you are specifically fishing for permit, he recommends orange on a size 2 3407 hook.

Ed Opler, see ED'S GREENIE GRASS SHRIMP, page 70.

Epoxy Shrimp • Tim Borski

EPOXY SHRIMP

A Tim Borski design. Sample in photo was tied by Tim Borski on a size 4 34007 hook and measures horizontally 2-1/16" in overall length. Fly rides hook-point down.

Hook: 34007 or equivalent; sizes 2, 4

Thread: White or tan Monocord 3/0

Tail: Tan craft fur

Eyes: Burnt mono

Body Hackle: Long soft brown hackle, palmered forward

Back: Craft fur, pulled forward over hackle and secured at head

Head: 5-Minute Epoxy over gold Mylar overwrap

Weed Guard: Mason mono

Location Notes: The Florida Keys.

Fishing Notes: This is a tailing fly. Tim says the shallower the water, the slower you want to start this fly. Then, if you get some interest, pick up the pace for a strip or two, drop it, and watch for a pick-up.

Prey Notes: Suggestive shrimp or crab pattern.

Tim Borski, see BRISTLE WORM, page 50.

Eric's Epoxy Crab • Eric Peterson

ERIC'S EPOXY CRAB

An Eric Peterson design. Sample in photo was tied by Eric Peterson on a size 4 34007 hook and measures horizontally 2-1/4" in length, including antennae. Fly rides hook-point down.

Hook: 34007; sizes 2, 4, 6

Thread: White Monocord 3/0

Eyes/Underbody: Burnt mono eyes, or beads on mono, figure-eighted; two flat strips lead lashed to front one-third underside of hook; then wrap pearlescent Mylar, then fine copper wire or 1-lb. or 2-lb. mono drawn tight, around perimeter to form diamond outline

Body: Modge Podge base, hand formed, left to harden, then coated with Devcon 2-Ton Epoxy; add 20-lb. mono weed/coral guards as it dries

Antennae: Two strands of black Krystal Flash two-and-one-half times shank length, or two times marabou length

Mouth/Claws/Walking Legs: Pearl Krystal Flash, then beige marabou, then cree saddle tips splayed at base (above barb)

Tying Notes: The body is formed by framing around the eyes with fine copper wire, or with 1-lb. or 2-lb. mono; fill the frame with Modge Podge and, when dry, coat the underside with Devcon 2-Ton Epoxy and let it dry. Soften the mono weed guards by heating and press them onto the as-yet-non-epoxied top side so they stick. Coat the top with epoxy and let it dry.

Location Notes: The Florida Keys, the Bahamas, Belize, Yucatan, and Christmas Island.

Fishing Notes: Good tailing or cruising pattern. Let it drop, strip once or twice until the fish sees, let it drop, and watch the fish's movement to see a pick-up.

Prey Notes: Generic crab suggestive of many species of swimming crabs (Portunidae) and spider crabs (Majidae). It may also suggest some common shrimps (Penaeidae) and mantis shrimps (Squillidae).

Eric Peterson is owner of The Fairfield Fly Shop in Connecticut. He has been a tier for twenty-five years and fishes salt water wherever and whenever he can.

Eric's Standing Shrimp • Eric Peterson

ERIC'S STANDING SHRIMP

An Eric Peterson design. Sample in photo was tied by Eric Peterson on a size 2 34007 hook and measures horizontally 2-7/8" in length, including antennae. Fly rides hook-point down.

Hook: 34007; sizes 2, 4, 6

Thread: Rust Monocord 3/0

Mouth/Claws/Walking Legs: Pearl Krystal Flash, then brown marabou, then cree saddle hackle wound two to three turns at base (above barb)

Antennae: Two strands of black Krystal Flash two-and-one-half times shank length, or two times marabou length

Eyes: Small (1/8") black plastic beads

Weed/Coral Guard: 20 lb. mono V figure-eighted to shank behind eyes

Weight: 1/8" lead barbell

Tail: Fine brown bucktail, laid in over back, tips extending 1/2" over eyes, butts tied and flared over barbell

Body/Feelers: Brown or gold tan Antron-type dubbing, then three or four strands orange Krystal flash extending to two-thirds length of antennae

Carapace/Back: Single strand of clear Larva Lace laid across back, extending 3/8" over eyes, and ribbed with tying thread

Tying Notes: The weed guard is cut extra long to stand the upper body at an upright angle when stopped.

Location Notes: The Florida Keys, the Bahamas, Belize, Yucatan, and Christmas Island.

Fishing Notes: Eric fishes this pattern on a loop. Strip it economically until the fish sees it, let it drop so it stands on its tail, and watch the fish's movement to see the pick-up.

Prey Notes: Generic shrimp suggestive of common shrimps (Penaeidae), snapping shrimps (Alpheidae), grass shrimps (Palaemonidae), and mantis shrimps (Squillidae).

Eric Peterson, see ERIC'S EPOXY CRAB, page 73.

Ference's Goby • Tom Ference

FERENCE'S GOBY

A Tom Ference design. Sample in photo was tied by Tom Ference on a size 2 34011 hook and measures horizontally 2-3/8" in length. At the shoulder fly measures 7/16" in width. Weighted fly rides hook-point up; unweighted, hook-point down.

Hook: 34011; size 2

Thread: Monocord 3/0, tan, olive, or brown color (to match body)

Eyes: 3/16" diameter stemmed glass eyes

Tail: Hen hackle or chamois

Weight: 1/36 oz. lead barbell under throat to invert fly; may tie without weight for hook-point-down, mid-water-column version

Body: Plushille, wrapped forward (as you would chenille) around shank and eyes; brush out with piece of Velcro; trim to shape (notch back to suggest double-dorsal look); color as naturals with markers

Tying Notes: Roman Moser's Plushille comes flat but is twisted at its string-like core into a very deep fibered, chenille-like material. (See the photo showing some of Moser's shrimp and crab patterns, and a description of Plushille, in chapter 6.)

Location Notes: The Bahamas, Mexico.

Fishing Notes: Tom fishes this fly for cruising or mudding fish (it's heavy for tailers). He lets it sink and rest on the bottom, then moves it in fast strips (naturals move in spurts) when bonefish are within sighting range. For mudding fish, get it deep, with a slower stripping motion. Tom says he prefers the up-riding version because this fly is always near the bottom.

Prey Notes: Suggests many species of gobies and toadfish (Gobidae and Batrachoididae) found throughout shallow tropical waters; this pattern can be shaped and colored to approximate just about any of them.

Tom Ferrence is the Owner and president of International Angler in Pittsburgh, Pennsylvania. He has fished most bonefish destinations around the world and has been creating fly patterns for over twenty-five years.

Flats Fodder • Bill Hunter

FLATS FODDER

A Bill Hunter design. Sample in photo was tied by Bill Hunter on a size 4 34007 hook and measures horizontally 1-1/8" in length. Fly rides hook-point up.

Hook: 34007; sizes 2, 4, 6

Thread: Brown 6/0

Eyes: Medium (1/8") bead chain

Tail: Olive Krystal Flash

Body: Olive and yellow Ultra Chenille

Wing/Legs: Yellow, then olive, calf tail; then three or four sprigs olive Krystal Flash

Tying Notes: The tail, eyes, and wing/legs are tied on top in one pass; then the body material is tied in, wrapped forward, and figure-eighted over the eyes; the wing/legs are then divided, folded back under the body, and secured with thread while also forming the head.

Location Notes: The Florida Keys, Andros, Deep Water Cay, Andros, Christmas Island, Kanton Island, Ambergris Caye.

Fishing Notes: Bill alters the eye type for the desired sink rate: unweighted for sizes 4 to 10; bead chain for sizes 2 to 6; and lead barbell for sizes 1 to 6.

For his retrieve pattern, Bill says he likes to pop the fly two to four hops away from the fish; then he hesitates for a count of six and (assuming the fish is now watching) gives the fly a couple more hops, watching for a pick-up.

Prey Notes: Generic pattern suggesting small shrimp species (such as Palaemonidae, Gnatophyllidae, and Hippolytidae), small crabs, and possibly errant seaworms (Polychaetes).

Anecdotes: Bill ties this simple, versatile pattern in three different styles and many colors to match the prey and flats he encounters at different destinations, and to fit local angling conditions. Shown is a striped "soft" olive Fodder with an olive/yellow body—a style he also ties in brown/tan, fluorescent orange/peach, and so on. He ties the "soft" in single-color versions, too. Thirdly, he constructs the Flats Fodder in a "hard" style, distinguished by a firm body of clear V-Rib over Krystal Flash.

Bill Hunter, see APRICOT CHARLIE, page 22.

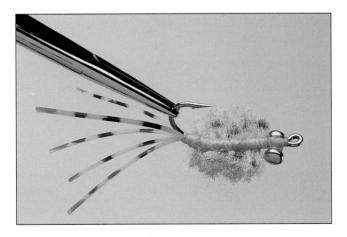

Fleeing Crab • Lenny Moffo

FLEEING CRAB

A Lenny Moffo design. Sample in photo was tied by Lenny Moffo on a size 4 34007 hook and measures horizontally about 1-7/8" in length. Fly rides hook-

point up.

Hook: 34007 or 3407; sizes 2, 4, 6, 8

Thread: Danville Flat Waxed Nylon 3/0, fluorescent pink (also chartreuse, tan, brown, or gray)

Legs: Sili Legs or other "rubber hackle," barred with brown and orange permanent markers

Body: Aunt Lydia's Craft & Rug Yarn, tan (or white, brown, or gray)

Weight: Lead barbell or bead chain, sized for sink rate and turnover (5/32" lead barbell in sample in photo)

Tying Notes: Figure-eight the yarn strips and eyes; Super Glue the joints; wrap the shank liberally with Flat Waxed Nylon thread.

Location Notes: Lenny fishes this pattern in the Keys in sizes 2 and 4, and in the Bahamas in sizes 4 and 6. He has taken fish with it at most other locations. It is also a good permit fly and, therefore, does double duty on mixed-species flats.

Fishing Notes: Alter the eye type for the desired sink rate. Strip until the fish sees, let it drop, and watch the fish's movement to see a pick-up.

Prey Notes: Generic swimming crab suggestive of many species of swimming and spider crabs (Portunidae and Majidae families). It mimics the profile of an escaping crab with swimming legs "propelling" from behind. Choose colors to complement flats tones or to match local species.

Anecdotes: In the old days when everybody fished the Keys with either a permit fly or a bonefish fly, this pattern was unusual because it would entice either species.

Lenny Moffo is a full-time guide, splitting his time between the flats near Big Pine Key in Florida and the rivers near Pray, Montana. He has been fishing and tying for twenty-five years.

Flint's Rubber Ducky • Dave Flint

FLINT'S RUBBER DUCKY

A Dave Flint design. Sample in photo was tied by Dave Flint on a size 4 34007 hook and measures horizontally 2" in length. Fly rides hook-point up.

Hook: 34007; sizes 2, 4, 6

Thread: Olive Flat-Waxed Nylon 3/0

Eyes: Medium (1/8") silver bead chain, or vary for desired sink rate

Underbody: Olive Flat Waxed Nylon 3/0

Tail: Brown or tan mottled marabou over feathers or fluff from tan or brown grizzly

Body: 1/4" wide strip of white latex, tapered to a point on tie-in end (cut from tourniquet or drug store "surgical" gloves); overlap when winding to form ridgelike ribs, and figure-eight over eyes

Tying Notes: Stretch the latex as you wind for the desired thickness and show-through.

Location Notes: Abaco, the Berry Islands, North Eleuthera.

Fishing Notes: Its non-reflective body makes this a good fly for bright, spooky conditions. With small bead-chain eyes or none, it's a good tailing fly; weight it heavier for mudding or cruising fish. Strip it until the fish sees it, stop it, and watch the fish for a pick-up.

Prey Notes: Generic small shrimp pattern suggestive of many species of Palaemonidae, Gnatophyllidae, and Hippolytidae. Vary the color of the tail and underbody to suggest local species.

Dave Flint, a commercial tier who lives in Spencer, Massachusetts, supplies fly shops and individual anglers with custom flies for salt water north and south.

Flutterbug • Jack Gartside

FLUTTERBUG

A Jack Gartside design. Sample in photo was tied by Jack Gartside on a size 6 34007 hook and measures horizontally 1-1/2" in length. Flared carapace measures

1-3/4" across its widest point. Weighted version rides hook-point up.

Hook: 34007; sizes 2, 4, 6

Thread: Tan or white 6/0

Tail: Orange, tan, or pearl Krystal Flash

Body: Same as tail

Wing: Tan or cream raccoon tail fur, splayed, and divided by wraps of Krystal Flash

Overwing: Short strands of Krystal Flash

Eyes: Bead chain, or none

Tying Notes: Splay and divide the wing with figure-eight wraps of Krystal Flash.

Location Notes: The Florida Keys, Andros, Yucatan.

Fishing Notes: Jack uses this fly as a shallow-water (under one foot deep) pattern when he wants a slow-sinking, fluttering descent. He fishes it fairly slow, crawling it across the bottom. He says it also fishes well in shallows if you tie it with no eyes so it lands very gently on the surface.

Prey Notes: The fly is tied flat to suggest the outline of a crab and portrays both swimming crabs (Portunidae) and spider crabs (Majidae).

Anecdotes: The design originated in Andros for use in the Fresh Creek area near Andros Town. Jack says he has since fished it successfully in many other areas and it's become one of his favorite flats patterns. *Author's note: It has also done well in Abaco and the Berrys.*

Jack Gartside, see BONEFISH EXPLORER, page 38.

Foxy Lady Crab • Bob Veverka

FOXY LADY CRAB

A Bob Veverka design. Sample in photo was tied by Bob Veverka on a size 4 34007 hook and, when flat, measures 1-3/8" in width, claw tip to claw tip; 2-1/8" in length. Fly rides hook-point up.

Hook: 34007; sizes 2, 4, 6

Thread: Clear mono

Tail: Krystal Flash, then brown bucktail, then orange wool butt (optional), then four matching variant hackles curving outward

Body: Opal Essence braid or pearlescent Mylar tubing

Legs: Rubber bands. Pinch into V and bind the point onto shank over body; spot with brown marker, tip with red

Wing/Carapace: Gray fox tail (brown hair from undertail), then shorter fox fur (brown fur from flanks), then Dazzle Link fur

Eyes/Weight: Medium (1/8") lead barbell with stick-on eyes

Body/Eye Coating: Devcon 5-Minute Epoxy

Location Notes: The Bahamas, the Keys.

Fishing Notes: Cast toward the fish, let it sink, then make slight strips as the fish approach. When the fish see it, stop, let it sink, and watch for a take. If there are no takers, give it a short strip and watch again.

Prey Notes: Generic crab shape suggestive of many species of swimming crabs (Portunidae), mud crabs (Xanthidae), and spider crabs (Majidae).

Bob Veverka, see CAPT. CRABBY, page 55.

Fur Charles • Will Myers

FUR CHARLES

A Will Myers design. Sample in photo was tied by Will Myers on a size 6 34007 hook and measures horizontally about 1-13/16" in length. Fly rides hook-point up.

Hook: 34007; sizes 6, 8

Thread: White Danville Plus

Weight Holder: Rubber band

Tail: White Westrim craft fur (brown for dark version)

Wing: White Westrim craft fur (brown for dark version); three or four sprigs Krystal Flash

Head Glue: Slo Zap C

Eyes/Weight: Various bead-chain or lead eyes slipped under holder—or none

Color: Berol Artmaker or other marking pens

Tying Notes: Tie on the rubber-band weight holder first, leaving no thread wraps on the hook shank underneath so you can easily slip different weights in and out.

Location Notes: You can color and weight for any destination.

Fishing Notes: The weight can be easily altered for different conditions. Strip until the fish sees, let it drop and watch the fish's movement to see a pick-up.

Prey Notes: The fly is designed to suggest many different shrimp species. By varying the color and size, you can suggest most members of the common shrimp (Penaeidae), snapping shrimp (Alpheidae), grass shrimp (Palaemonidae), and mantis shrimp (Squillidae) families.

Anecdotes: Will says he came up with this pattern because he got tired of arriving somewhere only to find all his shrimp patterns were the wrong color or weight. See also his variable weight/color crab pattern, the Buster Crab.

Will Myers, see BUSTER CRAB, page 53.

Fuzzy Hand • Allan Finkelman design based on A. J. Hand fly

FUZZY HAND

An Allan Finkelman design based on an A. J. Hand pattern. Sample in photo was tied by Allan Finkelman on a size 1/0 Eagle Claw 254 SS hook and measures horizontally 2-1/4" in length. Fly rides hook-point up.

Hook: Eagle Claw 254 SS; sizes 1/0, 1, 2, 4, 6

Thread: Yellow Flat Waxed Nylon

Eyes: 1/36 oz. lead barbells

Tail: Yellow marabou, flanked by pair of facing splayed cree neck hackle tips

Body: Tan medium chenille

Weed Guard: 15-lb. mono, V-style

Tying Notes: Sometimes Allan weights the fly with lead strips on the shank—as in his other listed pattern, Ben's Copper (page 27). He also ties it in tan/pink and tan/cree versions.

Location Notes: Florida, the Bahamas, Belize. Allan says it has worked everywhere he has fished it.

Fishing Notes: With light weight, this is a good tailing fly; weight heavier for mudding or cruising. Strip until the fish sees, stop, and watch for the fish to pick up.

Prey Notes: Generic crab suggestive of many species of swimming crabs (Portunidae), mud crabs (Xanthidae), and spider crabs (Majidae). It may also suggest the large claw profile of some mantis shrimps (Squillidae).

Anecdotes: This fly was adapted from A. J. Hand's Acrylic Flats Fly but eliminates all shiny elements to achieve a "fuzzy" look.

Allan Finkelman, see BEN'S COPPER, page 27.

Glass-Eyed Shrimp • Dr. Jonathan Slocum Design after Bob Boyle's Bonefish Shrimp.

GLASS-EYED SHRIMP

A Dr. Jonathan Slocum design, after Bob Boyle's more complicated Boyle Bonefish Shrimp (see page 43). Sample in photo was tied by Dr. Jonathan Slocum on a size 6 34007 hook and measures horizontally 3/4" in length. Fly rides hook-point up.

Hook: 34007; sizes 4, 6

Thread: Invisible sewing thread

Eyes: 3, 5, and 7mm glass eyes

Underbody: Single-strand red wool, tied along belly from "thorax" to above barb

Tail/Body: Pink bucktail, bound tightly to top of shank and three-quarters of the way down bend

Carapace: Narrow, clear Swannundaze, wound and liberally coated with Hard As Nails

Antennae: Pig or wild boar bristles, over back and hook eye

Hackle/Legs: White, pink, or brown hackle (tied in at midpoint), palmered, and trimmed on top and sides

Rostrum: Long, pointed section of plastic drinking straw

Tying Notes: Pull the legs down and lash the rostrum with the thread left hanging at the hook bend; be careful not to bind the hackle legs. The point of the rostrum extends over the hook eye. Trim the tail, flatten, and fix in a flat position with Zap-A-Gap.

Location Notes: Yucatán: Boca Paila, Ascencion Bay.

Fishing Notes: This fly works well on bright days. It should be allowed to sink, then retrieved in little jerks to stir up the marl into puffs. If the fish see it, they usually inspect it, and more often than not they'll take it. It works equally well on tailing and cruising fish.

Prey Notes: Not an exact likeness of anything, but suggestive of many prey. The eyes are very important. If they fall off, the fly is no longer anywhere near as effective. *Author's note: The fly may suggest some members of the common shrimp (Penaeidae), snapping shrimp (Alpheidae), and grass shrimp (Palaemonidae) families.*

Anecdotes: Dr. Slocum says he had six of these flies with him at Ascension Bay one year and gave two to a friend, Dr. Scott Boley, who was leaving for Boca Paila. Scott later told him he never experienced a single refusal on the pattern, and since it also consistently produced for its originator, it became a permanent resident of Slocum's box.

Dr. Jonathan Slocum started fly fishing with a Thomas and Thomas rod in 1924 when he was ten years old—and he hasn't stopped yet. He began tying flies in the 1950s. Now he routinely fishes for trout in the Catskills and Pennsylvania, and he normally goes salmon fishing three times a year and bonefishing twice a year.

GOLDEN SHRIMP

A Jim O'Neill design. Sample in photo was tied by Jim O'Neill on a size 4 34007 hook and measures horizontally 2-1/4" in length. Fly can ride hook-point up or down, depending on side of shank to which you attach eye weight.

Hook: 34007 or 3407; sizes 2, 4, 6, 8

Thread: Tan Monocord 3/0

Eyes: Medium (5/32") lead barbell, painted dark red (or 1/8" and 3/32" bead chain for sizes 6 and 8, respectively)

Tail/Antennae: Copper and gold Krystal Flash

Body: Golden tan medium chenille

Wing: Tan calf tail mixed with copper and gold Krystal Flash

Tying Notes: Jim sometimes ties this pattern on a Tiemco 800S but finds the wire a bit heavy. He says good fish will straighten out a size 8 hook anyway, so there seems to be little advantage to using a sturdier hook.

Location Notes: The fly has been good at Andros and Los Roques on both grassy flats and deep sandy bottoms.

Fishing Notes: Jim says he fishes the lead-eye version much as he does a Clouser Deep Minnow, letting it sink fast and then stripping it to bounce off the bottom. The bead-chain version he fishes as a Crazy Charlie, using a conventional jig action and increasing the speed of retrieve as the water depth decreases.

Prey Notes: Generic shrimp suggestive of many species, but in the golden tan color is probably most suggestive of the common shrimps (Penaeidae) and mantis shrimps (Squillidae)—especially *Pseudosquilla ciliata*, the golden mantis.

Anecdotes: Jim says this is a big-fish fly for him and has taken several double-digit specimens at the locations he frequents.

Jim O'Neill is a history professor at Wyoming's Casper College, and a former Pacific Northwest mountaineering guide. He has been an angler for over thirty years, often fishing over 100 days a year, and has stalked bonefish at Andros, Belize, Los Roques, Exuma, and Islamorada.

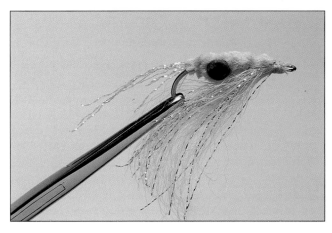

Golden Shrimp • Jim O'Neill

Gorell's Hackle Shrimp • Franklyn Gorell

GORELL'S HACKLE SHRIMP

A Franklyn Gorell design. Sample in photo was tied by Franklyn Gorell on a size 6 34007 hook and measures horizontally 7/8" in length; antennae are 1-1/2" in length from base. Fly rides hook-point up.

Hook: Mustad 34007; sizes 4, 6, 8 (usually ties in size 6)

Thread: Brown Flat Waxed Nylon (also black, pink, and others)

Eyes: 1/8" or 3/16" bead chain

Antennae/Head/Carapace/Tail: Krystal Flash, pearl (also black, pink, and others)

Hackle: Mottled brown or brown grizzly (also grizzly, beige, and others)

Tying Notes: Tie in the eyes at the bend. Wind *down* the bend and tie in the hackle butt and Krystal Flash. Wind the thread *over* the Flash and hackle to the bead chain, then wind the thread—followed by the hackle—to the hook eye. Trim the hackle flat across the spine of the fly, pull the flash forward across the spine, and tie off. Trim the hackle all around, leaving it longer at the hook point to serve as a weed guard. Trim the Krystal Flash, leaving two strands for the antennae.

Location Notes: Franklyn originally created this ingenious little pattern for Belize, but he has now taken fish with it in the Yucatan (Casa Blanca), the Bahamas (three locations), Los Roques, Christmas Island, the Florida Keys, the Cayman Islands, and most other major bonefishing destinations.

Fishing Notes: Franklyn ties the fly in size 8 with the smallest (3/16" or 5/32") bead chain for tailing fish, especially single tailers. The fly was designed for normal flats depths, not for deep water. It seems to work in all tide stages and in a variety of habitats (although you may have to vary the color).

For stripping action, Franklyn normally uses quick, short strips of two to four inches, until the fish turns onto the fly. Then he stops it and waits for a pick-up. You can also keep stripping, or use longer pulls, if you desire.

The fly was designed for cruising fish, but Franklyn says he's used it in muds and on tailing fisl. as well. Because of its light weight and hackle, it lands softly and works better on tailers than most other "eyed" patterns.

Author's note: This light, quiet pattern fishes well in shallow and medium depths. It is usually tied with 1/8" or 3/16" bead chain, but sometimes with lead eyes. A careful balance of flash and non-flash elements makes it effective for both low-light and bright-light conditions, an uncommon versatility for a flats fly. Also a low-impact pattern, the Hackle Shrimp is effective getting down to tailing fish fast. A good basic fly.

Prey Notes: Suggestive of some common and snapping shrimps, and many smaller species such as Palaemonidae, Gnatophyllidae, and Hippolytidae. The simple construction, which uses only two materials (hackle and Krystal Flash), makes it easy to carry everything you need to tie many different colored flies on location to portray local species.

Anecdotes: The idea for this fly occurred to Franklyn while he was snorkeling. He noticed how all the shrimp were translucent and gave off just the smallest suggestion of shape and color rather than a clear outline. He says they emitted tiny flashes as they moved.

Franklyn Gorell owned and ran a manufacturing company, which he sold in 1989. He retired in 1991 and now spends his summers in Idaho. He fishes for bonefish (and many other freshwater and saltwater species) all over the world.

Gotcha • Jim McVay

GOTCHA

A Jim McVay design. Sample in photo was tied by Jim McVay on a size 4 3407 hook; its outside dimension, hook-eye-to-tail, measures horizontally 1-3/8". The wing itself measures 1-3/4" in length. Fly rides hook-point up.

Hook: Mustad 3407 or 34007; sizes 2, 4

Thread: Fluorescent or Gotcha Pink Danville Flat Waxed Nylon

Eyes: 1/8" bead chain on size 4, or 5/32" bead chain on size 2, or 1/50 oz. (5/32") lead barbells for fast sink

Tail: Pearl Mylar tubing

Body: Pearl Diamond Braid

Wing: Yellow Krystal flash over blond craft fur

Tying Notes: The tail is as long as (or longer than) the body; the wing length reaches past the tail. McVay also ties the fly with an orange wing for dark flats (Fish Fuzz No. 13 Goldfish Orange). *Author's note: I've found that a Gotcha with an auburn brown wing (Mystic Bay No. 19 Rust) can work extremely well on mangrove flats and dark bottoms.*

Ted McVay, Jim's son, modifies the Gotcha when fishing calm, deep waters (in particular, those around Andros' Moxey Creek and Loggerhead Cay) for big fish that are often mixed in with schools so they have to be pulled out. He ties the Gotcha with a thinner wing than his father for fishing such calm conditions because he says the heavy dressing seems to suck up too much water, making it splat too much on impact.

Location Notes: Works everywhere. *Author's note: The first time I tried the Gotcha in Andros, twenty-seven fish ate it. It has since fooled fish in every Bahamian location I've tried it.*

Fishing Notes: Tied with 1/8" or 3/16" bead chain, this is a good medium-depth shrimp pattern, and with lead eyes it is often effective in deeper water. It is very productive in low light and—surprisingly—also in bright light. Apparently, small-faceted materials make this bright fly less prone to "bright-light spooking" than shinier Charlies. The Gotcha is especially effective in Andros, Abaco, the Berry Islands, and other Bahamas locations. It should be in every flats angler's box.

Prey Notes: The Gotcha is more sophisticated at portraying shrimp than its rather gaudy appearance might suggest. Its reflective body and tail take on some of the color and textured look of its surroundings, mimicking the naturally camouflaged appearance of many of the bonefish's favorite shrimps—including many members of the large, meaty Penaeidae family, as well as the snapping shrimps (Alpheidae). In smaller sizes the fly also mimics tinier shrimp families such as Palaemonidae, Gnatophyllidae, and Hippolytidae.

Anecdotes: Jim says, "I think Rupert Leadon [of the Andros Island bonefish club] named this pattern. Every time one of us would throw the fly and a fish would hit it, he would say 'Gotcha.' After a while, he'd said it so many times, it just seemed like that was the right name for it."

Jim McVay is a retired oil well driller and a fixture of the Andros Island Bonefish Club. He first tied this pattern while en route to Andros, using yellow carpet fibers he snipped out of the back of a Cargill Creek-bound taxicab. He later found a shade of blond craft fur that worked equally well. Jim estimates he has taken thousands of bonefish on this mirrored miracle, and credits it with more thirty- to fifty-fish days than he can remember. Many anglers consider it one of the best bonefish patterns ever devised.

Grassy Wonder • Winston Moore

GRASSY WONDER

A Winston Moore design. Sample in photo was tied by Winston Moore on a size 8 3407 hook and measures horizontally 1-1/8" in length. Fly rides hook-point up.

Hook: 3407; sizes 4, 6, 8

Thread: Black Monocord 3/0

Body: Light olive vernille (or yarn)

Wing: Peacock blue (No. 13-B) FisHair flanked by grizzly saddle tips. Can use kingfisher blue Partridge SLF in place of FisHair

Location Notes: Winston says this pattern works in Belize and the Yucatan when nothing else does—he's taken hundreds of fish with it on grassy flats when all the old faithfuls failed.

Fishing Notes: Winston uses very short strips for bonefish, never more than four inches. He says he often applies just enough strip to move the fly—almost a twitch of the stripping fingers—generally about two inches in length.

Prey Notes: Generic fly suggestive of many small shrimps that inhabit turtle grass and shoals, such as Palaemonidae, Gnatophyllidae, and Hippolytidae.

Winston Moore, see AGENT ORANGE, page 20.

Green Puff • Winston Moore

GREEN PUFF

A Winston Moore design. Sample in photo was tied by Winston Moore on a size 6 3407 hook and measures horizontally 1-1/2" in length. Fly rides hook-point down.

Hook: 3407; sizes 4, 6

Thread: Chartreuse Monocord 3/0

Tail: Pearl Krystal flash, then Peacock Blue (No. 13-B) FisHair, then pair of flanking grizzly hackle tips. Can use kingfisher blue Partridge SLF in place of FisHair.

Body: Light olive vernille or other fine chenille

Eyes: Smallest (3/32") bead chain, figure-eighted *under* shank (hook-point side)

Location Notes: Winston says this pattern has been very good on grassy flats at all locations fished. He has found it to work especially well at Los Roques, and to be deadly in Belize and the Yucatan.

Fishing Notes: Winston uses very short strips for bonefish, never more than four inches. He says he often applies just enough strip to move the fly—almost a twitch of the stripping fingers—generally about two inches in length.

Prey Notes: Generic shrimp suggestive of many members of such diminutive families as Palaemonidae, Gnatophyllidae, and Hippolytidae. The fly also suggests juvenile common shrimps (Penaeidae) and snapping shrimps (Alpheidae).

Winston Moore, see AGENT ORANGE, page 20.

Greg's Flats Fly • Greg Miheve

GREG'S FLATS FLY

A Greg Miheve design. Sample in photo, the Banded Tan version, was tied by Greg Miheve on a size 4 34007 hook and measures horizontally 1-3/4" in overall length. Span between splayed tips measures 3/4" to 1". Fly rides hook-point up.

Hook: 34007; sizes 2, 4, 6, 8

Thread: Tan 3/0 or 6/0 (or color to match tail or bands)

Eyes: Medium (1/8") bead chain (or 5/32" lead barbell)

Tail/Claws/Antennae: White calf tail hair (length to yield a tail one-and-one-quarter shank lengths long), splayed and flanked on each outer side by two strands Krystal Flash

Underbody: Wide pearl Flashabou over white thread base

Bands: Tan thread, wound to form four contrasting bands ending behind eyes

Outer Body: Clear (or, in other variations, colored) V-Rib, tapered to appear larger near eyes

Hackle: Extra long saddle, tan (or grizzly, or color to match banding in other versions), stripped of its left-side (shiny side facing you, butt down) fibers; tied in by *tip* at tail, and palmered forward

Tying Notes: Tie the hair on top of the shank to cover the full length of the shank to behind the eyes; wind the thread to cant the hair about 30° to 45° downward (when viewed in tying position, hook-point down) along the bend. Split the hair in half and splay with thread at about a 90° angle of separation. Add the underbody, bands, body wrap, and hackle.

You can also tie the fly in a non-banded version (just leave out banding steps), and a "live-heart" or LH version (overwrap the upper 1/4" of the body with bright fire orange or red Flat Waxed Nylon thread to suggest its heart).

Location Notes: The Florida Keys, the Bahamas, Christmas Island, Belize, Los Roques. Greg says the fly has been called the most productive pattern at Deep Water Cay in the Bahamas. Tan-banded is the most popular version, and works everywhere. Others: solid brown, golden tan, banded pink, chartreuse LH, white LH, and olive. A newer version, banded gray with a pink LH and barred cream (or light dun) hackle, is also finding great interest.

Fishing Notes: Alter the eye type for the desired sink rate. Strip until the fish sees, let it drop, and watch the fish's movement to see a pick-up.

Prey Notes: This generic shrimp is suggestive of many species, depending on bands and coloration. The banded style best mimics the banded snapping shrimp, *Alpheus armillatus;* solid colors suggest common shrimps (Penaeidae), grass shrimps (Palaemonidae), and mantis shrimps (Squillidae).

Anecdotes: Neal Rogers (author of *Fly Fishing Magic*) ties a version of Greg's fly he calls the "Man in Tan" with a conventional inverse wing of tan calf tail instead of the body hackle, and without a V-Rib outer body. He says it has been a fantastic performer for him in the Yucatan on many, many trips.

Greg Miheve is a retired intelligence officer living in Florida. He is a founder of the Emerald Coast Flyrodders in Fort Walton, Florida, and on the board of directors of the Fly Fishing Federation's SE Council. A tier for over forty years, Greg has been doing it professionally for ten. He supplies Deep Water Cay, Andros Island Bonefish Club, Casa Blanca, Urban Angler (New York City), Lure & Feather, and many individual anglers.

Greg's Tiny Shiny Shrimp • Greg Miheve

GREG'S TINY SHINY SHRIMP

A Greg Miheve design. Sample in photo, the Pink Banded version, was tied by Greg Miheve on a size 8 34007 hook and measures horizontally 1-3/8" in overall length. Fly rides hook-point down.

Hook: 34007; sizes 6, 8, 10

Thread: White 3/0 or 6/0; pink for bands, black for head

Tail/Antennae: Eight to ten strands Krystal Flash, wound down bend to cant 30° to 45°

Underbody: White thread base; then wide pearl Flashabou

Bands: Pink banding thread wound to form three or four equidistant contrasting bands ending behind eyes

Outer Body: V-Rib

Hackle: Palmered saddle

Tying Notes: The fly is tied in both banded and non-banded versions.

Location Notes: The Bahamas,Yucatan.

Fishing Notes: Greg says this pattern needs a shrimpy swimming motion, in addition to being allowed to freely drift if current is present. Remember, he cautions, this is a small fly—no six-inch or one-foot strips, please.

Prey Notes: Suggests smaller grass shrimps or glass shrimps. *Author's note: It may also suggest small translucent threadworms or Syllidae that live in the substrate of many sand and mud flats.*

Greg Miheve, see GREG'S FLATS FLY, page 91.

Hairy Legs Crab • Jack Montague

HAIRY LEGS CRAB

A Jack Montague design. Sample in photo was tied by Jack Montague on a size 2 34007 hook and measures horizontally 3-1/4" in overall length. Weighted fly rides hook-point up; unweighted, hook-point down.

Hook: 34007; sizes 2, 4

Thread: Tan Monocord 3/0

Underbody/Body: Deer hair underbody, spun, trimmed, and coated with epoxy; lay in pheasant or grouse breast/flank feather as carapace; let dry; then coat with epoxy again

Eyes: Black plastic beads; place two drops epoxy on body and poke beads into place

Legs: Tips of deer hair left by trimming flat of underbody

Tying Notes: Claws of pheasant or grouse feather may be added.

Location Notes: The Keys.

Fishing Notes: Jack works his pattern with a hand-twist retrieve while putting his rod tip in the water. Each hand twist moves the fly the amount retrieved. He also wiggles the rod to add more action.

Prey Notes: Depending on color, the fly is suggestive of many species of swimming crabs (Portunidae), mud crabs (Xanthidae), and spider crabs (Majidae).

Jack Montague is a representative for G. Loomis rods and STH reels. He lives in Punta Gorda, Florida.

Hallucination • Phil Chapman

HALLUCINATION

A Phil Chapman design. Sample in photo was tied by Phil Chapman on a size 4 34007 hook and measures horizontally 2-7/8" in length, including antennae. Body measures 1/2" in width at shoulders. Fly rides hook-point down.

Hook: 34007; sizes 2, 4, 6

Thread: Black Flat Waxed Nylon 3/0

Weight: 1/50 oz. lead barbell

Whiskers: Small clump (twelve to fourteen) natural tan deer hairs

Face/antennae: Clump (two long strands) root beer Krystal Flash

Eyes: Mono, melted and enlarged by dipping in epoxy

Claws: Matched pair brown grizzly hackles, flared outward

Head: Orange grizzly butt, palmered

Body/Legs: Brown Estaz, palmered, interspersed with rust Lumaflex legs (three or four pairs) barred with marker

Weed Guard: Add 15-lb. Mason guard before finishing head

Tying Notes: The fly can also be tied inverted.

Location Notes: The Keys.

Fishing Notes: For tailing and cruising fish. The fly stands erect on the bottom and has good leg and antenna animation.

Prey Notes: Generalized combination crab/shrimp fly suggestive of many species, depending on color and size.

Phil Chapman, see BONE-ZAI CRAB, page 35.

Harbour Island Charlie • Dr. Michael Holtzman

HARBOUR ISLAND CHARLIE

A Dr. Michael Holtzman design. Sample in photo was tied by Dr. Michael Holtzman on a size 8 34007 hook and measures horizontally 1-3/16" in length. Fly rides hook-point up.

Hook: 34007; sizes 4, 6, 8

Thread: Red Danville 6/0

Eyes: Small (3/32") bead chain for size 6 or 8, medium (1/8") for size 4, painted black over yellow; or extra small plated lead

Body: Tying thread overwrapped with 12-lb. to 20-lb. clear mono

Wing: Red fox squirrel tail

Tying Notes: You can further modify the sink rate and splash impact by the use of lead wire and different density eyes.

Location Notes: The northern outer Bahamas: North Eleuthera, Harbour Island, Abaco.

Fishing Notes: Michael developed this small and light pattern for Harbour Island's sometimes very spooky fish. He also ties it heavier and bulkier for either deep or muddy conditions. Strip until the fish sees, stop, and watch the fish's movement to see a pick-up.

Prey Notes: This generic pattern suggests many smaller species of shrimps and crabs. It may suggest *Lysmatta grabhami*, the red-back cleaning shrimp.

Dr. Michael Holtzman is a retired research scientist who lives in the Bahamian outislands, where he pursues *A. vulpes* every day that winds and tides will allow.

Harbour Island Clouser • Dr. Michael Holtzman

HARBOUR ISLAND CLOUSER

A Dr. Michael Holtzman design. Sample in photo was tied by Dr. Michael Holtzman on a size 4 34007 hook and measures horizontally 2-1/2" in length. Fly rides hook-point up.

Hook: 34007; sizes 2, 4, 6

Thread: Pink Danville Flat Waxed Nylon 3/0

Eyes: Medium (1/8") bead chain, painted black over yellow

Body: Pink tying thread, wrapped to cover shank

Wing: White bucktail, then rainbow Krystal Flash, then gray bucktail

Tying Notes: The fly can also be tied with chartreuse thread and a yellow-and-white wing. Michael developed this modification for especially spooky conditions after many years of fishing with his good friend Joe Cleare of Harbour Island. The "body" serves as a filter to eliminate the shine of the hook for bright days, skinny water, and spooky fish— long a concern of Joe's when fishing this area's more challenging quarry.

Location Notes: The northern outer Bahamas: North Eleuthera, Harbour Island, Abaco.

Fishing Notes: Michael says he usually fishes the size 2, finding the larger size elicits more strikes even on bright, clear-water days. But he cautions that this makes careful presentation critical, especially with tailers. Strip until the fish sees, let it drop, and watch the fish's movement to see a pick-up.

Prey Notes: Depending on color and stripping rhythm, suggestive of many prey species (see also the prey notes under Clouser Deep Minnow, page 60), including shrimps, crabs, polychaete swimming worms, and juvenile fish.

Anecdotes: Michael says that Joe Cleare had long liked the gray-and-white Clouser pattern but found its bare shank spooked fish, so he tied it with a thread-covered body and it has been a proven producer ever since.

Dr. Michael Holtzman, see HARBOUR ISLAND CHARLIE, page 95.

Hare Trigger • Dick Brown

HARE TRIGGER

Author's design. Sample in photo was tied by Dick Brown on a size 4 34007 hook and measures horizontally 1-5/8" in length. Fly rides hook-point down.

Hook: 34007; sizes 2, 4, 6, 8

Thread: Tan Danville Flat Waxed Nylon 3/0

Eyes: Two plastic hair brush bristles, figure-eighted to shank

Antennae: Krystal Flash, then a V-shaped segment of golden-pheasant tippet

Underbody: Natural or dyed-olive rabbit, palmered

Carapace: Golden-pheasant breast feather

Weed/Coral Guard (optional):   V of 12-lb. or 15-lb. Mason hard mono, figure-eighted to shank

Location Notes: Andros, Abaco, the Berry Islands, North Eleuthera, the Florida Keys, Belize.

Fishing Notes: Tailing fly. Cast close. Strip sparingly. When the fish sees, pause, and watch the fish's movement to see a pick-up.

Prey Notes: Suggests many members of the common shrimp (Penaeidae), snapping shrimp (Alpheidae), grass shrimp (Palaemonidae), and mantis shrimp (Squillidae) families.

Honey Lamb • Ellen Reed

HONEY LAMB

An Ellen Reed design. Sample in photo was tied by Ellen Reed on a size 4 3407 hook and measures horizontally 1-1/4" in length. Fly rides hook-point up.

Hook: 3407, size 4

Thread: Tan mono 3/0

Antennae: Golden-pheasant tippet

Eyes: Small (3/32") lead barbell (or bronze with black finish)

Body Hackle: Brown grizzly hackle

Body: Tan (honey-colored) chenille

Front Skirt or Collar: Lambswool over gold Krystal Flash

Weed/Coral Guard: Single strand of 20-lb. Mason mono

Tying Notes: Ellen uses lambswool from a duster, but says craft fur works fine too.

Location Notes: The Florida Keys; Ellen says it's a good pattern for both oceanside and backcountry. It seems to work when they're not eating anything else.

Fishing Notes: You can alter the eye type for the desired sink rate. Strip sparingly. When the fish sees, let it drop, and watch the fish's movement to see a pick-up.

Prey Notes: Suggests members of the common shrimp (Penaeidae) and mantis shrimp (Squillidae) families.

Ellen Reed and her husband Fred moved in 1985 to the Keys, where they own a small marine repair business. They sneak off to the flats "more often than they should," especially when the tide's good. *Author's note: Thanks to Tim Borski for alerting me to Ellen's very fetching patterns.*

Hoochy Caucci Fly • Al Caucci

HOOCHY CAUCCI FLY

An Al Caucci design. Sample in photo was tied by Al Caucci on a size 2 34007 hook and measures horizontally 2-1/8" in length. Fly rides hook-point up.

Hook: 34007 or TMC 800S; sizes 2, 4, 6

Thread: Tan Monocord 3/0 for size 2, 6/0 for smaller sizes

Eyes: Plated; for sizes 2 and 4 use 1/36 oz. or 1/50 oz. lead barbell; for size 6 use 1/100 oz. barbell

Tail: Tan marabou (or extra fine craft hair), same length as hook

Body: Pearlescent Flashabou, wrapped to behind eyes, then overwrapped with clear V-Rib or narrow Swannundaze No. 22

Wing: Tan craft hair or fine FisHair, with three or four strands gold Krystal Flash on each side

Tying Notes: Al ties in three other colors: white (white thread/tail/wing, No. 10 silver tinsel or Flashabou body, and pearl Krystal Flash); brown (brown thread/tail/wing, pearlescent Flashabou body, and gold Krystal Flash); and pink (pink thread/tail/wing, No. 10 silver tinsel or Flashabou body, and silver Krystal Flash).
Al Crazy Glues the eyes and winds many turns of thread to secure them, covering the area between and just behind the eyes. He also sometimes applies a coat of clear Super-T-Acrylic glue, or a teardrop of hot glue, filling the area between the lead eyes and forward to the hook eye for added durability and a shellfish-like glint.

Location Notes: Exuma, Andros, Belize, and the Caribbean. Also the Florida Keys, but Al says for Florida's big, smart fish, he leaves out the Krystal Flash, uses smaller (1/50 oz.) eyes, and adds the Super-T or hot-glue head.

Fishing Notes: Al says he intentionally designed the Hoochy to hit the water with a plunk—it gets the attention of big fish. The fly also dives to the bottom fast, and its fine-textured craft hair and marabou pulsate when retrieved at slow speeds and even when paused. It works well in sizes 2 and 4 for larger fish, and Al says he uses it primarily for deep sand, mud, and coral flats, where big fish cruise and feed in triples, doubles, or alone. For thinnest waters he ties a size 6 or size 8 version without the Krystal Flash.

Prey Notes: Depending on size and color, the fly can suggest many common shrimps (Penaeidae), snapping shrimps (Alpheidae), and mantis shrimps (Squillidae). It also mimics immature crabs.

Anecdotes: Al says one fall day in 1993, when he had some time off from teaching a class, he and friend Jerry Wolland were fishing in the bights of Andros with guide Charlie Neymour. He caught a nice eight- or nine-pound fish on this pattern, then Jerry took a turn on deck and threw at a pod of fish. A monster bonefish suddenly appeared out of the grass and took the tan Hoochy. Twenty minutes later, Charlie released Jerry's fish, estimating its weight at about sixteen pounds.

Al Caucci,   see AL'S GLASS MINNOW, page 21.

Hoover • Brian O'Keefe

HOOVER

A Brian O'Keefe design. Sample in photo was tied by Brian O'Keefe on a size 4 34007 hook and measures horizontally 2-5/8" in length. Fly rides hook-point up or down, depending on size of eyes and bulk of wing.

Hook: 34007; sizes 2, 4, 6

Thread: Tan Monocord 3/0

Eyes: Medium (1/8") bead chain

Underbody: Thread of same color as head and rabbit wing (or none)

Wing: Natural tan rabbit strip (the thinner the better)

Tying Notes: The rabbit can be pierced and poked onto the hook, then tied in at the head. Or you can tie it in above the hook point and then again at the head. Glue with Zap-A-Gap before tying it down. *Author's note: Angler Warren Brewster ties a pattern, Brewster's Rabbit Fly, that applies the rabbit strip upside down to the hook-point side of the shank. This lets the* *hair stick up when the fly inverts and makes for a very killing pattern for the Bahamas' Sandy Point area where Warren fishes 80 to 100 days a year.*

Location Notes: Christmas Island, South Andros, the Berry Islands, Belize.

Fishing Notes: Brian says this pattern is sometimes very hot and other times worthless. In size 6, it has worked well on the bigger fish at Christmas Island, and in larger sizes on redfish, snook, and tarpon as well.

For a retrieve Brian says he keeps this pattern moving with short and medium strips. At times when fishing for bones, he says that trevally, snappers, barracuda, and other jacks will attack it before the bonefish have a chance.

Prey Notes: Generic attractor pattern with a shape suggestive of several prey forms, including errant worms or polychaetes, small gobies (Gobiidae), toadfish (Batrachoididae), and small baitfish species.

Anecdotes: Brian named this pattern for the tendency of fish to come up behind and "Hoover" it in.

Brian O'Keefe, a professional photographer and a fly-fishing industry sales representative, single-handedly supplies about a third of all the feature photography in national fishing journals and travel brochures. An avid and pioneering flats angler, he has explored some of the most out-of-the-way bonefish hangouts, as well as all of their regular haunts.

Interceptor • Randall Kaufmann

INTERCEPTOR

> *A Randall Kaufmann design. Sample in photo was tied for Randall Kaufmann and to his specifications by Umpqua Feather Merchants on a size 6 3407 hook and measures 1-1/4" in length. Fly rides hook-point up.*

Hook: 3407; sizes 2, 4, 6, 8

Thread: Fluorescent pink 6/0

Eyes: Gold- or nickel-plated steel (size to match desired sink rate), painted pink, then white, then black, and coated with epoxy

Tail: Wine over fluorescent pink over pearl Krystal Flash

Body: Pearl flat braid

Wing: Same as tail, trimmed at angle (tail and wing both trimmed at same time so wing Krystal Flash is the shorter)

Tying Notes: Can be tied in other colors to suit; try yellow, orange, gold, or green.

Location Notes: The Bahamas.

Fishing Notes: This attractor pattern was designed by Randall on Grand Bahama in 1991 during a cold front that put fish down. "There were very few fish on the flats—if we saw ten fish in a day it was big news," he says. "Because it was important to make every shot count, we needed a fly that was exciting. This gaudy, flashy fly attracted fish from afar and made them curious enough to grab it." Randall notes this fly is not the normal match with or contrast to the bottom color, but says there are, after all, no absolutes in fishing—you must keep an open mind.

Prey Notes: Generalized shrimp attractor. As shown, it may suggest several members of the brighter common shrimp (Penaeidae) or snapping shrimp (Alpheidae) families. In gold and green versions it may portray some of the mantis shrimps (Squillidae).

Randall Kaufmann, see CHRISTMAS ISLAND SPECIAL, page 57.

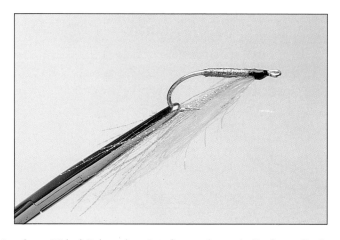

Intruder • Michael Bednar adaptation of pattern he saw in Kaufmann Catalog.

INTRUDER

A Michael Bednar adaptation of a pattern he saw in Randall Kaufmann's catalog. Sample in photo was tied by Michael Bednar on a size 2 3407 hook and measures horizontally 3-1/4" in overall length. Fly rides hook-point up.

Hook: 3407; sizes 2, 4, 6

Thread: Black Monocord 3/0

Body: Green Krystal Flash

Wing: Green Krystal Flash; then white FisHair; then Flashabou

Tying Notes: Tie in Krystal Flash at the bend, twist into a "rope," and wind forward to form the body. Secure at the eye, then double back to form the underwing.

Location Notes: The Keys, the Bahamas.

Fishing Notes: Michael is a big fan of fishing for bones at sunrise and sunset and in the Keys. He says that—barring a hurricane—there will always be some fish on the flats at these low-light times. He likes this fly, which has earned a permanent place in his box, because of its ability to catch light and attract fish.

Prey Notes: This fly has a worm-like movement and Michael believes it resembles the palolo worm, which twists and wiggles at night and looks like neon squiggles in the water.

Michael Bednar, see BONENANZA, page 42.

JT Special • Yvon Chouinard adaptation of John Torstenson design

J T S P E C I A L

An Yvon Chouinard adaptation of a John Torstenson design. Sample in photo was tied by Yvon Chouinard on a size 6 Gamakatsu hook and measures horizontally 1-1/2" in length.

Hook: Gamakatsu (or Mustad 3407/34007); sizes 6, 8, 10

Thread: Black Monocord 3/0

Eyes: Medium (1/8") or small (3/32") bead chain, or use smallest (3/32") lead barbell to alter sink rate and splash profile

Tail: Cree saddle hackles, shiny sides facing, and flared

Body/Wing: Tan marabou tips

Overwing: Brown bucktail, very sparse

Tying Notes: Tie the body quite full with marabou.

Location Notes: Belize, the Bahamas; effective everywhere.

Fishing Notes: When fished dead-stop, the fly emulates crabs. When stripped, it suggests juvenile fish or gobies.

Prey Notes: Generic crab or forage fish suggestive of many species.

Anecdotes: Yvon says this is his best pattern for Belize's spooky flats.

Yvon Chouinard, inventor, mountain climber, aggressive surfer, and founder of the innovative Patagonia Company, is a fanatical bonefisherman who stalks the flats of Belize, the Bahamas, Christmas Island, and other destinations several times a year.

Jim's Bonefish Puff • Jim Orthwein

JIM'S BONEFISH PUFF

A Jim Orthwein design. Sample in photo was tied by Jim Orthwein on a size 4 Mustad 34011 hook and measures horizontally 3" in length. Fly rides hook-point up when weighted with eyes, down when unweighted.

Hook: 34011; size 4

Thread: Chartreuse Monocord or Flat Waxed Nylon 3/0

Eyes: Small (3/32") gold bead chain

Body: Pearl Poly Flash

Wing/Tail: Chartreuse marabou, then pearl Krystal Flash, then white marabou

Tying Notes: Tie in the pearl body first and coat with Hard As Nails. Use prime marabou tips for the wings; tie in twelve strands of Krystal Flash between.

Location Notes: Bimini, Chub Cay, Andros.

Fishing Notes: Jim says bonefish often take this fly while it is sinking: Let it sink, then retrieve slowly, one foot at a time.

The fly is especially effective at medium and high tides, and when fish are mudding. It is very effective for tailing fish when tied with no eyes (and when so tied, reverse the color order because the hook will ride point-down): white marabou first, then Krystal Flash, then chartreuse marabou.

Prey Notes: Suggestive of many juvenile fish, worms, and possibly young gobies (Gobiidae).

Anecdotes: Jim has taken a number of double-digit bonefish with this fly, including his fourth world record (10 kg or 20-pound tippet class), a ten-pound, four-ounce fish caught on May 22, 1994 in Bimini with guide Rudy Dames.

Jim Orthwein, formerly chairman of DM&M Worldwide, one of the country's largest advertising agencies, is a partner in the investment firm Huntleigh Asset Partners L.P., a director of the Anheuser-Busch Companies, and the former owner of the New England Patriots football team. In angling circles, Jim is well known as the current holder of four IGFA fly-rod world records for bonefish. He is an avid bluewater angler as well, having caught a black marlin weighing over 1,000 pounds. He is also a serious oils painter.

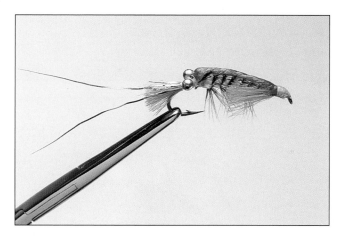

Jim's Golden Eye • Jim Orthwein

JIM'S GOLDEN EYE

A Jim Orthwein design. Sample in photo was tied by Jim Orthwein on a size 4 Mustad 9674 hook and measures horizontally 3" in length. Fly rides hook-point up.

Hook: Mustad 9674 or 38941; sizes 2, 4

Thread: Beige Monocord 3/0

Antennae: Peccary (or moose mane)

Eyes: Medium (1/8") gold bead chain

Head/Face: Nugget Gold synthetic hair ends (FisHair No. 15-B, 70 denier) over gold Mylar tubing ends, brushed out

Body: Slip section of Mylar tubing over shank so hook goes inside tubing (core removed);

tie down tubing and overwrap with clear Swannundaze or V-Rib

Legs: Brown saddle hackle, palmered into spiraled crevices of V-Rib and clipped on back and sides

Carapace/Tail: Nugget Gold FisHair twisted into rope and pulled over back, then doubled back alongside itself and lashed to one side as off-center tail or telson; coat back heavily with Hard As Nails

Tying Notes: The bronze hook must be humped by bending down at both ends when finished, making the back adhere tightly to the body.

Location Notes: Bimini, Andros, Chub Cay, Eleuthera, Spanish Wells, Abacos.

Fishing Notes: Alter the eye size for the desired sink rate. It has become popular among bonefish anglers to strip a fly only until the fish sees it and then stop the retrieve to watch for the fish to eat, but Jim says he finds it is often best to continue to strip steadily after the fish has seen the fly—a strategy that clearly works very well for him.

Prey Notes: Generic shrimp suggestive of common shrimps (Penaeidae) and mantis shrimps (Squillidae), especially *Pseudosquilla ciliata,* the golden mantis.

Anecdotes: Jim has taken three of his four IGFA world record bonefish on this fly, as well as many more double-digit fish.

Jim Orthwein, see JIM'S BONEFISH PUFF, page 104.

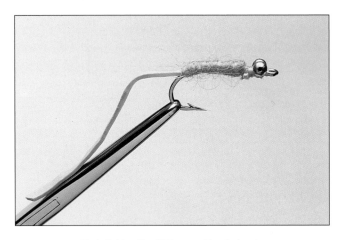

Jim's Rubber Band Worm • Jim Orthwein

JIM'S RUBBER BAND WORM

A Jim Orthwein design. Sample in photo was tied by Jim Orthwein on a size 4 Mustad 34007 hook and measures horizontally 2-7/8" in length. Fly rides hook-point up.

Hook: 34007 or 3407; sizes 4, 6

Thread: Beige Monocord 3/0

Eyes: Medium (1/8") gold bead chain

Tail: Walgreen, CVS, or similar beige rubber band (1/8" wide), trimmed to point at end

Body: Gold-colored rug wool or yarn. Color is almost exact match for Nugget Gold (FisHair No. 15-B) in Jim's Golden Eye

Location Notes: Bimini, Andros, Chub Cay, Eleuthera, Spanish Wells, Abacos.

Fishing Notes: See Jim's Golden Eye, page 105.

Prey Notes: Suggestive of several seaworms or polychaetes, especially errant or swimming worms such as members of the Syllidae and Arabellidae families. The fly may also suggest smaller gobies (Gobiidae) and some smaller shrimp species.

Anecdotes: Jim, who has taken three IGFA bonefish world records on his Jim's Golden Eye fly, and another on his Jim's Bonefish Puff, has also taken many double-digit fish on this one.

Jim Orthwein, see JIM'S BONEFISH PUFF, page 104.

Joe-To-Go • Steve Huff

JOE-TO-GO

A Steve Huff design. Sample in photo was tied by Steve Huff on a size 2 34007 hook and measures horizontally 1-15/16" in length. Fly rides hook-point down.

Hook: 34007; size 2

Thread: Fluorescent green floss

Tail: Grizzly hackle tips

Body: Root beer Ice Chenille

Eyes: Burnt 100-lb. mono

Hackle: Grizzly

Weed Guard: 15-lb. Ande mono

Tying Notes: Steve says he has tied this pattern with white chenille for early morning; he also occasionally weights it with lead wire under the body for getting deeper faster.

Location Notes: The Florida Keys.

Fishing Notes: The fly lands softly and remains almost suspended. It is good on calm, still days for tailing fish. Steve says to cast it close, make a short strip or two to get the fish's attention, and then clear your line.

Prey Notes: A generic prey pattern, this fly suggests many species of shrimps and crabs, and possibly some toadfish and goby species.

Anecdotes: Steve says the first fish caught on this fly weighed fourteen-and-one-quarter pounds.

Steve Huff was born in south Florida and has been guiding in the Keys and the Everglades for twenty-seven years. He's a member of the Orvis Saltwater Advisory Team.

Ken Bay Bonefish Shrimp • Ken Bay

KEN BAY BONEFISH SHRIMP

A Ken Bay design. Sample in photo was tied by Ken Bay on a size 2 34007 hook and measures horizontally 2-3/4" in overall length. Fly rides hook-point up.

Hook: 34007; sizes 2, 4

Thread: White Monocord 3/0

Eyes: 1/36 oz. lead eyes, painted yellow with black pupil

Tail: White bucktail

Body: White chenille

Wing: White marabou

Tying Notes: Use 1/50 oz. eyes for shallow water and tailing fish.

Location Notes: The Keys, the Bahamas.

Fishing Notes: Tie the fly in tan or white to match the bottom color.

Prey Notes: This suggestive design portrays a great variety of prey species across a diverse range of families, including shrimps, juvenile fish, worms, crabs, and gobies.

Anecdotes: Ken says he patterned this fly after the Clouser Deep Minnow but using marabou for action, and with a larger body profile.

Ken Bay lives in Daytona Beach, Florida, and is a professional tier. He has authored several tying books, including *Salt Water Flies,* published in 1972, which is probably the first book ever devoted to this subject.

Kraft Fur Worm • Tim Borski

KRAFT FUR WORM

A Tim Borski design. Sample in photo was tied by Tim Borski on a size 4 34007 hook and measures horizontally 2-3/8" in overall length. Fly rides hook-point up.

Hook: 34007; size 4

Thread: Brown Monocord

Tail: Tan craft fur, barred with marker

Body: 5-Minute Epoxy

Eyes: Burnt mono

Weed Guard: 15-lb. or 20-lb. Mason mono

Tying Notes: This fly is incredibly simple yet effective. It was designed with tailing fish in mind. Tim says he has no doubt it will also work on mudding and/or cruising fish when tied on a bit larger hook, and with lead eyes (rather than burnt mono).

Location Notes: The Florida Keys.

Fishing Notes: Tim says he likes to drop this fly in the fish's projected path, allow the fish to approach it, and then begin a long, slow glide. "I want the fly to rise from the bottom up into the water column, then glide back down. No sudden bumps, starts, twitches, etc. Nice and easy. Very effective on fish that have seen it all."

Prey Notes: Suggests medium-sized shrimp and mantis species (Penaeidae, Alpheidae, and Squillidae), and larger seaworms or polychaetes.

Tim Borski, see BRISTLE WORM, page 50.

Lefty's Clouser Deep Minnow • Lefty Kreh's version of Bob Clouser's fly.

LEFTY'S CLOUSER DEEP MINNOW

This is Lefty Kreh's version of his good friend Bob Clouser's excellent fly. Sample in photo was tied by Lefty Kreh on a size 4 hook and measures horizontally 2-7/8" in length. Fly rides hook-point up.

Hook: 34007; sizes 2, 4, 6

Thread: Tan Monocord 3/0

Eyes: 1/50 oz. or 1/36 oz. metallic, 1/4" behind eye of hook

Wing: With hook inverted, twenty strands white bucktail, then eight to ten strands rainbow Krystal Flash, then twenty strands tan bucktail

Tying Notes: The fly can be tied in chartreuse: chartreuse bucktail over rainbow Krystal Flash over white bucktail, with chartreuse tying thread.

Location Notes: Works everywhere.

Fishing Notes: Alter the eye type for the desired sink rate. Strip until the fish sees, let it drop, and watch the fish's movement to see a pick-up.

Prey Notes: Generic prey shape suggestive of many species. (See also the prey notes under the Clouser Deep Minnow, page 60.)

Lefty Kreh is one of the most experienced—and, without question, best-known—salt water fly fishermen in the world. He has taken over sixty species of fish on this pattern, and he also gave it its name.

Len's Hackle Merkin • Len Wright design after Del Brown Pattern.

LEN'S HACKLE MERKIN

A Len Wright design, after a Del Brown pattern. Sample in photo was tied by Len Wright on a size 4 34007 hook and measures horizontally 1-1/2" in length, and 1-3/4" in width across leg tips. Fly rides hook-point up.

Hook: 34007; sizes 4, 6, 8

Thread: Tan Monocord 3/0

Weight: Strips of lead (stacked in descending lengths like a flattened pyramid) glued to spine on bottom (non-point side) of hook to form keel; weight positioned toward hook eye to sink fly at this end first

Claws/Face: Two sprigs Krystal Flash, then two pairs tan grizzly hackles, splayed

Eyes: Two 1/8" brass bead-chain orbs strung on monofilament

Body: Alternating folded tan grizzly saddle hackle figure-eighted to shank, and tan rubber legs figure-eighted between

Tying Notes: Len uses Krystal Flash in this fly for the low light of early and late day, and switches to non-Krystal Flash versions during peak sunlight periods. He alters the keel weight (and also ties the fly sparser or bulkier) for the desired sink rate. The keel weight, he finds, ensures that the fly rides hook-point up, which bead chain does not.

Location Notes: The Florida Keys.

Fishing Notes: Strip until the fish sees, let it drop, and watch the fish's movement to see a pick-up. Len says for tailing fish and evening cruisers with their dorsals showing, he ties the fly on a heavily dressed size 6 or size 8 with minimal lead.

Prey Notes: Generic crab shape suggestive of many species of swimming crabs (Portunidae), mud crabs (Xanthidae), and spider crabs (Majidae).

Len Wright is perhaps best known in fishing circles for his far-thinking work on trout in *The Ways of the Trout* and *Fishing the Dry Fly as a Living Insect*. He is, however, also an avid flats angler who has been pursuing bonefish for many, many years in the Bahamas, Caymans, and (most recently) the Florida Keys—often with master guide Rick Ruoff (see his Absolute Flea and Deep Flea patterns, pages 19 and 65) at his side.

Len's Hackle Shrimp • Len Wright

LEN'S HACKLE SHRIMP

A Len Wright design. Sample in photo was tied by Len Wright on a size 4 34007 hook and measures horizontally 1-5/8" in length; body hackle is about 3/4" in width across middle. Fly rides hook-point up.

Hook: 34007; sizes 4, 6, 8

Thread: Gray Monocord 3/0

Weight: Strips of lead (stacked in descending lengths like flattened pyramid) glued to spine on bottom (non-point side) of hook to form keel; weight positioned toward hook eye to sink fly at this end first

Claws/Face: Pair of flared grizzly hackles flanked by pair of white hackles, then two sprigs Krystal Flash each side

Eyes: Two 1/8" bead-chain orbs strung on monofilament and painted black

Body: Grizzly saddle, closely palmered

Tying Notes: Len uses Krystal Flash in this fly for the low light of early and late day and switches to non-Krystal Flash versions during peak sunlight periods.

Location Notes: The Florida Keys.

Fishing Notes: Alter the keel weights for the desired sink rate: no weight and heavily dressed for shallow; four strips for six-inch to two-foot depths. Strip until the fish sees, let it drop, and watch the fish's movement to see a pick-up.

Prey Notes: This generic shrimp pattern suggests members of the common shrimp (Penaeidae), snapping shrimp (Alpheidae), and mantis shrimp (Squillidae) families.

Len Wright, see LEN'S HACKLE MERKIN, page 111.

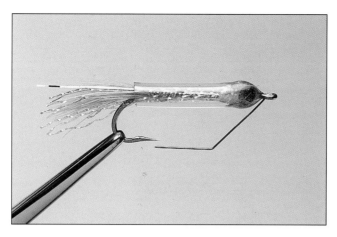

Lipstick Minnow • Scott Sanchez

LIPSTICK MINNOW

A Scott Sanchez design. Sample in photo was tied by Scott Sanchez on a size 2 34011 hook and measures horizontally 1-15/16" in overall length. Fly rides hook-point down.

Hook: Mustad 34011; sizes 1/0, 1, 2, 4, 6

Thread: Gray Monocord 3/0

Tail: Gray marabou or rabbit hair

Tube Holder: Pearl or silver Mylar braid, or Poly Flash

Underbody: Rainbow Krystal Flash

Weed/Coral Guard: No. 4 or No. 5 wire, inserted through hook eye, lashed to shank, bent 45°, then horizontal to point

Overbody: 1/8" ID x 3/16" OD clear vinyl tubing

Eyes: 3/16" stick-on

Head: Clear 5-Minute Epoxy (or Aquaseal or Goop)

Tying Notes: To reduce flash, use Ultra Hair instead of Krystal Flash; Lureflash Translucent also makes a great tail.

Location Notes: Both Turneffe Flats and the outer flats in Belize, Boca Paila, the Virgin Islands.

Fishing Notes: The fly works well in shallow reef areas where bonefish are preying on small juvenile fish. It lands more softly and has more subtle action than lead-eye minnow or epoxy minnow patterns.

Prey Notes: Generic small fish suggestive of many species of minnows, *Jenkinsia lamprotaenia*, or *Anchoa mitchelli*. It is also suggestive of juveniles of larger gamefish—such as snappers (Lutjanidae)—that spend their first years in the shallows.

Anecdotes: The fly was named by Larry Sunderland of Austin Angler.

Scott Sanchez is a professional tier, an assistant manager of the Jack Dennis Outdoor Shop in Jackson Hole, Wyoming, and a consultant for Dan Bailey's Fly Shop. He fishes fresh and salt water for many species.

Livebody Crab • Ben Estes

LIVEBODY CRAB

An experimental Ben Estes design. Sample in photo was tied by Ben Estes on a size 2 3407 hook and measures horizontally 2-1/2" in length. Carapace measures 1/2" in diameter. Fly rides hook-point down.

Hook: Mustad 3407; sizes 1, 2

Thread: Clear 1-lb. or 2-lb. Fenwick Light Line mono

Underbody: Build up with white gift-wrap yarn or other, and trim to flat disk

Weight: Lead dumbbell tied in behind eye of hook

Legs: Tan Sili Legs, knotted and tipped with fluorescent marker

Antennae: Krystal Flash

Claws: Cree hackle tips

Eyes: V-shaped mono with burnt ends

Carapace/Back: Disk cut from Livebody material

Belly Plate: White vinyl Plasti-dip

Weed Guard: 12-lb. or 15-lb. Mason hard mono loop

Tying Notes: Place legs, claws, antennae, and eyes on a yarn base and saturate with Crazy Glue, then press on the Livebody carapace.

Location Notes: Mexico, the Bahamas, the Keys.

Fishing Notes: This is a very light crab and is almost impossible to sink upside down—

it dives headfirst. Fish as any crab. Cast in front of the fish, move slowly, and drop it to the bottom when the fish spots it. Keep a tight line to the fly and watch the fish take the fly before striking.

Prey Notes: Generic pattern suggestive of many swimming (Portunidae) and spider (Majidae) crab species found in reef and flats habitats.

Anecdotes: Ben says both bonefish and permit will take this fly. Once he cast it to three permit he spotted at Esperanza. The first one picked it up, but the fish took the fly sideways and it fell out ... only to have another come up from behind and pick it up again!

Ben Estes, see BEN'S EPOXY BONEFISH FLY, page 28.

Magic Mantis • *Dick Brown*

MAGIC MANTIS

Author's design. Sample in photo was tied by the author on a size 4 34011 hook and measures horizontally 2-1/4" in length. Fly rides hook-point up.

Hook: 34011; sizes 2, 4, 6; bent down to hump fly

Thread: Tan Monocord 3/0

Weight: 1/36 oz. or 1/24 oz. lead barbell tied in at hump

Eyestalk Holder: Two wraps fine chenille forming ball around barbell

Tail: Mottled tan deer hair, then brown marabou tips

Eyes: Plastic hair-brush bristles, splayed forward on top of chenille ball; flatten eyestalks at base and lash to shank just behind weight/chenille

Antennae/Forelegs: Copper Krystal Flash, leaving two long strands

Body: Tan and brown Long Flash Chenille spiraled together up to eyes, then figure-eighted through eyes and tied off

Tying Notes: The fly also works well with an olive and gray Flash Chenille body, an olive marabou tail, and chartreuse Krystal Flash antennae/forelegs; and in an all-golden-tan version.

Location Notes: Andros, Abaco, the Berry Islands, North Eleuthera, the Keys.

Fishing Notes: Alter the eye type for the desired sink rate. Strip in spurts with pauses until the fish sees; stop and watch the fish's movement for a pick-up. You can also strip in continuous spurts.

Prey Notes: Generic mantis shrimp suggestive of many species of Squillidae, such as golden mantises and rock mantises depending on size and color.

Magnum Mantis • Bill Catherwood

MAGNUM MANTIS

A Bill Catherwood design. Sample in photo was tied by Bill Catherwood on a size 2 hook and measures horizontally 2-1/2" in length and 1-1/2" in width. Fly rides hook-point down.

Hook: 9082 S 3X long kink-shaped popper hook, or 34011; sizes 1, 2 (either should be bent upward just behind eye)

Thread: Tan cotton-coated polyester

Tail/Telson: Pyle-hen neck hackle (outer plate) over hen eider, mallard, or black duck (center or main telson plates), over pyle-hen neck hackle (under telson plate)

Underbody: Light beaver, dubbed

Gills: Emu, palmered through underbody

Killing Claws: Two long ginger variant cock hackles, bent twice each into opposing N shapes

Clubbing Claws: Pyle-hen neck, over ginger variant cock neck, over rose-dyed saddle hackle

Legs: Two matched (but opposing) sets of four each ginger variant hackles tied in at base of claws

Eyes: Short hen eider quill with hackle tip

Antennae: Long hen eider quill with hackle tip

Carapace or Back: Game-hen body feathers, then cock ring-necked pheasant

Tying Notes: Admittedly one of the most unusual designs in this book, Bill has woven his artistic hackle magic to produce an innovative, lifelike mantis shape.

Location Notes: The Bahamas.

Fishing Notes: Let the fly sink, and make a slow, crawling strip until the fish sees it. Then watch the fish's movement to see a pick-up.

Prey Notes: Stomatopod; *Squilla empusa*.

Bill Catherwood, see ARTICULATED CRAB, page 23.

Manjack Cay Charlie • Ed Mitchell

MANJACK CAY CHARLIE

An Ed Mitchell design. Sample in photo was tied by Ed Mitchell on a size 4 34007 hook and measures horizontally about 1-3/8" in length. Fly rides hook-point up.

Hook: 34007; sizes 1, 2, 4, 6

Thread: Brown Danville Flat Waxed Nylon 3/0

Eyes: Medium (1/8") silver bead chain

Tail: Eight strands Flashabou

Body: Red/brown or root beer Crystal Chenille

Wing: Cinnamon Bear Fish Fuzz (Gehrke), then twelve strands gold Krystal Flash

Location Notes: The Bahamas; the pattern has taken a ten- and a twelve-pound fish on Green Turtle Cay.

Fishing Notes: Ed says he likes this fly for cruising fish in shallow water and finds it works well on all colors of bottom. He finds it especially effective on sand. You can alter the eye size and type for the desired sink rate. Strip until the fish sees, let it drop, and watch the fish's movement to see a pick-up.

Prey Notes: Generalized shrimp attractor suggestive of members of the common shrimp (Penaeidae), snapping shrimp (Alpheidae), and mantis shrimp (Squillidae) families.

Ed Mitchell writes for *Fly Fisherman, Salt Water Sportsman, Saltwater Fly Fishing,* and *Field & Stream.* He is author of *Fly Rodding the Coast*, 1995, Stackpole.

Marabou Shrimp (Tan) • Randall Kaufmann

MARABOU SHRIMP

A Randall Kaufmann design. Sample in photo was tied for Randall Kaufmann and to his specifications by Umpqua Feather Merchants on a size 6 3407 hook and measures horizontally 1-1/2" in length. Fly rides hook-point up

Hook: 3407; sizes 2, 4, 6, 8

Thread: Tan 6/0

Eyes: Gold- or nickel-plated steel (size to match desired sink rate), painted tan, then black, then coated with epoxy. Size and weight depend on depth

Body: Orange or fluorescent orange Diamond Braid

Wing: Tan marabou over Krystal Flash (fluorescent orange, pearl, and orange), with tan grizzly tied along each side; should be about twice the length of hook shank

Tying Notes: You can also tie this fly in yellow, pink, and white. It was designed to attract in deep, low-light conditions, with marabou for animation, and grizzly and Krystal Flash for visibility.

Location Notes: The Bahamas, Christmas Island, Los Roques.

Fishing Notes: Randall designed this fly for large fish cruising deep—for instance, along drop-offs, or on deeper flats during high tides. He says large fish are sometimes found in deeper waters and if you can't get your fly down to them quickly, the window of opportunity passes. Lead eyes (this was one of the first bonefish patterns to use them) get this one down fast. Randall says he likes to see all bonefish flies sink to fish level by a count of three.

Prey Notes: Colors suggest many juveniles of the common shrimp (Penaeidae), snapping shrimp (Alpheidae), and mantis shrimp (Squillidae) families.

Randall Kaufmann, see CHRISTMAS ISLAND SPECIAL, page 57.

McCrab • George Anderson

McCRAB

A George Anderson design. Sample in photo was tied by Highland Flies on a size 6 34007 hook and measures horizontally 1-3/4" in length. Carapace measures 9/16" in diameter. The fly rides hook-point up.

Hook: 34007; sizes 4, 6

Thread: Tan Monocord 3/0

Tail: Two cree hackle tips, flared with three or four sprigs Flashabou; then tan marabou

Body: Off-white deer body hair, spun and clipped to carapace shape

Eyes: Small black mono or burnt mono, painted black and Super Glued to underside of body

Legs: Three pairs rubber legs, knotted and Super Glued to underside of body

Belly plate: Small pancake of lead putty or Orvis Heavy Metal, Super Glued to belly and covering legs; coat with cream-colored Plasti-dip

Weight: Smallest (1/100 oz.) lead barbell, tied to underside of carapace and just behind hook eye

Markings: Use markers to bar legs and spot carapace

Tying Notes: The fly is also tied in two other colors: mottled brown and jade green. For permit, George ties the McCrab in sizes 2 and 1/0 with much larger barbells to sink it deep and fast.

Location Notes: The Florida Keys, Belize, the Bahamas, Yucatan. George says he often uses a size 4 in the Keys for delicate presentation to larger tailing fish, and he sometimes goes up to a size 2—which will make a little splat, like an epoxy fly—to get the attention of larger cruising fish. For spooky bonefish in thin water, however, such as those in Belize, he chooses the smaller size 6 with minimal weight and splash.

Fishing Notes: George fishes this pattern for bonefish much the way he does for permit. He puts it two to three feet in front of the lead fish, strips it a few times to get the attention of the fish, then lets it drop to the bottom. If the fish tail on it, he strip-strikes; if they don't, he'll twitch strip it just enough to make it look like it's trying to burrow for cover.

Prey Notes: George uses McCrabs to suggest immature stone crabs and other small cream-colored species (e.g., juvenile spotted decorator crabs, *Microphrys bicornutus*) in the Keys, the Yucatan, and Belize. Tied in jade green, the pattern suggests the popular bonefish prey *Mithrax sculptus*, or green reef crabs.

Anecdotes: George says novelist Tom McGuane (see his Sea Flea pattern, page 147) named the McCrab on a trip to Belize. He says he originally intended the fly specifically as a permit pattern, but then one of his earliest experiences changed his mind. He put the McCrab in front of a pair of twenty-pound permit, got an immediate take, and set the hook. But when the fight was over, he discovered an aggressive six-pound bonefish had rushed in to steal the crab! He decided then that the McCrab—in smaller sizes—would work well for bonefish, and tied several in size 4, which proved deadly the following day.

George Anderson lives in Livingston, Montana, where he owns and operates Yellowstone Angler. He spends six to seven weeks a year stalking the flats for bonefish, permit, and tarpon throughout the Bahamas, the Keys, and the Caribbean. His articles appear frequently in *Fly Fisherman* and other angling journals.

MINI CRAB FLY

A Charlie Gowen design. Sample in photo was tied by Charlie Gowen on a size 4 34007 hook and measures horizontally 1" in length. It also measures 1" across leg tips. Fly rides hook-point up.

Hook: 34007; sizes 4, 6

Thread: Olive Monocord 3/0

Eyes: Small lead barbell, unpainted

Legs: Three strips olive thin Swannundaze or V-Rib, lashed to shank in crisscross fashion; Zap-A-Gap

Body: Olive Mylar Cactus Chenille or (for non-reflective version) medium Ultra Chenille

Wing: Sparse olive or pearl Krystal Flash over sparse hair-wing of elk or calf tail

Mini Crab Fly • Charlie Gowen

Tying Notes: Vary the color—coordinating thread, legs, body, and wing—for species of other colors: olive (shown), light tan, and cream are very effective. Trim the front legs shorter than the mid- and back legs to smooth the movement when stripped. When weighted with the smallest lead eyes, the wing helps invert the fly into a point-up position. *Author's note: You can adjust to the brightness of conditions by carrying both Mylar chenille and non-reflective chenille versions.*

Location Notes: The fly has fished very well at Great Exuma, Long Island, the Berry Islands, Abaco, and Andros. It was developed to fish over sandy and coral rock bottoms where crabs and small urchins abound.

Fishing Notes: Charlie says this is not a deepwater fly, as its bulk slows the sink rate. But the Mini Crab lands gently—ideal for one-and-one-half-foot depths and shallower. Fish it the way a crab moves: Strip once or twice in short bursts until the fish sees, let it drop, and watch the fish's movement to see a pick-up.

Prey Notes: Generic crab suggestive of many species of swimming crabs (Portunidae), mud crabs (Xanthidae), and spider crabs (Majidae).

Anecdotes: Charlie says he was once stalking an eight-pound fish feeding in water so thin its dorsal broke the surface. "It took me twenty minutes to stalk this fish in such skinny water. But when the cast put the Mini Crab three feet off his nose, he absolutely charged it, and then he roared away, kicking up a rooster tail all the way off the flat. It still brings a smile to my face."

Charlie Gowen, who spent several years in Miami where he caught the bonefish bug, now lives in southern Connecticut. He has been bonefishing for eighteen years and has fished most of the Bahamas destinations (often with Doug Schlink—see the Moxey Creek Shrimp, page 125). Charlie is also an avid trout angler who makes annual treks to Montana, and he's an expert rock climber.

Missing Link • Brian O'Keefe

MISSING LINK

A Brian O'Keefe design. Sample in photo was tied by Brian O'Keefe on a size 2 34007 hook and measures horizontally about 2-1/4" in length. Fly rides hook-point up.

Hook: 34007; sizes 2, 4, 6

Thread: Tan Monocord 3/0

Eyes: Medium (1/8") bead chain

Tail: Ten strands gold Krystal Flash, then blond or beige craft fur, then two flanking cree saddle tips

Body: Grizzly (or ginger) saddle palmered and clipped to leave legs, over tan vernille wound forward and figure-eighted at eyes

Tying Notes: Brian says he often ties the fly more tapered than this sample, and with a more ginger-colored body and hackle.

Location Notes: The fly has worked well in South Andros, the Keys, and the Berry Islands for bonefish, and in Belize for permit.

Fishing Notes: Brian says he likes this fly because it fools big bonefish, and because it works also on permit and muttons so no fly change is required.

For the retrieve, he suggests you strip until the fish sees, let it drop, and watch the fish's movement to see a pick-up.

Prey Notes: Generic attractor pattern with a shape suggestive of several larger prey forms including gobies (Gobiidae), toadfish (Batrachoididae), and larger shrimps, such as the Penaeidae and Squillidae families.

Anecdotes: Brian named this pattern for the Missing Link Flat in the Berry Islands, where it took an eight-pound and a twelve-and-one-half-pound fish on its maiden voyage.

Brian O'Keefe, see HOOVER, page 100.

MOE (Mother Of Epoxy) Shrimp • Harry Spear

MOE (MOTHER OF EPOXY) SHRIMP

A Harry Spear design. Sample in photo was tied by Harry Spear on a size 2 34007 hook and measures horizontally 2-3/4" in length. Fly rides hook-point down.

Hook: 34007; sizes 2, 4

Thread: Chartreuse Monocord or Flat Waxed Nylon 3/0

Tail/Claws/Legs: White marabou fibers (one side of marabou blood feather pulled from quill), then tan marabou fibers (same amount), then pair furnace neck or saddle hackles flanking marabou and flared out; next pull one wrap thread under and behind entire tail to kick it up from shank; then resume normal wraps

Eyes: Burnt 60-lb. or 80-lb. Ande pre-stretched mono, figure-eighted to shank

Body: Fasco Fas-Stick Epoxy Glue No. 110 or similar tub epoxy, mixed in exactly equal parts and mixed thoroughly for one full minute (or it comes out tacky and won't harden). Do not let mix begin to set before applying or it will develop memory and will not retain shaping. Apply with toothpick or dental tool to form flat diamond shape over "cross" formed by mono eye shaft and shank. Thin body as you work to outer edges, and form edges into crescent-shaped, concave curves between each point on body's outline. *Keep body thin*—fish don't seem to like fat bodies.

Weed Guard: Pair clear mono spikes (15-lb. hard mason for size 2 hook; 12-lb. for size 4 hook); prepare by passing butt ends near flame to slightly fatten and, when hard, sink "anchors" into epoxy body

Finishing: Place in fishing orientation (body up, hook down) into oven preheated to 140°F *with heat turned off.* Leave in oven to remove moisture and set epoxy.

Tying Notes: Prepare the mono eyes by cutting a 3/4" piece of mono; then, holding it in a forceps, put its end into a sooty candle flame, melt and blacken it, and invert it to the vertical to allow a round eye to form as a droplet. Repeat for the other side. You should have an eye shaft about 7/16" to 9/16" long when you're finished.

Harry also ties another version using olive over white marabou, flanked by splayed grizzly tips.

Location Notes: The Florida Keys (size 2), the Bahamas (size 4).

Fishing Notes: Harry says you should fish this fly as a shrimp (in spurts): Drop it when the fish sees it, and strip it again if needed.

Prey Notes: Generic shrimp suggestive of many common shrimps (Penaeidae), snapping shrimps (Alpheidae), grass shrimps (Palaemonidae), and possibly even mantis shrimps (Squillidae).

Anecdotes: Harry says this pattern works extremely well if you can get it into the bonefish's window of vision without scaring him. The light epoxies can usually be cast closer to fish, and work best for tailers in calm water.

Harry Spear is one of the legends of Florida Keys flats fishing and fly tying. When I once asked Rick Ruoff whose flies he liked most, he mentioned only two names, Steve Huff's (see his Joe-To-Go, page 107) and Harry's. It was Harry who pioneered the use of epoxy in bonefish flies with his original MOE prototype, which took a twenty-three-and-one-half-pound permit the first day angler Bill Levy fished it off Harry's skiff in 1978. Epoxy is now a staple ingredient of many of the most successful Keys patterns. See also Harry's Tasty Toad, page 166.

Morning Hatch Shrimp • O'Keefe's adaptation of Morning Hatch Fly Shop pattern

MORNING HATCH SHRIMP

A Brian O'Keefe adaptation of a Morning Hatch Fly Shop (Tacoma, Washington) design. Sample in photo was tied by Brian O'Keefe on a size 6 34007 hook and measures horizontally about 1-1/4" in length. Fly rides hook-point down.

Hook: 34007; sizes 6, 8, 10

Thread: White Monocord 3/0

Eyes: Burnt 12-lb. or 15-lb. Mason mono

Tail: Six strands pearlescent Krystal Flash

Underbody: Pearlescent Krystal Flash

Body: White or cream saddle hackle, palmered from base of tail to hook eye and clipped along body (except for collar). Overwind head to angle collar back toward eyes.

Tying Notes: Brian says a couple of pink Krystal Flash strands in the tail are sometimes nice on this one.

Location Notes: Good at Christmas Island (size 10); also at South Andros, the Berry Islands, and Belize.

Fishing Notes: Brian says hits come very easy on this one as it sinks after each pull in the retrieve. Strip until the fish sees it, and watch the fish's movement to see a pick-up.

Prey Notes: Small shrimp suggestive of juvenile members of the common shrimp (Penaeidae), snapping shrimp (Alpheidae), and grass shrimp (Palaemonidae) families.

Brian O'Keefe, see HOOVER, page 100.

Moxey Creek Shrimp • Doug Schlink

MOXEY CREEK SHRIMP

A Doug Schlink design. Sample in photo was tied by Doug Schlink on a size 4 34011 hook and measures horizontally 2-5/8" in length, including antennae. Fly rides hook-point up.

Hook: 34011; sizes 2, 4; put a 15° bend in shank similar to bend-back style, and bend eye slightly downward (toward point side); flatten barb, sharpen, and slightly offset point

Thread: Yellow Danville Flymaster 6/0

Forelegs: Barred lemon wood duck, tied in by tip, folded and wrapped as a wet-fly hackle

Antennae: Argentine wild boar guard hairs (or moose mane)

Weight: 1/36 oz. or 1/24 oz. (5/32" or 7/32") plated barbell

Eyes: Burnt mono painted black, or black plastic bead eyes (on latter cut five eyes from string and crush out middle three)

Underbody: Gold Sparkle Chenille

Body: Dubbed blend of hare's ear and Argentine boar underfur (or other spiky dubbing such as seal or dark brown Sealex); apply loosely so gold shows through

Location Notes: The fly was designed for Andros and first fished in Moxey Creek Flats. It has also been effective in Great Harbour Cay (Berry Islands) creeks and outer grass flats.

Fishing Notes: The fly has worked well on cruising fish in a brisk moving tide. It's also good for mudding fish.

Prey Notes: Suggestive of common shrimps (Penaeidae) and mantis shrimps (Squillidae), especially *Pseudosquilla ciliata*, the golden mantis.

Anecdotes: Doug says he originally went to the trouble of tying a carapace covering of plastic from a Ziploc bag with gold wire, but the first fish that took the fly ripped off the covering and the fly still worked fine, so he declared the carapace "window dressing" and now fishes the fly as described and pictured.

Doug Schlink is an expert angler who works with Chip Bates at Angler Adventures. He has fished the Yucatan, Los Roques, and all major (and some not so major) Bahamian destinations. He considers bonefish his second favorite quarry, after Atlantic salmon.

Myers' Shrimp • Will Myers

MYERS' SHRIMP

A Will Myers design. Sample in photo was tied by Will Myers on a size 6 34011 hook and measures horizontally about 1-7/8" in length. Fly rides hook-point down.

Hook: 34011; sizes 6, 8

Thread: White Danville Plus

Weed Guard: 12-lb. Mason hard mono

Legs: Ten strands white bucktail

Body/Tail: White Big Fly Fiber

Eyes: 50-lb. mono with epoxy

Overbody: Marine Goop

Colors: Berol Artmaker or other marking pens

Tying Notes: When Will builds the body of this fly, he applies a gob of Goop along the top of the hook shank; moistens his fingers with Kodak Photo-Flo or saliva; shapes the Goop as desired; and applies a second coat if needed (Goop shrinks).

Location Notes: The fly fishes well at all locations that have larger shrimps.

Fishing Notes: This pattern can be easily adapted to look like local shrimp varieties if you carry different sizes and add color on-site. You can alter the weight by adding Orvis putty to the weed guard.
Strip until the fish sees, stop, and watch the fish's movement to see a pick-up. Or you can just cast, leave the fly still in front of the fish, and wait for a take.

Prey Notes: Will's pattern, when tied with different coloration (brown is shown), suggests many different shrimp species. By varying its color and size, you can use it to suggest many of the common shrimps (Penaeidae), snapping shrimps (Alpheidae), grass shrimps (Palaemonidae), and mantis shrimps (Squillidae).

Will Myers, see BUSTER CRAB, page 53.

Nacho • Nick Curcione

NACHO

> *A Nick Curcione design. Sample in photo was tied by Nick Curcione on a size 4 3407 hook and measures horizontally 1-1/2" in length. Fly rides hook-point up.*

Hook: 3407; size 4

Thread: Tan Monocord 3/0

Eyes: 4/32" (1/8") lead barbell, painted black

Body: Mylar braid, light copper color

Underwing: Gray craft fur; then a dozen strands copper-colored Krystal Flash

Overwing: Copper-dyed wool; combed out

Location Notes: Nick says he originally tied this fly for the Mexican Yucatan Peninsula, and its color and the destination gave it the name. The pattern has also fished extremely well in Christmas Island, where not only bonefish but also trevally and sharks found it much to their liking. Nick says he hooked his largest permit ever on this fly: a thirty-plus-pounder in the Yucatan that was later lost—but still vividly remembered—when the leader fouled on a lobster trap.

Fishing Notes: Strip the fly until the fish sees, let it drop, and watch the fish's movement for a pick-up. Resume if there's no interest.

Prey Notes: Suggests small shrimp species from the Palaemonidae, Gnatophyllidae, and Hippolytidae families.

Nick Curcione, see BONE BUG, page 34.

Nasty Gilbert • Tim Merrihew

NASTY GILBERT

A Tim Merrihew design. Sample in photo was tied by Tim Merrihew on a size 4 3407 hook and measures horizontally 1-3/8" in overall length, including antennae. Fly rides hook-point up.

Hook: 3407; size 4, crimped and triangulated

Thread: Pale yellow Monocord 3/0

Eyes: Medium (1/8") gold-colored or brass bead chain

Tail: Pale Gold Crystal Hair No. 22 (not Krystal Flash), cut short to look shrimp-like

Underbody: Pale Gold Crystal Hair

Overwrap/Carapace: Clear Swannundaze No. 82, coated with clear nail polish or thin epoxy

Legs: Pale Gold Crystal Hair

Cephalothorax: Pale yellow rabbit dubbing

Tying Notes: Lay Swannundaze from the eyes to the tail before overwrapping to avoid a reverse taper and enhance translucency. Begin bodywrapping on the bend, to give the body a natural curved shape. Alter the color of the cephalothorax by applying different dubbing colors. Wrap the dubbing behind the Crystal Hair legs/antennae, then figure-eight the dubbing ahead of the eyes and forward of the legs/antennae. Trim the legs to just past the hook point. Leave two strands of Crystal Hair longer for the antennae. The fly can be tied in pale yellow, light tan, or bright yellow by changing only the dubbing color, or by blending in some yellow Krystal Flash. Other variations: Color the head with bright orange head cement; spiral the body with a shade-darker thread, for a rib; darken the fly for tan bottoms with a light brown thread underbody.

Material Notes: Tim prefers Crystal Hair No. 22 over the Krystal Flash equivalent because he finds it finer and more tightly crimped and because the color just seems to work better. Unfortunately, distributor Umpqua says Crystal Hair is no longer made, but Tim says the following technique will come very close to his original: Substitute clear Krystal Flash for the legs and tail, winding a layer of *pale* yellow thread as an underbody to supply the color under the Swannundaze. Much of the overall color, he notes, comes from the cephalothorax dubbing reflected in the Krystal Flash.

Location Notes: Christmas Island. Tim says this pattern, which he developed specifically for Christmas Island, usually performs best in the pale yellow that approximates a lot of the coral bottoms. On the oceanside flats reef areas, which are darker in color, a light brown version does better. He also notes that in some years, bright yellow makes the fish almost suicidal.

Fishing Notes: Tim says in his experience, bonefish eat more selectively in terms of color, size, and shape than most people believe. He says that as long as he is fishing something close to what the fish are eating, he strips very economically. "I only need to move the fly enough so they can see it. Once they've spotted it, I can stop my retrieve, and they will pick it up dead. If you doubt that bonefish are observant," he adds, "just try fishing a dark-colored leader at Christmas."

Prey Notes: Depending on color, the fly is suggestive of many smaller shrimps, such as juvenile common shrimps (Penaeidae) and snapping shrimps (Alpheidae), as well as members of such diminutive families as Palaemonidae, Gnatophyllidae, and Hippolytidae.

Tim Merrihew is a medical microbiologist by education who's spent the last twenty years in electronic security. He lives in Tualatin, Oregon, and he enjoys all types of fishing, from long-range tuna boats out of San Diego to float tubing for trout in British Columbia. He's a fixture at Christmas Island where others say he catches an awful lot of bonefish.

Ouch • Dr. Jonathan Slocum

OUCH

A Dr. Jonathan Slocum design. Sample in photo was tied by Dr. Jonathan Slocum on a size 12 3406 hook and measures horizontally 1/2" in length, including hook bend. Fly rides hook-point down.

Hook: 7957 1X short or 3406 heavy wire; size 12

Thread: Invisible sewing thread for tying; then fluorescent orange for head

Body: Light gray dubbing, or very thin chenille

Hackle: Grizzly

Tying Notes: Trim the hackle to leave a short bristle.

Location Notes: This fly is fished only in Belize, where small sea lice are plentiful.

Fishing Notes: Strip the fly until the fish sees, pause, and watch the fish's movement to see a pick-up.

Prey Notes: Gribble, *Limnoria tripunctata*, sea roach, *Ligia exotica*.

Anecdotes: Dr. Slocum says one day he was fishing in the grass beds in Belize and little sea lice were stinging his legs. A guide said the fish eat them regularly, picking them off the grass blades. Dr. Slocum tied this pattern to look like a small louse, and he began taking fish on it. He says he only uses it when the lice begin biting him.

Dr. Jonathan Slocum, see GLASS-EYED SHRIMP, page 83.

Palmered Crab • Jeffrey Cardenas

PALMERED CRAB

A Jeffrey Cardenas design. Sample in photo was tied by Jeffrey Cardenas on a size 4 34007 hook and measures horizontally 1-5/8" in overall length. Fly rides hook-point up.

Hook: 34007; sizes 2, 4, 6

Thread: Monocord 3/0

Tail: Tan marabou, flanked by dry-fly-quality hackle tips for claws, then two long strands Krystal Flash for antennae

Eyes: Medium (5/32") Orvis black lead barbell

Body/Legs: Three wide saddles (leave fluff at base), palmered heavily with bottom fluff wound in; trim flat across back to shape legs

Tying Notes: You can palmer all three hackles at once if you're careful. Heavy palmering is essential—you may even want to compress the turns to pack the body bulk. Also, use wide hackles to provide long legs (3/4" fibers on a size 4 hook). The fly can be tied in rust, white, and other hues to suggest coloration of local prey and habitat.

Location Notes: The Florida Keys.

Fishing Notes: Use a size 6 for tailing, and a size 2 for situations where permit as well as bones are present. Cast close, read the fish, twitch strip as necessary … and hang on.

Prey Notes: Generic crab shape suggestive of many species of swimming crabs (Portunidae), mud crabs (Xanthidae), and spider crabs (Majidae).

Anecdotes: Jeffrey developed this pattern to take advantage of the importance of crabs in the diets of bonefish in the Keys. He feels marabou and hackle make for livelier action than do rubber legs—they move even when the fly is still. The hackle provides bulk and buoyancy that tend to keep the hook point riding up, a critical advantage when you're over Keys grassy bottoms.

Jeffrey Cardenas, see BUNNY BONE, page 52.

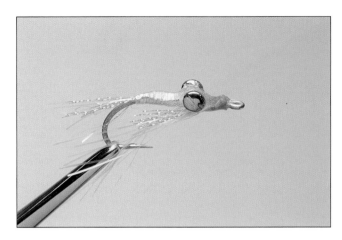

Paris Flat Special • Eddie Corrie

PARIS FLAT SPECIAL

An Eddie Corrie design. Sample in photo was tied by Eddie Corrie on a size 2 3407 hook and measures horizontally 1-5/8" in length. Fly rides hook-point up.

Hook: 3407; sizes 2, 4, 6

Thread: Single-strand orange 6/0

Eyes: Large (3/16") gold Dazl eyes

Tail: Orange Krystal Flash, then three or four sprigs pearlescent Flashabou

Body: Pearlescent Flashabou wound over orange thread underbody

Wing: Short orange Krystal Flash, then long pearlescent Flashabou, then four or five white calf tail hairs for legs

Overcoat: Epoxy

Head: Orange thread coated with epoxy; oversized (1/4" long)

Tying Notes: To represent other shrimps found at Christmas Island, Eddie also uses other colors of thread and Krystal Flash, including fluorescent green, yellow, and light tan.

Location Notes: Christmas Island. Eddie has guided fly fishers there for over ten years. He designed this fly specifically for the atoll's Paris Flat during after-full-moon tides. The fly sinks very fast and represents shrimps found in the lagoon around rock structure (coral). The fly also looks like the shrimps found on ocean flats such as Korean Flat, Robert Plantation, and Puka Flat.

Fishing Notes: Eddie says he fishes the fly by retrieving in one-foot strips to get the fish's attention. When the fish sees it, he makes a few quick six-inch strips and watches the fish. If the fish hesitates and its body goes vertical, he stops … pauses … and then strip-strikes. If he feels nothing, he resumes the original stripping pattern.

Prey Notes: Generic shrimp suggestive of many species of common shrimps (Penaeidae), snapping shrimps (Alpheidae), and grass shrimps (Palaemonidae).

Big **Eddie Corrie** is head guide and manager of bonefishing operations at Christmas

Island. He was born and raised on this island atoll and has fished and guided there for more than a decade.

Pearl Flash • Neal Rogers

PEARL FLASH

A Neal Rogers design. Sample in photo was tied by Neal Rogers on a size 4 Tiemco 800S hook and measures horizontally 1-7/8" in length. Fly rides hook-point up.

Hook: Tiemco 800S; sizes 2, 4, 6

Thread: White Monocord 3/0

Eyes: Medium (5/32") lead barbell, plated

Tail: Pearl Krystal Flash

Body: Pearl Poly Flash

Wing: White calf tail flanked by grizzly hackle tips

Tying Notes: Light green pearlescent Poly Flash is also very effective for the body. Tie the fly with bead chain for thin water/spooky conditions; add a weed guard for grass habitats.

Location Notes: The Florida Keys, Yucatan.

Fishing Notes: Alter the eye type for the desired sink rate. Neal retrieves in one- to two-inch quick strips. The fly works well in chum slicks.

Prey Notes: Suggestive of some common shrimps (Penaeidae) and snapping shrimps (Alpheidae). The fly may also suggest some swimming worms or polychaetes such as sand-worms (Nereidae) and errant threadworms (Syllidae).

Anecdotes: Neal says in several instances he has had fish refuse as many as four or five other flies and then take this one. In addition to bonefish, Neal has taken two permit on the pattern.

Neal Rogers is coauthor—with his wife and fishing partner, Linda—of *Saltwater Fly*

Fishing Magic. An avid saltwater angler, he bonefishes several times a year in the Keys, Yucatan, and elsewhere.

Perdi Shrimp • Doug Brewer

PERDI SHRIMP

A Doug Brewer design. Sample in photo was tied by Doug Brewer on a size 4 3407 hook and measures horizontally 2" in overall length. Fly rides hook-point down.

Hook: 3407; sizes 2, 4, 6, 8

Thread: Brown Danville Plus

Tail: Tan Widow's Web or sparkle yarn

Body: Brown thread

Rib: Orange Krystal Flash

Face: Tan Widow's Web or sparkle yarn

Feelers: Brown rubber hackle

Overbody: "Hot Head" material, amber (see description under Standard MOE, page 161)

Eyes: Black, painted next to feelers

Tying Notes: Other color options: pink, white, olive, coral, and orange. Change the thread, Widow's Web, rubber hackle, and Hot Head to match.

Location Notes: Use the larger sizes in the Bahamas and Christmas Island; use the small size 8 in Belize, in skinny water, and for spooky fish.

Fishing Notes: Strip the fly for movement. It is tied and fished mainly for cruising fish, and retrieved as a spooked shrimp. Movement is important.

Prey Notes: In all its colors the fly suggests members of many small shrimp families such as Palaemonidae, Gnatophyllidae, and Hippolytidae.

Anecdotes: The fly was named after Doug's puppy, who's always on the move ...

Doug Brewer, see BREWER'S AMBER, page 49.

Pflueger Hoy • Bob Hyde

PFLUEGER HOY

A Bob Hyde design. Sample in photo was tied by Bob Hyde on a size 6 3407 hook and measures horizontally 1-3/8" in overall length. Fly rides hook-point up.

Hook: 3407; sizes 4, 6

Thread: Tan Monocord 3/0

Tail: Pink marabou tips

Body: Fuzzy Nymph leech yarn; then pink, long-fibered, soft hackle palmered to head

Wing: Tan marabou

Tying Notes: The fly can also be tied with a royal blue marabou tail and a cream-colored hackle, palmered.

Location Notes: The Bahamas; the pattern is especially effective for tailers on Exuma's shallow flats.

Fishing Notes: Bump the fly until it's seen, then make six- to eight-inch strips, watching for a pick-up.

Prey Notes: Generic prey form suggestive of both crab and shrimp species. It may also suggest some swimming seaworms or sandworms.

Anecdotes: This very effective tailing fly was named by Peace and Plenty manager Charlie Pflueger, who offers a complementary fishing trip to the first angler to guess the definition of "HOY."

Bob Hyde, previously a Florida Keys guide, is part owner and operator of the Peace and Plenty Lodge in Exuma, Bahamas.

Pink Epoxy Charlie • George Hommell

PINK EPOXY CHARLIE

A George Hommell design. Sample in photo was tied for George Hommell by Highland Flies on a size 4 3407 hook and measures horizontally 1-3/8" in length. Fly rides hook-point up.

Hook: 3407; size 4

Thread: Pink Gudebrod

Eyes: Medium (1/8") bead chain

Body: 5-Minute Epoxy mixed with pink dye (Rit or Tintex fabric dye, or rubber-worm dye) over rainbow pearlescent Krystal Flash

Wing: Multicolor pearlescent Krystal Flash over pink-dyed bucktail

Tying Notes: Variations: You can also tie the fly with a brown or white epoxy body and a matching wing color.

Location Notes: All of the Bahamas; the Florida Keys' oceanside flats.

Fishing Notes: Work the fly very slowly, bouncing it on the bottom. It is good for two- to six-foot depths on any tide; and for both mudding and tailing fish.

Prey Notes: This generic shrimp suggests many species.

George Hommell is the owner of World Wide Sportsman in Islamorada, a former Keys guide, and a pivotal figure in the emergence of bonefishing. He has fished everywhere: the Bahamas, Mexico, Belize, Venezuela.

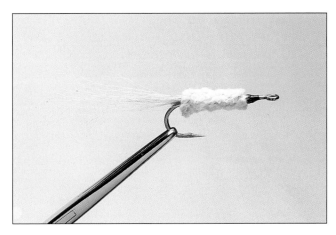

Pipe Cleaner Fly • Dick Berry

PIPE CLEANER FLY

A Dick Berry design. Sample in photo was tied by Dick Berry on a size 4 34007 hook and measures horizontally 2-1/4" in length. Fly rides hook-point down.

Hook: 34007; sizes 2, 4

Thread: Black Prewaxed Monocord

Eyes: None

Tail: Buff white bucktail one-and-one-half times length of hook

Body: White pipe cleaner

Location Notes: Eleuthera, Harbour Island, the Bahamas.

Fishing Notes: The original fly pattern, with its heavy hook as well as the wire in its pipe cleaner, is too heavy for thin, calm water, but it gets down fast at medium depths on choppy days. You can tie the fly with a smaller hook and standard chenille for spookier conditions.

Prey Notes: White polychaete seaworm pattern suggestive of many swimming polychaetes, such as sandworms (Nereidae) and errant threadworms (Syllidae), that burrow just under the surface, as well as errant tubeworms (Onuphidae) that live on the surface.

Anecdotes: Several years ago Dick needed a white fly so he took a streamer, cut off everything on it that was not white, and wrapped one of fellow guest George Fisher's white pipe cleaners around the shank for a body. He says he caught his two largest fish on this fly—a nine-pounder and another of about eleven-and-one-half pounds, both on Harbour Island's Girls Bank flat.

Dick Berry is a retired executive of the Olin Company, and now plays golf, chases bonefish, and collects pipe cleaners.

Pop Hill Special • Edmond G. Hill

POP HILL SPECIAL

An Edmond G. Hill design. Sample in photo was tied by Dr. Gordon Hill, Pop's son, on a size 4 hook; it measures horizontally 1-5/8" in length. Fly rides hook-point down.

Hook: 34007 or Eagle Claw 254SS; size 4

Thread: Light green or white Flat Waxed Nylon 3/0

Body: Plain clear 15-lb. Ande mono

Wing: Four white saddle hackles

Tying Notes: The wing is tied up so the hook point rides down—unlike most bonefish patterns.

Location Notes: The fly is successful on white sand flats in the Florida Keys and Bahamas; also Belize and Mexico. It has worked especially well on light-colored flats in Exuma and Andros.

Fishing Notes: Lead a school of bonefish and allow the fly to sink to the sandy bottom. Your fly-rod tip should be lowered to water level or even into the water. Retrieve with jerky "puffs," made by one- to three-foot strips. The fly hook should dip into and puff the sand.

Prey Notes: Gordon says the Pop Hill Special mimics tiny crustaceans, which by their nature can't easily be seen, since they've whitened to camouflage themselves against the natural white sandy bottoms of their habitat. *Author's note: The fly may also be fished to suggest some of the errant seaworms or polychaetes such as sandworms (Nereidae), errant threadworms (Syllidae), and tubeworms (Onuphidae).*

Anecdotes: According to Gordon, "Many years ago while fishing on the crystal-bright white flats on the west side of Andros, we were having trouble getting bones to hit our usual patterns. Pop noted that the fish were not spooky, and that he could wade close to them. He observed them feeding on 'invisible' creatures. A fine dip net came up with some small white and clear crustaceans. He figured that if he could tie a fly the same color as these (and of the flat itself) and then retrieve it so it puffed the sand, it might work. He caught eleven bones on it that morning! I've since used it successfully for years, and I've won the bonefish tournament at Georgetown, Exuma, six times in a row with the pattern."

Dr. Gordon Hill, a retired surgeon, lives on Big Pine Key where he is a charter member of the S.O.B.'s (Sport Fishermen Of Broward) with the rank of Supreme Angler. He fishes for tarpon, permit, and bonefish and has fished the Keys, the Bahamas, Yucatan, and Belize for thirty-two years. His father, "Pop," pioneered saltwater fly fishing in the 1920s. Gordon says he and his dad were not just father and son, but also fishing buddies who shared many waters and many fish until Pop passed away in 1985.

Pop's Bonefish Bitters (Hermit Crab Bitters in Photo) • *Craig Mathews*

POP'S BONEFISH BITTERS

A Craig Mathews design. Sample in photo, the Hermit Crab Bitters variation, was tied by Craig Mathews on a size 8 3407 hook in a "Tears of Keys" blank; it measures horizontally 3/4" in length, and 1" in width. Fly rides hook-point up.

Hook/Body/Eyes: Tears of Keys blank (Tiemco 800S or Mustad 3407); sizes 4, 6, 8, 10; amber shown, also olive, chartreuse, orange, pink, white

Thread: Uni-Thread 6/0; white, cream, camel to match or complement T.O.K. blank

Legs: Sili Legs or round rubber (color to match body)

Weed/Coral Guard: Natural mottled deer hair over Zelon underwing; Zelon should match T.O.K. in color

Tying Notes: Figure-eight four sets of rubber legs onto the shank behind the head, then tie in a section of Zelon reaching to the hook point, and trim the excess. Tie the deer hair over the Zelon—the deer hair should be short and coarse so that it flares and cups the pattern around the hook point.

Special Variation: Craig ties the Hermit Crab Bitters—a very successful new Bitters version—using amber, olive, or lime T.O.K. blanks and dyed Spandex rubber legs, clipped short; he mottles the legs with Sanford markers. Common leg colors for this variation: blue with red and dark blue mottling, to suggest the three-colored hermit; olive green with brown mottling, for smooth-clawed hermit species; red mottling on cream, for the red bar-eyed hermit; and green-brown mottling on cream or light olive, for the green-striped hermit.

Location Notes: The original Pop's Bitters was developed for the reef flats of Belize but has since been fished successfully all over the bonefish world. *Author's note: I've had several reports of this pattern fishing particularly well at Sandy Point in the Bahamas.*

Fishing Notes: Pop's Bitters lands quietly and fishes well for mudding, tailing, and cruising fish in shallow water. Craig describes his retrieve for this pattern as a single, slow two- to six-inch strip; then two slow two- to six-inch strips; followed by six- to twelve-inch strips, or sometimes no strip at all. A chartreuse version works best in the P.M., an amber in the A.M. Olive works well in turtle grass. Orange has been a good Bahamas color. Pink and white are very effective in extreme shallows.

Craig fishes the Hermit Crab Bitters variation on the lee side of cays and near short mangroves and mangrove shoots, where these crabs crawl with a slow, short strip and many pauses. Used primarily for tailing and shoreline-cruising fish, this newer fly worked well on Craig's last trip to Belize after guides tipped him off to the naturals there, and the need for imitations. *Author's note: Craig told me recently that after his initial trials, several anglers reported great success with this fly at both Ascencion Bay and Belize.*

Prey Notes: Pop's Bitters suggests many swimming, spider, mud, shore, fiddler, and land crabs from Belize and the Bahamas, including the common blue crab (*Callinectes sapidus*), the green reef crab (*Mithrax sculptus*), and the spotted decorator crab (*Microphrys bicornutus*). The Hermit Bitters variation portrays the three-colored hermit (*Clibanarius tricolor*); the smooth-clawed hermit (*Calcinus tibicen*); the red bar-eyed hermit (*Dardanus fucosus*); and the green-striped hermit (*Clibanarius vittatus*).

Anecdotes: Craig named this pattern for Belizian Pops Winston Cabral, considered by many to be one of the best bonefish guides in the world.

Craig Mathews, see CLAM BEFORE THE STORM, page 59.

Ralph's Hackled Epoxy Bonefish Fly • Ralph Woodbine

RALPH'S HACKLED EPOXY BONEFISH FLY

A Ralph Woodbine design. Sample in photo was tied by Ralph Woodbine on a size 6 34007 hook and measures horizontally 1-3/8" in length. Fly rides hook-point up.

Hook: 34007; sizes 2, 4, 6

Thread: White 6/0

Eyes: Medium (1/8") bead chain for sizes 4 and 6, or large (3/8") bead chain for size 2, painted black

Tail: Tan marabou, tied short and full

Body: Wind white yarn, saturated with cement, tapering body to long triangular shape; then cover with pearl braid such as Kreinik Tyer's Ribbon, Poly Flash, or Diamond Braid and flatten body horizontally; darken top (side facing point) with brown permanent marker

Hackle: Cree saddle, palmered

Coating: Coat body with Zap-A-Gap, palmer hackle to eyes, spray with Zap-A-Gap Kicker. Trim hackle of bottom of body and coat bottom and head with Devcon 5-Minute Epoxy

Tying Notes: Ralph ties the fly with lead barbell eyes for deep water.

Location Notes: The Florida Keys, Yucatan, Christmas Island, the Caribbean.

Fishing Notes: Very durable. Ralph reports he has taken as many as twenty fish on a single fly. Strip until the fish sees, let it drop, and watch the fish's movement to see a pick-up.

Prey Notes: Generic shrimp suggestive of many common shrimps (Penaeidae), snapping shrimps (Alpheidae), and mantis shrimps (Squillidae). The larger sizes may also suggest toadfish (Batrachoididae).

Anecdotes: Ralph's frequent fishing partner, J. Watt Shroyer, used a size 2 to take half a dozen small permit (five to fifteen pounds) at Ascencion Bay in 1994; he says it worked better there than conventional crab flies. The only drawback was that the fish took it deeply.

Ralph Woodbine, see CHRISTMAS ISLAND FLASH CHARLIE, page 57.

Rock Mantis • Carl Richards

ROCK MANTIS

A Carl Richards design. Sample in photo was tied by Carl Richards on a size 4 Dai-Riki 700B hook and measures horizontally 2-1/4" in length, including antennae.

Hook: Dai-Riki 700B; sizes 2, 4, 6

Thread: Olive Dynacord 3/0

Eyes: Mono, painted green

Antennae: Four boar bristles

Ears: Olive-dyed hackle tips glued to eyestalks

Raptorial Legs: Olive after feathers or marabou fibers

Walking Legs: Long, stiff, cream cock hackle

Carapace/Abdomen: Olive after feathers or marabou fibers

Swimmerets or Pleopods: Short, webby badger hackle

Tail: Olive after feathers or marabou fibers

Weight: Lead strips under and behind eyes, or lead barbell under tail

Location Notes: Belize, Abaco, the Berry Islands, North Eleuthera.

Fishing Notes: Alter the weight type for the desired sink rate. Fish close to the bottom with a hopping retrieve at varying speeds.

Prey Notes: Rock mantis, *Gonodactylus oerstedii,* which often inhabit the inside slope of outer reefs and coral keys.

Anecdotes: Carl has taken fish with this pattern in both the Bahamas and Belize. On one expedition to the Berry Islands it was—in tan—the most productive fly of the trip.

Carl Richards, see BLACK URCHIN, page 32.

Ron's MOE • Ron Leyzen

RON'S MOE

A Ron Leyzen design. Sample in photo was tied by Ron Leyzen on a size 4 3407 hook and measures horizontally 1-7/8" in length. Fly rides hook-point up.

Hook: 34007, 3407 Partridge Sea Prince, or TMC 811S; sizes 2, 4, 6

Thread: Color to match body, 6/0

Underbody/Frame: Square of flexible plastic (such as report-folder cover) cut to fit hook size (3/16" for size 4)

Eyes: Soft lead split shot, pinched onto (cut-off) corners of underbody

Tail: Marabou flanked by grizzly hackle tips

Wing: Fox squirrel, then Krystal Flash

Outer Coating: 5-Minute or 20-Minute Epoxy

Tying Notes: With the hook right-side up in the vise, and the thread wound to the bend, cut off two opposite corners of the plastic square; cut small slits in the two other corners. Lay the square atop the thread-covered shank, with the slits on top of the shank. Slide the rear slit around the thread and bind the slit corner to the shank. Lift the plastic and wind the thread forward. Then insert the thread into the forward slit and bind it to the shank. Invert the hook, crimp on the eyes, and epoxy the fly's "top," adding glitter if desired. Once the epoxy's set, apply a second coat to the entire body and rotate it regularly until the epoxy is set. Tie in the tail and wing, and finish.

Location Notes: Yucatan, Mexico (white is good); Ambergris Caye, Belize (tan/gold and pink are good); the Florida Keys; Placencia, Belize.

Fishing Notes: Good for tailing and cruising fish. Strip until the fish sees, let it drop, and watch the fish's movement to see a pick-up. Leave the fly motionless occasionally for a few seconds.

Prey Notes: Generic shrimp suggestive of many species of common, grass, and snapping shrimps, depending on color. The fly can also suggest swimming crabs.

Anecdotes: The fly was named by Al Beatty at Fly Fair '92 in Holland. A pink version caught Ron's first permit.

Ron Leyzen, see CRAPOXY, page 61.

Salsa Shrimp • Craig Mathews

SALSA SHRIMP

A Craig Mathews design. Sample in photo was tied by Craig Mathews on a size 2 3407 hook and measures horizontally 1-1/2" in length. Fly rides hook-point down.

Hook: TMC 800S, Mustad 34007 or 3407; sizes 1, 2, 6

Thread: White Uni-Thread 6/0

Rostrum/Chelipeds: Red deer hair or elk hair

Claws: Two grizzly hackles with tips removed

Eyes: Large plastic beads

Shellback: Dun-dyed Zelon (represents cephalopods, thorax, and top of abdomen); pull Zelon over back and tie off at hook eye. This also represents tail (uropod and telson) when trimmed to shape

Body: Gray and pink Zelon cut up, blended, dubbed into rough body, then picked out

Weight: None

Rib: Grizzly hackle palmered and trimmed to represent swimmerets (pleopods)

Tying Notes: Other color options: olive, orange, and brownish-white. Normally no weight is used, but in two to three feet of water, you can add a nontoxic lead substitute.

Location Notes: The fly was designed for Belize; it has since been fished successfully in Bimini, Kanton, and Christmas Island.

Fishing Notes: The fly should be fished with a rapid, long retrieve. Stop only after the fish has followed without taking for ten to twenty feet; pause and let it drop to bottom, then quickly strip one to three feet. Craig says he favors a special "swim-away" technique for this pattern. He throws a downtide (or downcurrent) belly into the line while placing the fly in front of the fish. The water movement carries the fly away from both fish and angler for the first several feet of the retrieve. Once the belly is stripped out, the fly swings back toward the angler.

Prey Notes: Mimics Mexican shrimps and other subtle gray/brown/pink shrimps found on reefs and in shallow, subtidal areas, including the pink shrimp, *Penaeus duorarum*, and the pink spotted shrimp, *Penaeus brasilensis*.

Anecdotes: Craig says he was broken off on the retrieve with this fly by his first four fish. He named the pattern for the salsa Belizians serve as an hors d'oeuvre before a shrimp dinner.

Craig Mathews, see CLAM BEFORE THE STORM, page 59.

Sand Bandit • Terry Baird

SAND BANDIT

A Terry Baird design. Sample in photo was tied by Terry Baird on a size 6 Gamakatsu hook and measures horizontally 2" in length. Fly rides hook-point up.

Hook: Gamakatsu O'Shaughnessy; sizes 1, 2, 4, 6, 8

Thread: 2-lb. Ande mono

Eyes: Medium bead chain, or lead

Tail: Pink (or yellow, chartreuse, or brown) marabou

Body: 1/8" pearl Flashabou overwrapped on shank

Wing: Two stacks Super hair; bottom stack clear, top stack pink (or color to match tail)

Feelers (optional): Two strands Krystal Flash, one-and-one-quarter times wing length and straddling wing

Claws: Sili Legs or round rubber, one-and-one-half times hook length; angled up and splayed out to sides; barred with red, black, or other marker

Tying Notes: Terry says that he designed this one to be a *style* of tying, and that many materials can be substituted. The key is to have the legs angled off the bottom, allowing constant movement of the claws when the fly is fished.

Location Notes: Christmas Island, Fanning Island, the Hawaiian Islands, Belize, the Bahamas, the Keys.

Fishing Notes: This is a good fly for calm shallows and spooky fish. Its sparse profile is quiet but sinks fast. The legs give movement even when it's at rest. Strip gently.

Prey Notes: In different colors, the fly suggests many members of the snapping shrimp (Alpheidae) and grass shrimp (Palaemonidae) families. It also portrays some of the smaller spider crabs or Majidae.

Terry Baird, who lives in Portland, Oregon, grew up in Hawaii and has fished the South Pacific as well as Mexico, the Bahamas, the Turks and Caicos, and the Virgin Islands.

Scott's Tube Shrimp (Copper) • Scott Sanchez

SCOTT'S TUBE SHRIMP

A Scott Sanchez design. Sample in photo was tied by Scott Sanchez on a size 4 34007 hook and measures horizontally 1-1/2" in length to marabou tips, 2-5/8" overall to antennae tips. Fly rides hook-point down.

Hook: 34007; sizes 2, 4, 6

Thread: Brown Monocord 3/0

Weight: Three wraps .025" lead, slightly behind hook eye

Forelegs: Brown marabou

Eyes: Plastic hair-brush bristles (or burnt mono) tied alongside marabou, then figure-eighted at base to separate, and glued

Antennae/Underbody/Telson: Two strands brown Ultra Hair and six strands root beer Krystal Flash

Body: Copper brown Short Flash Chenille

Hackle: Brown Long Flash Chenille

Carapace: Clear vinyl tubing (found in aquarium stores) cut to shape (slice an elongated, curved, diamond-shaped section from tubing)

Rib: Doubled 3/0 brown Monocord, used as "dubbing loop" rib to lash down carapace

Weed/Coral Guard: 6-lb. to 7-lb. Mason V with ends flattened and figure-eighted to shank

Tying Notes: The Ultra Hair and Krystal Flash that form the back of the underbody should extend past the bend for the antennae, and past the hook eye for the tail or telson. The pattern can also be tied in olive, tan, hot pink, pink, orange, and gray. You can color the tubing with Dip-an-Glo worm dye from the Spike-It Bait Company.

Location Notes: Belize, Andros, Venezuela, Posada Del Sol (Honduras), St. John (Virgin Islands).

Fishing Notes: Best fished in shallow water with short strips. The fly works well in thick turtle grass. For fishing in deeper water—two feet or more—Scott uses a small split shot (size B) on a fluorocarbon tippet. The fly is good for tailing and cruising fish. Alter the eye type for the desired sink rate.

Prey Notes: Generic shrimp suggestive of many species of the common shrimps (Penaeidae), snapping shrimps (Alpheidae), and grass shrimps (Palaemonidae).

Scott Sanchez, see LIPSTICK MINNOW, page 113.

Sea Flea • Tom McGuane

SEA FLEA

A Tom McGuane design. Sample in photo was tied by Tom McGuane on a size 10 3407 hook and measures horizontally about 7/8" in length. Tom sent a second, even sparser and shorter (5/8") sample, and a third with a green-dubbed body and deer-hair-only wing. Fly rides hook-point up.

Hook: 3407; size 10

Thread: Green Kevlar or olive Uni-Thread

Eyes: Stainless 1/8" bead chain or 5/32" lead barbell

Body: Swannundaze No. 78 (Light Transparent Olive)

Wing: Emerald-green dyed deer hair and/or green Krystal Flash

Tying Notes: Tom says, "This is low-tech fly tying or it wouldn't survive my skills. The essentials are that it must be *very* small and *very* green (emerald green)." He included two other versions, one with a body of Salmo Web No. 25 (Green Highlander), the other with green Larva Lace No. 62, and he says olive chenille works too.

Location Notes: This fly's design, according to Tom, is based on the observation that Atlantic flats with any grass on them harbor a good many tiny green crabs, which bonefish prefer. This fly has worked really well for him in the Keys, Belize, and the northern Bahamas.

Fishing Notes: Tom fishes the Sea Flea on a long (twelve- to fourteen-foot) leader so he can cast *across* smaller fish and *into* pods. He fishes it dead-sink or with minimal creeping movement.

Prey Notes: Tiny green crabs. *Author's note:* Mithrax sculptus, *often called a "reef" crab, frequently inhabits grass beds. The fly also suggests the blue crab* Callinectes sapidus, *a favored bonefish prey that is green as a small juvenile.*

Anecdotes: Tom says, "I caught thirty-seven bonefish the first day I ever used this fly in Belize fishing with the great Winston 'Pops' Cabral."

Tom McGuane was born in Michigan and has lived in Montana for the last twenty-seven years. He has been a novelist all his life and is author of such highly acclaimed works as *Ninety-Two in the Shade* (the first major novel to feature bonefishing), *Keep the Money,* and *The Bushwhacked Piano.* He also wrote the essay collection *An Outside Chance,* and has made occasional forays into journalism and film. Tom has bonefished for thirty years. Apart from angling, his great passion is training cutting horses. He was the 1994 Montana Cutting Champion.

See-Bone • Saul Greenspan

SEE-BONE

A Saul Greenspan design. Sample in photo was tied by Saul Greenspan on a size 4 34007 hook and measures horizontally 1-3/4" in length. Fly rides hook-point up.

Hook: 34007; sizes 2, 4

Thread: Danville Plus or Flat Waxed Nylon 3/0

Underbody: White spun polyester thread as base for lead head

Head: 3/0 or BB split shot

Body: Brown wool yarn (also white, yellow, pink, or chartreuse)

Wing: Brown impala (also white, yellow, pink, or chartreuse), bushy

Hackle: Stiff gray grizzly, two turns

Eyes: Painted with enamel, applied with round toothpick

Tying Notes: Over a 5/8"-wide thread underbody (Crazy Glued), pinch split shot, using pliers with soft, covered haws. Prep the shot by widening the base of the slit with a Dreml drill, then apply epoxy glue and crimp. Then file and sand the lead until it is round, paint it with oil enamel over enamel primer (white, yellow, pink, brown, or chartreuse), apply the eyes, and finish the fly with two-part polymer varnish.

Location Notes: The Florida Keys, Islamorada, Key Largo, Florida Bay.

Fishing Notes: Saul developed this pattern for fish mudding and cruising in deep water—the largest version is for the deepest areas, and he emphasizes this is not a tailing fly. He retrieves the See-Bone with short strips. When a fish follows, he pauses so the fly drops to the bottom, then waits two seconds, and strikes with his stripping hand.

Prey Notes: Generic shrimp shape suggestive of many species that inhabit deeper waters. The fly may also suggest some of the swimming crabs and reef crabs that inhabit deeper waters.

Anecdotes: The fly has won two major fly-fishing tournaments in Islamorada for other anglers.

Saul Greenspan is a retired industrialist who was born in New York City and now lives in New Hampshire. He bonefishes in the Florida Keys and fishes with Eddie Wightman.

Shallow H₂O • Lefty Kreh

SHALLOW H₂O FLY

A Lefty Kreh design. Sample in photo was tied by Lefty Kreh on a size 4 34007 hook and measures horizontally 2-1/8" in length. Fly rides hook-point up.

Hook: 34007; sizes 2, 4, 6

Thread: White Monocord 3/0

Body: Fluorescent orange medium chenille, one turn

Wing: About twenty strands chartreuse over twenty strands white bucktail

Location Notes: The Florida Keys, Belize, the Bahamas, Christmas Island, Yucatan.

Fishing Notes: Alter the eye type for the desired sink rate. Strip until the fish sees, let it drop, and watch the fish's movement to see a pick-up.

Prey Notes: Generic shrimp shape suggestive of many species; the orange chenille suggests the eggs of the spawning females of many species.

Lefty Kreh, see LEFTY'S CLOUSER DEEP MINNOW, page 110.

Shimmering Shrimp • Page Rogers

SHIMMERING SHRIMP

A Page Rogers design. Sample in photo (gray) was tied by Page Rogers on a size 2 811S hook and measures horizontally 2-1/2" in length. Fly rides hook-point down.

Hook: Tiemco 811S; sizes 2, 4

Thread: Clear Danville mono

Mouth: Small hank gray Ultra Hair ("Smoke") bound to spine of shank and splayed at bend, then a few strands pearl, gunmetal, and silver Flashabou dubbing, mixed

Underbody: Livebody Foam (size W 565; color No. 03), slotted lengthwise and bound loosely with thread (no cement)

Eyes: 20-lb. Mason mono, burned and painted black

Body Covering: Dubbing (in a loop) of gray Mystic Bay Fly Fur (No. 09) mixed with pearl, gunmetal, and silver Flashabou dubbing

Carapace: Smoke Ultra Hair fibers, topped with wide strip transparent pearl or transparent glitter Witchcraft Tape

Rib: Clear Danville mono

Weight: Can add smallest (1/100 oz. or 3/32") barbell under tail

Weed/Coral Guard: Can add mono V-shaped guard behind eyes before dubbing body

Tying Notes: Cut the Livebody Foam cylinder in thirds at a 45° angle (like this:"/"), and cut a slot lengthwise in the bottom of the cylinder to slip over the shank; cut the carapace from Witchcraft Tape with a very long point in front, to form a rostrum over the eyes, and with a fan shape over the rear (over the hook eye).

Location Notes: The Bahamas.

Fishing Notes: This fly sinks slowly by design. Strip sparingly or not at all. Watch the fish's movement to see a pick-up.

Prey Notes: In this color (and other colors: white, pink, gold, or olive), this generic shrimp suggests many species of the common shrimps (Penaeidae), snapping shrimps (Alpheidae), and grass shrimps (Palaemonidae).

Anecdotes: Page came up with this pattern while giving tying demonstrations at the International Fly Tyers Symposium in New Jersey one year when the heat prevented her from tying the epoxy patterns she'd intended.

Page Rogers an Episcopal priest from Connecticut, fishes for stripers, false albacore, bonito, and blues. When she is not busy saving souls, she also creates some of the most innovative saltwater patterns on the scene today.

Shimmerskin Mantis • Terry Baird

SHIMMERSKIN MANTIS

A Terry Baird design. Sample in photo was tied by Terry Baird on a size 4 Tiemco 9374 hook and measures horizontally 2-1/2" in length. Carapace measures 3/8" in width. Fly rides hook-point up.

Hook: Mustad 34011 or Tiemco 9374; sizes 2, 4, 6, 8

Thread: 2-lb. Ande mono

Eyes: Small-sized mono eyes, or 30-lb. mono with burnt ends figure-eighted to eye-brace stalk

Eye Brace: Ten to fifteen strands clear or tan Super Hair

Claws: Five to ten strands clear Super Hair, knotted at joints (glue knots)

Body: Clear mono "thread" on base, then bulk up by stacking Antron

Weight: Bead chain or lead barbell

Legs: Sili Legs or natural latex, tipped with black marker

Carapace: Shimmerskin (or pearlescent clear Mylar sheet) cut into long oval, and notched with long channel at one end. Attach unnotched end of carapace behind eye of hook and pull it back so it straddles eye brace and hook bend, then tie over it a small bunch rust-colored Antron (or SLF or Polar Aire or similar semitransparent material).

Feelers: Two strands tan or gold Krystal Flash or Holographic Flash, extending beyond eyes

Tying Notes: The fly was designed to show a large profile to the fish yet cast well in wind. Terry says he uses mono for the thread, then strengthens all the joints with Hard As Nails to create a light but durable body. He warns to not overdress this pattern.

Location Notes: Fanning Island, Andros.

Fishing Notes: Terry says he fishes this pattern in long, undulating strips along the bottom.

Prey Notes: Suggests many members of the mantis shrimp (Squillidae) family, especially *Squilla empusa* and *Gonodactylus oerstedii*.

Terry Baird, see SAND BANDIT, page 145.

Shroyer's Yellow Charlie • J.Watt Shroyer design after Nauheim's Charlie

SHROYER'S YELLOW CHARLIE

A J.Watt Shroyer design derived, but different, from Nauheim's original Nasty Charlie. Sample in photo was tied by J.Watt Shroyer on a size 4 34007 hook and

measures horizontally 2-1/2" in length. Fly rides hook-point up.

Hook: 34007; sizes 2, 4, 6

Thread: Chartreuse Monocord 3/0

Eyes: Medium (1/8") bead chain, ends painted red

Tail: Yellow Krystal Flash

Body: Yellow Krystal Flash

Wing: Yellow over pink Krystal Flash

Tying Notes: Jay ties both sparse and fatter bodies.

Location Notes: Christmas Island, Belize, the Bahamas, and Yucatan.

Fishing Notes: Good for shallow water over a clear bottom. When sparsely tied, the fly is also good for tailing fish. It is not effective for mudding fish or deeper water unless you use lead eyes.

Prey Notes: Suggestive of many smaller shrimps such as immature common shrimps (Penaeidae) and members of the diminutive Palaemonidae, Gnatophyllidae, and Hippolytidae families. But Jay says it may also suggest some Pacific seaworms (polychaetes). Jay says at Christmas the stomach contents of a fish cut in half by a shark revealed many small yellow and brown worms about the size of this fly.

Anecdotes: Jay says over the years this has always been the fly the guides at Christmas Island eyed in his box, usually in yellow, pink, and brown (see also Ralph Woodbine's Christmas Island Flash Charlie, page 57, and Yvon Chouinard's Yellow Clouser, page 177).

J. Watt Shroyer, a dental surgeon located on Florida's west coast, says he doesn't have an original bone in his body, but this little Charlie variation of his is a very good one. He fishes it often at Christmas Island in the company of Ralph Woodbine, whose patterns he also likes (see Ralphs' Hackled Epoxy Bonefish Fly, page 141).

SILLY LEGS BONEFISH FLY

A Barry and Cathy Beck design. Sample in photo was tied by Barry Beck on a size 4 Orvis SW hook and measures horizontally 1-3/4" in overall length. Legs measure 1-1/2" across tips. Fly rides hook-point up.

Hook: Orvis SW; sizes 2, 4, 6

Thread: White Monocord 3/0

Eyes: Clouser lead eyes, 1/24 oz. to 1/32 oz., midshank

Tail: Chartreuse calf tail and pearl Krystal Flash

Legs: Chartreuse Sili Legs material

Body: Kreinik 1/8" Tyer's Ribbon

Throat: Krystal Flash over chartreuse calf tail

Tying Notes: Other color combinations: white legs/pink calf; orange legs/fuchsia calf; tan legs/tan calf. You can also substitute dull vernille for the flashy Kreinik Ribbon for bright, spooky conditions, and substitute marabou for the calf to achieve more life.

Location Notes: The fly has been effective in the Bahamas and Mexico.

Fishing Notes: This pattern was designed to fish flats in relatively low water on both incoming and outcoming tides. Stripping action should start out slowly and increase when the bonefish show interest. The pattern can be used in all situations—mudding, cruising, and tailing.

Prey Notes: The wide rubber-leg profile of this pattern produces lifelike motion, cushions presentation, and reduces fish-spooking splash. It suggests common (Peneidae), snapping (Alpheidae), and mantis shrimps (Squillidae), as well as swimming crabs (Portunidae).

Former owners of Becky's Fly Shop and now principals of Raven Creek Photography, **Barry** and **Cathy Beck** fish around the world, host angling trips, write about (and photograph) fishing adventures, and appear at shows and seminars around the country. Their work has appeared in *Fly Fisherman, Field & Stream, Outdoor Life,* and most other angling journals. Cathy is author of *Cathy Beck's Fly-Fishing Handbook.*

Silly Legs Bonefish Fly • Barry and Cathy Beck

SIR MANTIS SHRIMP

A Craig Mathews design. Sample in photo was tied by Craig Mathews on a size 2 3407 hook and measures horizontally 1-7/8" in length. Fly rides hook-point down.

Hook: TMC 800S, Mustad 34007 or 3407; sizes 1, 2, 4, 6

Thread: Olive or white Uni-Thread 6/0

Raptorial Legs: Clumps or tufts of olive or gold rabbit fur tied on at hook bend, one-half body length or hook-shank length, with two to four Krystal Flash fibers (in color to match body) laid alongside each leg; rabbit clumps are divided by thread into two bulky legs

Rostrum: Olive- or gold-dyed deer tied between legs

Eyes: Large black plastic beads

Shellback: Olive or gold Zelon, to represent cephalothorax and top of abdomen; pull Zelon over back and tie off at hook eye. This also represents tail (uropod and telson) when trimmed to shape

Body: Olive or gold Zelon cut up and blended, wound in dubbing loop and picked out

Weight: None

Rib: Rusty "Flagstaff brown" dyed variant, or grizzly saddle hackle, palmered and trimmed to length to represent swimmerets (pleopods and walking legs)

Tying Notes: For the body, you can substitute a strip of olive or gold rabbit fur, wound. No weight is added to this pattern.

Location Notes: The fly has been successfully fished in Belize, Ascension Bay, and Exuma. It is especially effective in Belize.

Fishing Notes: The fly works best on reefs when the tide is in and when fish are holding around cays, cruising and patrolling for prey. Cast downtide or downcurrent well in front of the fish, throwing some belly into your line *beyond* your targets. This allows the water's movement to pull the line belly and the fly *away* from the fish. Your shrimp will appear to be running away from attackers. The more belly you throw, the longer the "swim-away" lasts. Once the belly is stripped out, the fly will swing back toward you. Use a rapid long retrieve. Stop only after a fish has followed without taking for ten to twenty feet; then pause, let the fly drop to bottom, and quickly strip one to three feet.

Prey Notes: The fly mimics the mantis shrimp, *Squilla empusa*, the golden mantis, *Pseudosquilla ciliata*, and other mantis species.

Anecdotes: Craig says the name comes from his first encounter with one of these nasty little creatures, when he found one in an abandoned conch shell. He picked it up and brought it to the guides to show them, but they all ran away. Then it suddenly "clicked" and cut his middle finger. Now, he says, he's learned to call these mean little buggers "Sir."

Craig Mathews, see CLAM BEFORE THE STORM, page 59.

Sir Mantis Shrimp • Craig Mathews

Slamaroo • Lenny Moffo

SLAMAROO

A Lenny Moffo design. Sample in photo was tied by Lenny Moffo on a size 4 34007 hook and measures horizontally about 1-5/8" in length. Fly rides hook-point up.

Hook: 34007 or 3407; sizes 2, 4, 6

Thread: Brown Monocord 3/0 (also chartreuse, tan, brown, or gray)

Tail: Six to eight short strands Krystal Flash

Body: Six to eight strands Krystal Flash, wrapped on shank

Wing/Legs: Four to eight strands tan Sili Legs and two to four strands white or natural rubber legs (or other "rubber hackle"), barred with brown and orange permanent markers

Eyes: Lead barbell or bead chain, sized for sink rate and turnover (5/32" lead barbell in sample in photo)

Head: Tan medium chenille

Tying Notes: Lenny says he uses gray Krystal Flash on the body, or sometimes brown. When he figure-eights the chenille head, he pulls one wrap underneath the rubber legs to separate them from the shank. You can vary the chenille color to your choice, or to match local prey colors. Lenny uses small chenille for the size 6, medium for sizes 2 and 4.

Location Notes: The pattern has taken fish in the Keys in sizes 2 and 4, and in the Bahamas in sizes 4 and 6.

Fishing Notes: Alter the eye type for the desired sink rate. Strip until the fish sees, let it drop, and watch the fish's movement to see a pick-up.

Prey Notes: Impressionistic prey form suggestive of both shrimps (Penaeidae and Alpheidae families) and crabs (Portunidae and Majidae families).

Anecdotes: Lenny says, "We have grand-slammed several times with this fly. Permit will eat it as well as small tarpon—thus the name."

Lenny Moffo, see FLEEING CRAB, page 77.

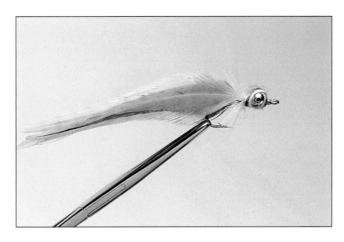

Slinky • Dick Brown

SLINKY

Author's design. Sample in photo was tied by the author on a size 4 34007 hook and measures horizontally 3-1/8" in length. Fly rides hook-point up.

Hook: 34007; sizes 4, 6, 8

Thread: Tan Flat Waxed Nylon 3/0

Eyes: Medium bead chain

Tail: Two long cream or bleached grizzly hackles flanked by two light badger saddle hackles, tied to bend tarpon-fly-style

Head: Fine cream and tan yarn, figure-eighted around eyes

Weed/Coral Guard (optional): V of 12-lb. or 15-lb Mason hard mono, figure-eighted to shank

Tying Notes: Leech yarn, speckled crystal chenille, and Kreinik Micro Ice Chenille also work well for the head.

Location Notes: Andros, Abaco, the Berry Islands, North Eleuthera, the Florida Keys, Belize.

Fishing Notes: Cast close. Strip sparingly. When the fish sees, let it drop, and watch the fish's movement to see a pick-up.

Prey Notes: Generic pattern suggestive of gobies (Gobiidae) and errant seaworms or polychaetes such as sandworms (Nereidae) and errant threadworms (Syllidae).

Anecdotes: This fly has taken several fish of over ten pounds.

Sneaky Snake • Ellen Reed

SNEAKY SNAKE

*An Ellen Reed design. Sample in photo was tied by Ellen Reed on a size 4 3407
hook and measures horizontally 1-7/8" in length. Fly rides hook-point down.*

Hook: 3407; size 4

Thread: Tan mono

Tail: 1/2" strip gray rabbit, over gold Krystal Flash and white calf tail

Body: Light tan Sparkle Chenille

Collar: Tan deer body hair

Eyes: Small (3/32") lead barbell (or bronze with black finish)

Weed/Coral Guard: Single strand of 20-lb. Mason mono

Location Notes: The Florida Keys; the fly is usually fished oceanside, but it is also good
in heavy grass in the backcountry.

Fishing Notes: Alter the eye type for the desired sink rate. Strip until the fish sees, let it
drop, and watch the fish's movement to see a pick-up.

Prey Notes: Large-headed profile suggests gobies and toadfish (Gobiidae and
Batrachoididae) and some shrimp species.

Ellen Reed, see HONEY LAMB, page 98.

Spot • Bob Nauheim

SPOT

A Bob Nauheim design. Sample in photo (Orange Spot) was tied by Bob Nauheim on a size 4 34007 hook and measures horizontally about 1-3/8" in length. Fly rides hook-point up.

Hook: 34007; sizes 2, 4, 6

Thread: White Monocord 3/0, or color to match body

Body: Orange chenille, then long brown hackle palmered and clipped, leaving "spiky" fibers one-and-one-quarter times hook gape

Wing: Brown bucktail from natural white tail

Tying Notes: In addition to orange, the fly is tied in brown, yellow, pink, and chartreuse. All have produced.

Location Notes: The Bahamas, Yucatan, Belize, the Florida Keys.

Fishing Notes: Strip once or twice until the fish sees, let it drop, and watch the fish's movement to see a pick-up.

Prey Notes: Generic prey shape suggestive of both crabs and shrimps.

Anecdotes: This was Bob's regular fly before he came up with the prototype for the Crazy Charlie.

Bob Nauheim, see CRAZY CHARLIE, page 62.

Squimp • Cary Marcus

SQUIMP

A Cary Marcus design. Sample in photo was tied by Cary Marcus on a size 2 811S hook and measures horizontally about 3" in length. Fly rides hook-point up.

Hook: Tiemco 811S; sizes 2, 4, 6

Thread: Tan or white Flat Waxed Nylon, or Monocord 3/0

Eyes: Umpqua's nontoxic 1/8" black-on-yellow metal eyes (Bestco #1) for size 4; tie on top of shank midway between point and barb. Use 3/16" (1/36 oz.) lead eyes for deep water

Antennae/Tentacles: Two doubled strands of Sili Legs; color to suit but usually matching body or wing (tan or white)

Mouth Parts: Small bunch tan or white craft fur

Body: Pearl Poly Flash or Diamond Braid; tie in tag end as underbody on weighted-eye end of shank to add bulk to upper torso of Squimp, creating a tapered body

Wing: Medium to small bunch craft fur, color to suit (optional: add four to six strands Krystal Flash)

Legs: Two strands of Sili Legs tied to each side of hook shank. Trim the two that angle along body to body length; trim the two at hook eye shorter

Hackle (optional): Palmer a cree or barred sandy dun saddle hackle, then apply wing and trim "bottom" flush to body

Tying Notes: Cary says his pattern owes a bow to Robert McCurdy and his Baited Breath pattern for getting the eye weight placed properly—on the bend, where it offsets the heaviest part of the hook, and allows the wing to keel over the fly so that it always rides hook-point up. Cary ties it in brown and white versions and says he has been experimenting with dying pearl Poly Flash with tan Rit Dye—this looks good but he's not sure if it will hold.

Location Notes: Andros, Bimini, Exuma, the Berry Islands, Belize, Los Roques.

Fishing Notes: Alter the eye type for the desired sink rate. Strip the fly until the fish sees, let it drop, and watch the fish's movement to see a pick-up.

Prey Notes: Generalized shrimp attractor suggestive of several members of the common shrimp (Penaeidae), snapping shrimp (Alpheidae), and mantis shrimp (Squillidae) families.

Anecdotes: Cary says the first time he fished the Squimp (at Christmas Island), it hooked a huge fish that broke him off on coral. He reports that it has since taken many fish at all major bonefish locations, and that it has seduced several specimens of over ten pounds.

Cary Marcus is a Sage Rod representative and has stalked bonefish all over the Bahamas, Belize, Venezuela, and Christmas Island.

Standard MOE (Brewer's) • Doug Brewer

STANDARD MOE (BREWER'S)

A Doug Brewer design. Sample in photo was tied by Doug Brewer on a size 4 3407 hook and measures horizontally 1-3/4" in overall length. Fly rides hook-point up.

Hook: 3407; sizes 2, 4, 6, 8

Thread: Pink Danville Plus

Eyes: Medium (1/8") silver bead chain

Tail: Five or six strands Krystal Flash; then two strands pink rubber hackle; then shrimp pink marabou

Head: Coral "Hot Head" material

Tying Notes: Other color options: Change the marabou to tan, shrimp orange, sunrise, or grizzly (dyed pink, amber, yellow, or olive); change the Hot Head and rubber hackle to match. You can also change the eye size or use lead eyes to vary the sink rate.

Doug uses a material he calls "Hot Head," which is more buoyant than epoxy and doesn't smack the water as hard. In seminars and demonstrations at shows, he has also found it easier to work with than most epoxy and glue materials—even for new users. The glue gun and glue sticks are available through dealers. Contact his company for names—see chapter 7.

Location Notes: This is a very effective fly at Christmas Island and the Bahamas; the best colors are yellow, coral, and amber.

Fishing Notes: Use a strip-and-stop action. The pattern works for cruising and tailing fish.

Prey Notes: Attractor pattern suggestive in color and action of many small decapods such as swimming crabs (Portunidae) and common and snapping shrimps (Penaeidae and Alpheidae).

Doug Brewer, see BREWER'S AMBER, page 49.

Stealth Crab • Terry Baird

STEALTH CRAB

A Terry Baird design. Sample in photo was tied by Terry Baird on a size 4 Gamakatsu hook and measures horizontally 2-1/2" in length. Carapace measures 1/2" in width. Fly rides hook-point up.

Hook: Gamakatsu O'Shaughnessy; sizes 2, 4, 6, 8

Thread: 2-lb. mono

Large Claw: Furnace hackle

Body/Wing: Orange calf tail over shank, wrapped with gold tinsel

Eye Brace: Ten to fifteen strands Super Hair (or bucktail or squirrel)

Eyes: Medium mono secured to eye brace with 2-lb. mono

Small Claw: One-inch-long furnace hackle tip

Weight: Medium (1/8") bead chain or lead barbell

Carapace: Orange Guinea hackle

Tying Notes: The unique combination of the hackle carapace and the eyes on the synthetic hair "brace" provide not only a good profile, but also low wind resistance. The eyes and claws should sit up when the fly rests on its bead-chain or barbell-weighted bottom.

Location Notes: The Florida Keys, Andros, Belize, the Fanning Islands, the Hawaiian Islands.

Fishing Notes: Strip with a crab retrieve, swimming or crawling the fly until it's noticed then dropping it to the bottom and watching the fish for a take.

Prey Notes: Generic crab shape suggestive of many species of hermit, spider, and fiddler crabs, including the three-colored hermit, *Clibanarius tricolor*, the green reef crab, *Mithrax sculptus*, and the spotted decorator crab, *Microphrys bicornutus*.

Terry Baird, see SAND BANDIT, page 145.

Super Shrimp • George Warren

SUPER SHRIMP

A George Warren design. Sample in photo was tied by George Warren on a size 4 34011 hook and measures horizontally 1-15/16" in length. Fly rides hook-point down.

Hook: 34011; sizes 4, 6, 8

Thread: Tan Monocord 3/0

Eyes: Section of 80-lb. mono, 1/2" to 3/4" long, ends melted and dipped in black enamel

Claws/Forelegs/Feelers: Barred grizzly hackle tips plus Krystal Flash; one or two turns of hackle at base

Body: Tan, gray, or gold chenille, or Ice Chenille

Hackle Legs: Barred grizzly saddle hackle; leave normal on one side, but on second side trim to stubble, palmer to hook eye, and trim backside

Carapace: Strip of polyethylene sheeting, pulled over back and segmented with tying thread; add black enamel dots on humps of carapace, then two coats varnish

Tying Notes: The carapace is cut from a polyethylene sheet (e.g., a fly-material storage bag) in the shape of an elongated diamond with the wide part at the hook-bend end, and the narrow part at the hook eye. The point of the tail end (telson) should extend over the hook eye.

Location Notes: The Florida Keys, the Bahamas.

Fishing Notes: George says he has tied and fished any number of patterns over the years, but he now fishes this one exclusively, sometimes up to size 8, and varies colors and tones. Strip the pattern until the fish sees, stop, and watch the fish's movement to see a pick-up.

Prey Notes: Suggests members of the common shrimp (Penaeidae), snapping shrimp (Alpheidae), and mantis shrimp (Squillidae) families.

Anecdotes: George caught a nine-pound bonefish on this long-shanked shrimp pattern (in size 4) off Long Key in the Florida Keys.

George Warren, a retired educator and—most recently—director of admissions of the Rhode Island School of Design, is a painter (watercolor), woodcarver, and designer of furniture and houses. His carvings include wood sculptures of bonefish (one of which ended up in the Oval Office of then-president George Bush), and his work has appeared in galleries from Maine to Florida. He has been fly fishing all his life and bonefishing for over fifteen years.

Tabory's Bonefish Fly • Lou Tabory

TABORY'S BONEFISH FLY

A Lou Tabory design. Sample in photo was tied by Lou Tabory on a size 4 34007 hook and measures horizontally 1-1/2" in length. Fly rides hook-point up.

Hook: 34007; sizes 2, 4, 6, 8

Thread: Tan or beige Monocord 3/0

Eyes/Cushion (optional): Medium (1/8") bead chain; flare bucktail butts over eyes to cushion impact

Body: Pearl or light green Krystal Flash wound around shank; can leave a few strands long to blend with wing

Wing: Bleach brown deer tail to tan and tie near hook eye as inverted wing

Tying Notes: Lou ties this fly with and without eyes, and with and without Krystal Flash in the wing; he also constructs it with three different wing colors: tan (shown), white, and dark brown.

Location Notes: The Bahamas.

Fishing Notes: Lou says he adjusts the splash and sink rate in the fly by tying it in three styles: with eyes to sink fast; with no eyes, in a bend back style, for silent landings with a medium sink rate; and with eyes cushioned by a flared head for a quieter entry and slow sink rate.

Prey Notes: Generic shrimp suggestive of many species, including smaller Alpheidae and Penaeidae.

Anecdotes: Lou says this pattern has been a good producer over the years when he and his wife fish in the Bahamas.

Lou Tabory is the godfather of saltwater flats fly fishing in northern waters, a topic he frequently writes about and lectures on to groups around the country. He is the author of the pioneering *Inshore Fly Fishing* and *Lou Tabory's Guide to Saltwater Baits and Their Imitations*, and a member of the Orvis Saltwater Advisory Team.

Tan Chenille Charlie • Yvon Chouinard

TAN CHENILLE CHARLIE

An Yvon Chouinard design. Sample in photo was tied by Yvon Chouinard on a size 6 34007 hook and measures horizontally 1-1/2" in length. Fly rides hook-point up.

Hook: Gamakatsu (or Mustad 3407/34007); sizes 6, 8, 10

Thread: Yellow Monocord or Danville Flat Waxed Nylon 3/0

Eyes: Smallest (3/32") lead (plated) barbell

Tail: Gold Krystal Flash

Body: Tan chenille

Wing: Brown bucktail

Location Notes: Christmas Island.

Fishing Notes: When fished dead-stop, the fly emulates crabs. When stripped, it suggests small juvenile fish or gobies.

Prey Notes: Generic shrimp suggestive of many smaller members of the common shrimp (Penaeidae), snapping shrimp (Alpheidae), grass shrimp (Palaemonidae), and mantis shrimp (Squillidae) families.

Anecdotes: Yvon says this is one of his best patterns for Christmas Island's sand-covered flats.

Yvon Chouinard, see J T SPECIAL, page 103.

Tasty Toad • Harry Spear

TASTY TOAD

A Harry Spear design. Sample in photo was tied by Harry Spear on a size 1 34007 hook and measures horizontally 2-9/16" in length. Tied as shown, fly rides hook-point down.

Hook: 34007; size 1

Thread: Chartreuse Monocord, or Flat Waxed Nylon 3/0

Tail: White marabou fibers (one side of marabou blood feather pulled from quill), then tan marabou fibers (same amount), then pair of grizzly saddle hackles flanking marabou and flared out; pull one wrap of thread under and behind entire tail to kick it up from shank, and resume normal wraps

Body: White poly yarn, about eight small clumps, figure-eighted to shank and tightly packed; rough trim with curved surgical scissors, add color with Pantone or similar markers (e.g., dark green edges and black stripe down dorsal line); rub curved edges of yarn body with Hard As Nails or head cement, then pinch to flatten as they harden; trim edges

Weight: Lead barbell, 1/50 oz. or 1/36 oz., figure-eighted to shank and coated with liquid rod-builders' epoxy

Weed/Coral Guard: V-shaped piece of 16-lb. Mason hard mono (.020" dia.) figure-eighted to shank ahead of weight

Tying Notes: At the outset, lay down the thread base on the shank, and coat with liquid rod-builders' epoxy.

Location Notes: The Florida Keys.

Fishing Notes: Harry recommends fishing this one by showing it to the fish with a twelve- to eighteen-inch strip, then bumping it again, and letting it drop to the bottom. Strip as needed if the strike is not immediate. For tailing fish, lighten the weight; for mudding fish, increase the eye weight for increased depth. More weight will invert the fly.

Prey Notes: Suggestive of many species of toadfish (Batrachoididae)—which recent Florida Keys research shows to be a favorite bonefish prey. The fly may also mimic some gobies (Gobiidae).

Harry Spear, see MOE SHRIMP, page 123.

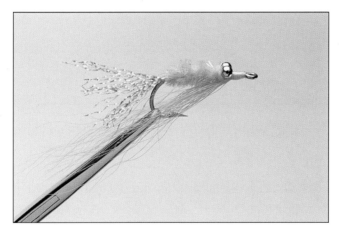

Tropical Shrimp • John Goddard

TROPICAL SHRIMP

A John Goddard design. Sample in photo was tied by John Goddard on a size 2 Partridge Sea Prince hook and measures horizontally 2-3/8" in length. Fly rides hook-point up.

Hook: Partridge Sea Prince (or other stainless wide gape); sizes 2, 4

Thread: Gotcha Pink Flat Waxed Nylon

Eyes: Medium (1/8") silver-colored bead chain

Tail: Dozen or so strands rainbow Lureflash (or Krystal Flash)

Body: Glo-Brite Chenille, Shocking Pink (GB No. 07)

Wing: Chartreuse bucktail

Location Notes: Very successful in Christmas Island, Yucatan, and the Bahamas.

Fishing Notes: Alter the eye size for the desired sink rate. Strip until the fish sees, let it drop, and watch the fish's movement to see a pick-up.

Prey Notes: Generic shrimp attractor pattern suggestive of snapping shrimps (Alpheidae) and some common shrimps (Penaeidae).

John Goddard, coauthor of *The Trout and the Fly*, and author of several other fly-fishing texts, is a lifelong, world-class international angler in fresh and salt water.

Turd Fly • Brian O'Keefe

TURD FLY

> *A Brian O'Keefe design. Sample in photo was tied by Brian O'Keefe on a size 6 34007 hook and measures horizontally 1-3/8" in length. Fly rides hook-point up.*

Hook: 34007; sizes 6, 8, 10

Thread: Tan Monocord 3/0

Tail: Pale tan or cream marabou, four strands pearl Krystal Flash

Eyes: Medium (1/8") bead chain, or none

Body: Tan vernille

Tying Notes: Brian says he likes this fly small—down to size 10—and that he usually ties it leaving the Krystal Flash strands twice as long as the marabou, so they extend like antennae. He also likes tying it with sparse ginger marabou and gold eyes. It can be tied with or without eyes.

Location Notes: The fly has worked very well everywhere, but especially in Christmas Island, the Bahamas, and Belize.

Fishing Notes: This pattern can be dropped on tailers and left on the sand. It has its own movement.

Prey Notes: Suggestive of several worm prey, including errant worms and fanworms. The fly also suggests smaller gobies (Gobiidae) and toadfish (Batrachoididae), and some smaller shrim species.

Anecdotes: Brian says he got the idea for this fly from tying the Missing Link fly smaller and smaller. He also mentions that it is quite similar to the Baited Breath pattern (a Bob McCurdy design), which he saw in Randall Kaufmann's *Bonefishing with a Fly*.

Brian O'Keefe, see HOOVER, page 100.

Turneffe Crab • Craig Mathews

TURNEFFE CRAB

A Craig Mathews design. Sample in photo was tied by Craig Mathews on a size 6 3407 hook and measures horizontally 7/16" in length; span across legs is 1". Fly rides hook-point up.

Hook: TMC 800S, Mustad 34007 or 3407; sizes 4, 6, 8, 10, 12, 14

Thread: Uni-Thread 6/0, color to match body

Weight: 3/32" bead chain, or mini nontoxic "lead" Lite Brite eyes

Body: Cream, tan, brown, olive (shown), green, or dun gray Furry Foam

Legs: Round rubber, mottled with Sanford marking pens (e.g., red-tipped with green or brown mottling)

Coral/Weed Guard: Natural mottled deer hair

Tying Notes: The fly is sometimes tied with no weight for very shallow water. The legs are tied on top of a bead-chain platform (or lead-substitute barbell eyes) to splay them out. When no weight is used, form the platform with plastic bead eyes. The foam must be tied in behind and beyond the hook point. *Important:* The hook must then be bent outward a few degrees—*both* upward away from shank, *and* to the left or right (away from the fly's center axis), to allow for a better hook-up rate.

Location Notes: Very effective in Belize where it was developed, the Turneffe Crab has now been successfully fished at most locations. *Author's note: It has worked well in white on*

Bahamas sand flats.

Fishing Notes: This crab casts better, lands more quietly, and sinks faster than deer hair crab flies. Craig suggests very slow short strips, or none at all.

Prey Notes: Depending on color and size, the fly mimics small reef crabs and flats crabs, including *Mithrax sculptus*, the green reef crab, *Microphrys bicornutus*, the spotted decorator crab, and others found in the Bahamas, Belize, and other locations.

Anecdotes: Craig says he named this one for the crabs so often seen in and on the reefs in Belize.

Craig Mathews, see CLAM BEFORE THE STORM, page 59.

Ultra Shrimp • Bob Popovics

ULTRA SHRIMP

A Bob Popovics design. Sample in photo was tied by Bob Popovics on a size 4 Tiemco 800S hook and measures horizontally 1-1/2" in length. Fly rides hook-point down.

Hook: Tiemco 800S; sizes 2, 4, 6

Thread: Beige Monocord, or Larva Lace

Forelegs: Ultra Hair tied on *underside* of shank

Mouth Parts: Small wad Ultra hair on top of shank

Eyes: Mono

Rear Legs: Neck hackle palmered in open spiral to hook eye

Carapace/Tail: Ultra hair, trimmed to shape; pointed rostrum over eyes and flared at eye for tail

Outer Coat: 5-Minute Epoxy

Location Notes: The Bahamas, Belize, Boca Paila, Los Roques.

Fishing Notes: Slow-strip and pause. Watch the fish's movement to see a pick-up.

Prey Notes: Primarily suggests grass shrimps (Palaemonidae), juvenile common shrimps (Penaeidae), and juvenile snapping shrimps (Alpheidae).

Anecdotes: The fly was named for its Ultra Hair material. It was designed for striped bass and weakfish but is now a reliable flats producer as well.

Bob Popovics, see BEAD MINNOW, page 25.

Vernille Sparkle Worm • Ben Estes

VERNILLE SPARKLE WORM

A Ben Estes design. Sample in photo was tied by Ben Estes on a size 4 3407 hook and measures horizontally 3" in length. Weighted, fly rides hook-point up; unweighted, hook-point down.

Hook: 3407 or 34007; sizes 2, 4

Thread: Brown Monocord 3/0, or clear 2-lb. mono

Weight/Eyes: Lead wire wrapped on shank, or medium (1/8") chrome bead chain

Undertail: Four to six short sprigs rootbeer Krystal Flash

Tail: Brown vernille, tipped with four to six short sprigs Krystal Flash

Body/Head: Rootbeer Arizona sparkle yarn or vernille; optional head of Kreinik Micro Ice chenille

Weed Guard: 12-lb. Mason

Tying Notes: Use a needle, bodkin, pin vise, or bent-open paper clip to whip-finish the Krystal Flash to the end of the vernille tail. Also ties pattern in cream. Sometimes adds head of Micro Ice Chenille (see tying sequences in chapter 4).

Location Notes: The Berry Islands, Abaco, Eleuthera.

Fishing Notes: Alter the eye type (or omit the eye) for the desired sink rate. Strip once or twice until the fish sees, stop, and watch the fish's movement for a pick-up. Resume if there's no interest.

Prey Notes: Seaworm pattern suggestive of many swimming polychaetes, such as sandworms (Nereidae) and errant threadworms (Syllidae), that burrow just under the surface; it also suggests errant tubeworms (Onuphidae).

Anecdotes: *Author's note: Ben sent me some of these to try, and I found them very effective on a recent trip to Abaco and the Berrys.*

Ben Estes, see BEN'S EPOXY BONEFISH FLY, page 28.

Victor's Candy • Bill Hunter

VICTOR'S CANDY

A Bill Hunter design. Sample in photo was tied by Bill Hunter on a size 4 34007 hook and measures horizontally 1-3/4" in length. Fly rides hook-point up.

Hook: 34007; sizes 1, 2, 4, 6

Thread: Rusty brown 6/0

Tail: Small clump orange marabou

Body: Tan/brown Ultra Chenille (fine)

Wing: Mixture of four strands barred gold golden-pheasant tippet, black-tipped elk neck hairs or bucktail, and four strands Krystal Flash

Eyes: Black marking pen

Tying Notes: The wing is tied in reverse fashion, before the body chenille is wound on. The tips of the wing point away from the hook point. The chenille is then wound tightly against the wing root and brought in front of the wing, folding it rearward.

Location Notes: Yucatan, the Florida Keys, Deep Water Cay, Andros.

Fishing Notes: Good tailing fly.

Prey Notes: Suggests snapping shrimps (Alpheidae) and smaller mantis shrimps (Squillidae).

Bill Hunter, see APRICOT CHARLIE, page 22.

Whitlock's Marabou & Pearl Glass Minnow • Dave Whitlock

WHITLOCK'S MARABOU & PEARL GLASS MINNOW

A Dave Whitlock design. Sample in photo was tied by Dave Whitlock on a size 4 34007 hook and measures horizontally 2-1/8" in length. Fly rides hook-point up.

Hook: 34007 or TMC 811S; sizes 2, 4, 6, 8 (hook eye turned down)

Thread: Fluorescent white, unwaxed single-strand nylon floss

Eyes: Plated lead barbell

Body: White and silver-gray marabou

Body Flash: Two strands pearl Saltwater Flashabou flanking four strands pearl Fire Fly

Cement: Dave's Flexament and Zap-A-Gap

Tying Notes: The white marabou is tied in over the eyes, Clouser-style (see Clouser Deep Minnow, page 60). Then invert the fly and tie in the Fire Fly, then the gray marabou. Flank with the Flashabou.

Location Notes: The Florida Keys, Belize, the Bahamas, Christmas Island, Yucatan, Los Roques.

Fishing Notes: Retrieve the fly as a frightened or crippled minnow, working it erratically with longish, sporadic strips, along sandy beaches or on flats with hard, sandy bottoms.

Prey Notes: Glass minnows, *Jenkinsia lamprotaenia*, or *Anchoa mitchelli*; the fly also suggests juveniles of larger gamefish that spend their first years in the shallows, such as members of the snapper (Lutjanidae) family.

Anecdotes: This fly was designed during a "Walker's Cay Chronicle" shoot at Los Roques. It imitates the billions of small silvery minnows that bonefish prey upon either collectively or alone as they eat along the shoreline there. This fly figured in the program that featured Dave tying it on the dock; Flip Pallot "stole" it from him and caught fish with it in the next scene.

Dave Whitlock, see DAVE'S SHRIMP, page 64.

Whitlock's Near Nuff Snapping Shrimp • Dave Whitlock

WHITLOCK'S NEAR NUFF SNAPPING SHRIMP

> *A Dave Whitlock design. Sample in photo was tied by Dave Whitlock on a size 4 34011 hook and measures horizontally 1-5/8" face-to-claw-tip, and 2-3/4" in overall length. Fly rides hook-point up.*

Hook: 34011; sizes 4, 6, 8

Thread: Tan, unwaxed, single-strand nylon floss

Weight: Chrome lead barbell, painted gold

Eyes: Black Mason nylon mono

Antennae: Silicone rubber strands and Krystal Flash

Pincers: Gold-dyed grizzly chicken back feathers

Legs: Gold-dyed grizzly saddle hackle

Body Dubbing: Rabbit hair, gold-dyed African goat, and brass Flashabou dubbing

Tail: Same as body dubbing

Cement: Dave's Flexament and Zap-A-Gap

Tying Notes: Turn down the hook eye and then reverse the center of gravity by adding the cast eyes to the hook shank (on the top of the hook shank—on its spine). The shrimp swims, jigs, and rests with its hook point up ... avoiding most hang-ups and avoiding fouling on underwater objects.

Location Notes: The Florida Keys, Belize, the Bahamas, Christmas Island, Yucatan, Los Roques.

Fishing Notes: Dave says he originally developed this pattern for fishing to tailers in the Florida Keys, but he has found it also works nicely on some flats fished blind. You may alter the weight size for the desired sink rate. Retrieve the fly sparingly, with a short strip. When the fish sees it, let it drop, and watch the fish's movement for a pick-up.

Prey Notes: This is one pattern that really looks like a shrimp. Depending on coloration, it suggests many of the snapping shrimps (Alpheidae), including *Alpheus heterochaelis, A. armatus*, and *A. armillatus*.

Dave Whitlock, see DAVE'S SHRIMP, page 64.

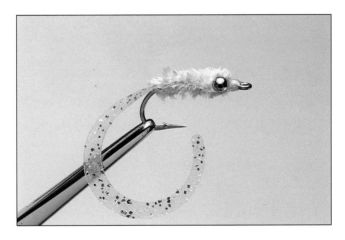

Wiggle Worm • Bill Sullivan

WIGGLE WORM

A Bill Sullivan design. Sample in photo was tied by Bill Sullivan on a size 4 34007 hook and, with tail extended, measures horizontally 3-1/16" in length. Fly rides hook-point up.

Hook: 34007; sizes 2, 4, 6

Thread: Tan, white, or pink Monocord 3/0 (color to match body)

Eyes: Medium (1/8") or small (3/32") bead chain, or lead barbells, to vary sink rate

Tail: Tan, white, or pink Wapsi Sili-Twister Tail

Body: Tan, white, or pink medium chenille

Location Notes: The Keys, Andros, Abaco, the Berry Islands, North Eleuthera.

Fishing Notes: Use long crawling strips until the fish sees the fly; pause, strip it again, and watch the fish's movement for a pick-up.

Prey Notes: Generic errant seaworm suggestive of many swimming polychaetes such as sandworms (Nereidae), errant threadworms (Syllidae), and tubeworms (Onuphidae).

Anecdotes: *Author's note: I first fished this pattern in Abaco's marls and the fish charged it, racing long distances and shouldering podmates out of the way to reach it first.*

Bill Sullivan is a founder and partner of Wellesley Outdoors, a Boston-area Orvis dealership. An avid salmon and trout angler for many years, he has lately been exploring saltwater species north and south, and recently bought his first flats boat.

Woolly Crab • Bill Tapply and Andy Gill

WOOLLY CRAB

A Bill Tapply and Andy Gill design. Sample in photo was tied by Bill Tapply on a size 4 34007 hook and measures horizontally 1-5/8" in length. Carapace is 5/8" in width. Fly rides hook-point up.

Hook: 34007; sizes 4, 6

Thread: Tan Monocord 3/0

Eyes: Medium (1/8") bead chain, blackened

Claws/Antennae/Face: Krystal Flash, then olive marabou; flank with pair matched grizzly or cree saddle tips, splayed

Body: Tan wool, spun onto shank and clipped to flat shape, colored with Pantone (or similar) pens, and hardened with head cement

Legs: Rubber legs, two sets; knotted, split at ends, colored with markers, and glued to belly plate

Belly Plate: Lead disk cut from wine bottle neck wrapper, flattened, Super Glued, and painted

Tying Notes: Bill and Andy sometimes use bucktail, Ultra Hair, or whatever else is lying around to build the claw/antennae/face assembly. Bill says he has tried using barbell weights on the crab, but they mess up the way it sinks. He says he's still working on a larger version for permit, but so far none seem to look or sink right.

Location Notes: Belize.

Fishing Notes: Bill says the Woolly Crab—because its body absorbs water—is easier to cast than buoyant deer-hair crabs that require heavy weights to sink. When tied right, the Woolly Crab sinks belly-down and hook-up, and it kicks up dust when it's twitched. Strip it until the fish sees it, let it drop, twitch, and watch the fish's movement to see a pick-up.

Prey Notes: Generic crab shape. Depending on color and action suggests many species of swimming crabs (Portunidae), mud crabs (Xanthidae), and spider crabs (Majidae).

Mystery novelist and outdoor writer **Bill Tapply**, and psychiatrist **Andy Gill**, both live in small towns west of Boston. They appear often in the pages of Bill's angling books (*Home Water, Opening Day and Other Neuroses*) and in his stories in outdoor journals such as *Field & Stream*. Those who know the two well say they will fish anywhere, anytime, for anything with fins.

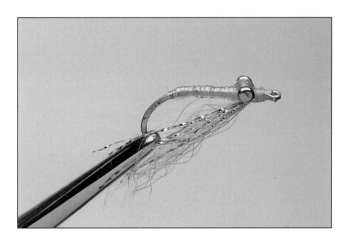

Yellow Clouser • Yvon Chouinard

YELLOW CLOUSER

An Yvon Chouinard design. Sample in photo was tied by Yvon Chouinard on a size 6 34007 hook and measures horizontally 1-1/2" in length. Fly rides hook-point up.

Hook: Gamakatsu (or Mustad 3407/34007); sizes 6, 8, 10

Thread: Yellow Monocord or Danville Flat Waxed Nylon 3/0

Eyes: Smallest (3/32") lead barbell, plated

Body: Yellow Larva Lace, Swannundaze, or V-Rib over yellow thread

Wing: Tan bucktail, over white bucktail, over gold Krystal Flash

Tying Notes: Yvon prefers Gamakatsu hooks for these patterns because he finds other models straighten out in small sizes. He ties a second version of this fly, which he calls the Green Clouser, with chartreuse tying thread for a body (no vinyl body wrapping) and a wing of white bucktail, then pearl Krystal Flash, then chartreuse bucktail. He says in size 6, this Green Clouser is deadly for Andros; in size 8, for Christmas Island.

Location Notes: The Yellow Clouser is Yvon's best pattern (along with his Tan Chenille Charlie) for Christmas Island. It's also his best fly for Belize's spooky flats.

Fishing Notes: Yvon says, "The lead-plated eyes get it down quickly in front of the fish so the fly is on the bottom when the fish gets close to it. Then I strip it once and leave it alone."

Prey Notes: Generic pattern suggestive of many species of shrimps and small worms or polychaetes.

Yvon Chouinard, see J T SPECIAL, page 103.

SELECTING BONEFISH FLIES

◆ ◆ ◆

For Major Locations and Prey, and for Different Depths, Light Levels, and Wind Conditions

Does fly pattern matter in bonefishing? The answer depends on where you fish, how you fish, the angling conditions, and the nature of the fish you pursue.

If you stalk wild bonefish in remote areas that have never seen anglers before, pattern choice won't matter much—the fish will hit any reasonable fly you throw, as long as you present it well.

Similarly, if you fish a single destination with a stable prey population and with constant wind, depth, and light conditions, you shouldn't need much of a selection of fly patterns either. A small number of local favorites will likely do you very well.

But if you're a typical flats angler—one who stalks bonefish in different places under different conditions—you'll need some variety in your box to give you flexibility. You'll want low-profile flies for casting in wind, quiet-landing flies for calm days, dull patterns for bright days, and bright patterns for dull conditions. And you will want a few different choices for tailing, cruising, and mudding fish.

Furthermore, if you stalk heavily pressured areas or pursue bonefish that seem to be stressed in some way (and it seems to me they always are), the fly you tie on your tippet will be carefully and nervously evaluated. You may find you need to widen your assortment with different "prey looks" to come up with one that passes muster. In these situations, fly choice may be as important as presentation. That is not to say that you can slack off on your delivery—it will still have to be perfect. But so will your fly choice.

Whatever your circumstances, four variables should govern your selection of bonefish flies: your destination, the local angling conditions, the disposition of the fish, and the prey that they are eating. Of these, destination and prey will most shape the overall look and color of your fly box. Then you can adjust your selection to daily conditions and to the disposition of the fish.

SELECTING FLIES FOR DIFFERENT DESTINATIONS

Fly boxes bound for different bonefishing locales reveal their destinations with characteristic "looks"—in terms of both fly sizes and colors—reflecting the different prey that reside in each site.

Florida Flies

Florida's rich waters nurture big fish and big prey. And Florida-bound bonefish flies portray the big crabs, shrimps, and toadfish that dominate bonefish diet there. Keys flies come large—in sizes 1, 2, 4, or even bigger. Tan, brown, white, beige, and olive dominate their colors, with occasional bits of pink, chartreuse, gold, or orange appearing. Examine the patterns of Harry Spear, Rick Ruoff, Steve Huff, Tim Borski, Jeffrey Cardenas, Ellen Reed, Lenny Moffo, and George Hommell—these typify Keys-style patterns. Specific Florida flies appear in Table 3.1

TABLE 3.1	FLIES FOR FLORIDA AND THE KEYS
LOCATIONS	**PATTERNS**
Biscayne Bay, Key Largo, Islamorada, Marathon, Big Pine Key, Key West	Absolute Flea, Apricot Charlie, Backcountry Bonefish Fly, Ben's Copper, Ben's Epoxy Bonefish Fly, Bone-Zai Crab, Bonefish Explorer, Bonefish Joe, Bonenanza, Bunny Bone, Brain Teaser, Branham's Epoxy Shrimp, Branham's Swimming Crab, Bristle Worm, Capt. Crabby, Clouser Deep Minnow, Dave's (Whitlock) Shrimp, Deep Flea, Deer Hair Critter, Del Brown Bonefish Fly, Epoxy Shrimp (Borski), Eric's Epoxy Crab, Eric's Standing Shrimp, Flats Fodder, Fleeing Crab, Flutterbug, Foxy Lady Crab, Fur Charles, Fuzzy Hand, Gorell's Hackle Shrimp, Greg's Flats Fly, Hairy Legs Crab, Hallucination, Hare Trigger, Honey Lamb, Hoochy Caucci Fly, Intruder, Joe-to-Go, J T Special, Ken Bay Bonefish Shrimp, Kraft Fur Worm, Lefty's Clouser Deep Minnow, Len's Hackle Merkin, Len's Hackle Shrimp, Livebody Crab, McCrab, Missing Link, MOE Shrimp (Spear), Palmered Crab, Pearl Flash, Pink Epoxy Charlie, Pop Hill Special, Ralph's Hackled Epoxy Bonefish Fly, Ron's MOE, Sand Bandit, Sea Flea, See-Bone, Shallow H2O Fly, Slamaroo, Slinky, Sneaky Snake, Spot, Stealth Crab, Super Shrimp, Tasty Toad, Victor's Candy, Whitlock's Near Nuff Snapping Shrimp
SIZES	
1/0, 1, 2, 4	
COLORS	
Tan, brown, gold, cream, olive; some pink and chartreuse	

Florida flies are inclined to be large, earth-toned, and snag proof. Many contain epoxy because of this material's attractive translucency and excellent sink rate.

Bahamas Flies

Bahamas patterns come in many more colors than Florida flies, reflecting both broader diversity of species and a wider color variation among species—even *within* them. In salt water, prey of exactly the same species can vary greatly in color from locale to locale (they are called "polychromatic"). So the mantis shrimp, *Gonodactylus oerstedii,* found in the Berry Islands may be tan and white, while the *G. oerstedii* found in the Marls west of Abaco may be brown and ocher.

Hook sizes run smaller in the Bahamas too (sizes 2 to 8), reflecting Bahamian prey that range from half to three-quarters the size of Keys species. When in big-fish areas, however, such as Bimini or the Berrys, flies of up to size 1 will produce.

While such diversity makes typifying Bahamian patterns difficult, you will gain a sense of this variety by looking through the flies of tiers such as Jim Orthwein, Winston Moore, Brian O'Keefe, John Goddard, Barry and Cathy Beck, Doug Brewer, Joe Branham, Al Caucci, Bob Nauheim, Ralph Bird, Eric Peterson, Doug Brewer, Ed Opler, Franklyn Gorell, Michael Holtzman, Bob Hyde, Greg Miheve, Ed Mitchell, Charlie Gowen, and Doug Schlink. Their flies are but a few reflecting the characteristic Bahamian look. Specific Bahamas flies appear in Table 3.2.

TABLE 3.2		
	FLIES FOR THE BAHAMAS	
LOCATIONS	**PATTERNS**	

LOCATIONS	PATTERNS
Abaco, Andros, Bimini, Berrys, Chub, Deep Water Cay, Eleuthera, Exuma, Harbour Island, Mores Island Sandy Point, Walker's Cay	Agent Orange, Al's Glass Minnow, Apricot Charlie, Articulated Crab, Backcountry Bonefish Fly, Bead Minnow, Beady Crab, Ben's Copper, Ben's Epoxy Bonefish Fly, Bill's Mantis, Bird's Bonefish Fly, Black Urchin, Blue Crab, Bobby, Bone Bug, Bone-Zai Crab, Bonefish Bunny, Bonefish Crab, Bonefish Explorer, Bonefish In-Furriator, Bonefish Joe, Bonefish Joe Chicken Fly, Bonenanza, Boyle Bonefish Shrimp, Branham's Epoxy Shrimp, Branham's Swimming Crab, Brewer's Amber, Bugskin Crab, Bunny Bone, Camera's Crab, Capt. Crabby, Clam Before the Storm, Clouser Deep Minnow, Crazy Charlie, Dave's (Whitlock) Shrimp, Deep Flea, Deepwater Bonefish Fly, Del Brown Bonefish Fly, Dr. Taylor Special, Ed's Greenie Grass Shrimp, Ed's Sassy Shrimp, Eric's Epoxy Crab, Eric's Standing Shrimp, Ference's Goby, Flats Fodder, Fleeing Crab, Flint's Rubber Ducky, Foxy Lady Crab, Flutterbug, Fur Charles, Fuzzy Hand, Golden Shrimp, Gorell's Hackle Shrimp, Gotcha, Green Clouser (see under Yellow Clouser), Green Puff, Greg's Flats Fly, Greg's Tiny Shiny Shrimp, Harbour Island Charlie, Harbour Island Clouser, Hare Trigger, Honey Lamb, Hoochy Caucci Fly, Hoover, Interceptor, Intruder, Jim's Bonefish Puff, Jim's Golden Eye, Jim's Rubber Band Worm, Joe-to-Go, Ken Bay Bonefish Shrimp, Lefty's Clouser Deep Minnow, Len's Hackle Merkin, Len's Hackle Shrimp, Livebody Crab, Magic Mantis, Magnum Mantis, Manjack Cay Charlie, Marabou Shrimp, McCrab, Mini Crab Fly, Missing Link, Morning Hatch Shrimp, Moxey Creek Shrimp, Myers' Shrimp, Nacho, Nasty Gilbert, Perdi Shrimp, Pflueger HOY, Pipe Cleaner Fly, Pop Hill Special, Pop's Bonefish Bitters, Sand Bandit, Sea Flea, Shallow H$_2$O Fly, Shimmerskin Mantis, Shroyer's Yellow Charlie, Silly Legs Bonefish Fly, Sir Mantis Shrimp, Slamaroo, Slinky, Spot, Standard MOE (Brewer's), Super Shrimp, Tabory's Bonefish Fly, Tropical Shrimp, Turd Fly, Turneffe Crab, Ultra Shrimp, Vernille Sparkle Worm, Victor's Candy, Wiggle Worm, Woolly Crab
SIZES	
1, 2, 4, 6, 8	
COLORS	
Orange, pink, gold, char-treuse, yellow, blue	

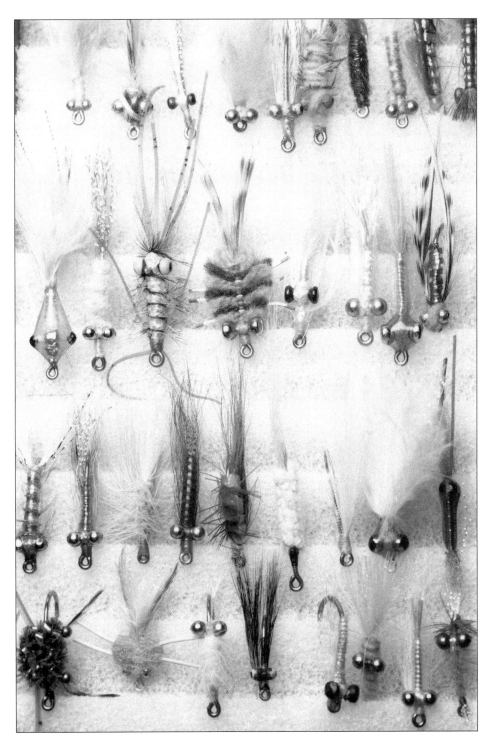

Popular Bahamas patterns tend toward medium sizes of 2 to 6 and come in many shapes and colors, reflecting the great assortment of prey and bottom tones found in this island. Orange, pink, and chartreuse are favored attractor colors.

Belize and Mexico Flies

Fish of Belize and the Yucatan share many of the prey-color preferences of Bahamas fish, but with an emphasis on greens, chartreuses, and yellows, consistent with local prey and bottom colors. Emerald green, as seen in Tom McGuane's Sea Flea and Craig Mathews' Turneffe Crab, fishes especially well. Medium or peacock blue also has an unusual attraction here, evidenced by such productive patterns as Winston Moore's Green Puff and his Grassy Wonder. Craig Mathews' Hermit Crab Bitters with blue legs works well too, and Ben Estes ties a version of his Ben's Epoxy Bonefish Fly with a blue tail and a blue-green cast to its body for these locales.

Table 3.3 lists patterns for Belize; Table 3.4 for Mexico. Note that hook sizes run smaller here—smallest, in fact, of all bonefish destinations. This in part reflects fish and prey size, at least in the case of Mexico. But for Belize, smaller profiles also yield the quieter presentations required by large fish on very shallow flats.

TABLE 3.3

FLIES FOR BELIZE

LOCATIONS	SIZES	COLORS	PATTERNS
Turneffe Islands, Glover's Reef, Ambergris Caye, Honduras	1, 6, 8, 10, 12	yellow, char-treuse, emerald, blue	Agent Orange, Beady Crab, Black Urchin, Bobby, Bonefish Crab, Brad's Tailbone, Branham's Swimming Crab, Brewer's Amber, Buster Crab, Camera's Crab, Clam Before the Storm, Clouser Deep Minnow, Crapoxy, Crazy Charlie, Dave's (Whitlock) Shrimp, Ed's Sassy Shrimp, Eric's Epoxy Crab, Fuzzy Hand, Gorell's Hackle Shrimp, Grassy Wonder, Green Puff, Greg's Flats Fly, Hermit Crab Bitters, Hare Trigger, Hoochy Caucci Fly, Hoover, J T Special, Lipstick Minnow, McCrab, Missing Link, Morning Hatch Shrimp, Ouch, Perdi Shrimp, Pink Epoxy Charlie, Pop's Bonefish Bitters, Rock Mantis, Ron's MOE, Salsa Shrimp, Sand Bandit, Scott's Tube Shrimp, Sea Flea, Shallow H$_2$O Fly, Shroyer's Yellow Charlie, Sir Mantis Shrimp, Slinky, Spot, Squimp, Stealth Crab, Turd Fly, Turneffe Crab, Ultra Shrimp, Whitlock's Marabou & Pearl Glass Minnow, Whitlock's Near Nuff Snapping Shrimp, Woolly Crab, Yellow Clouser

Yucatan and Belize patterns run smaller than flies used at other destinations. Sizes 6, 8, and 10 are common, although some anglers succeed with size 2, 4, and even larger profiles in the reefs. Many bright colors reflect prey diversity, but duller hues that match bottoms have become popular too. Veterans of this area find yellow, emerald green, chartreuse, and bright blue effective.

TABLE 3.4

FLIES FOR MEXICO'S YUCATAN

LOCATIONS	SIZES	COLORS	PATTERNS
Mexico	6, 8, 10	Yellow, chartreuse, blue	Agent Orange, Bead Minnow, Ben's Epoxy Bonefish Fly, Bobby, Bonefish Crab, Bonefish Explorer, Bonefish Joe, Brain Teaser, Brewer's Amber, Buster Crab, Crapoxy, Crazy Charlie, Dave's (Whitlock) Shrimp, Ed's Sassy Shrimp, Eric's Epoxy Crab, Ference's Goby, Flats Fodder, Flutterbug, Glass-Eyed Shrimp, Gorell's Hackle Shrimp, Grassy Wonder, Green Puff, Greg's Flats Fly, Greg's Tiny Shiny Shrimp, Livebody Crab, Man in Tan, McCrab, Nacho, Pearl Flash, Pop Hill Special, Ralph's Hackled Epoxy Bonefish Fly, Ron's MOE, Shallow H2O Fly, Shroyer's Yellow Charlie, Silly Legs Bonefish Fly, Spot, Tropical Shrimp, Victor's Candy, Whitlock's Marabou & Pearl Glass Minnow, Whitlock's Near Nuff Snapping Shrimp

Venezuela Flies

Los Roques' unpressured Venezuela flats attract large schools of wild fish with ample and diverse prey. Many patterns developed for other destinations work well here, and the colors and sizes common in the Bahamas seem most effective. On thinnest tides, however, even small size 8s and 10s may be necessary. Also Winston Moore says this is one place where his Agent Orange sends fish flying. Dave Whitlock developed his Whitlock's Marabou & Pearl Glass Minnow here. Jim O'Neill, who fishes these unspoiled flats often, has found his Golden Shrimp particularly effective, along with McVay Gotchas, gold Charlies, and tan and white Clousers. Productive patterns are listed in Table 3.5.

TABLE 3.5

FLIES FOR VENEZUELA'S LOS ROQUES

LOCATIONS	SIZES	COLORS	PATTERNS
Los Roques	2, 4, 6, 8	white, tan, gold, green, blue	Bobby, Bonefish Crab, Bonefish In-Furriator, Brewer's Amber, Clouser Deep Minnow, Crazy Charlie, Dave's (Whitlock) Shrimp, Deepwater Bonefish Fly, Del Brown Bonefish Fly, Flats Fodder, Golden Shrimp, Gorell's Hackle Shrimp, Gotcha, Green Puff, Greg's Flats Fly, Hermit Bitters, Horror, Marabou Shrimp, Nasty Charlie, Sea Flea, Silly Legs, Shallow H2O Fly, Squimp, Tan Mini-Puff, Whitlock's Marabou & Pearl Glass Minnow, Whitlock's Near Nuff Snapping Shrimp

Pacific and Christmas Island Flies

The world's major Pacific bonefish destination, Christmas Island, has its own distinct terrain, prey, and flies. Light tan, beige, and a peculiar tan-gold (see the golden Nasty Gilbert, page 128, and the Paris Flat Special, page 132) do well on this sprawling atoll, and yellow and chartreuse also seem particularly effective at times. Red attracts interest here too, probably because several Pacific species of crabs and shrimps display red claws. There is even a Pacific mantis—always a favorite on the bonefish daily menu—that has red legs. Other novel colors may produce equally well, as we learn more about the Pacific prey.

If you are Kiribati bound, study in particular the flies of Randall Kaufmann, Tim Merrihew, Ralph Woodbine, J. Watt Shroyer, Yvon Chouinard, Eddie Corrie, Bill Hunter (his Flats Fodder series), and Terry Baird.

TABLE 3.6		FLIES FOR CHRISTMAS ISLAND AND THE PACIFIC	
LOCATIONS	**SIZES**	**COLORS**	**PATTERNS**
Christmas Island, Kanton, Hawaii	2, 4, 6	White, pale tan, pale gray, pale gold, yellow, green, red	Ben's Epoxy Bonefish Fly, Bird's Bonefish Fly, Bobby, Bone Bug, Bunny Bone, Camera's Crab, Christmas Island Flash Charlie, Christmas Island Special, Clouser Deep Minnow, Crazy Charlie, Dave's (Whitlock) Shrimp, Deep Flea, Del Brown Bonefish Fly, Ed's Sassy Shrimp, Eric's Epoxy Crab, Eric's Standing Shrimp, Flats Fodder, Fur Charles, Golden Shrimp, Gorell's Hackle Shrimp, Gotcha, Greg's Flats Fly, Hoover, Lefty's Clouser Deep Minnow, Marabou Shrimp, Morning Hatch Shrimp, Myers' Shrimp, Nacho, Nasty Charlie, Nasty Gilbert, Paris Flat Special, Perdi Shrimp, Pop's Bonefish Bitters, Ralph's Hackled Epoxy Bonefish Fly, Salsa Shrimp, Sand Bandit, Shallow H$_2$O Fly, Shroyer's Yellow Charlie, Standard MOE (Brewer's), Tan Chenille Charlie, Tropical Shrimp, Turd Fly, Whitlock's Marabou & Pearl Glass Minnow, Yellow Clouser

Typical Christmas Island flies range in sizes 4, 6, 8, and sometimes smaller. White, beige, pale yellow, and gold tones reflect natural prey and bottom colors. Bright red, yellow, and orange-pink sometimes attract too, and larger patterns such as Eddie Corrie's Paris Flat Special also produce well.

A Note on Selecting Fly Color

As indicated earlier (see the discussion of fly color in chapter 1), many bonefish prey conceal themselves with camouflage patterns and with colors that match their surroundings—the sand, coral, turtle grass, and mangrove bottoms they inhabit. Anglers, therefore, should select most of their flies in earth-tone colors that approximate the hues of the bottoms where they fish. This general rule will serve you well as long as you bear in mind a couple of additional observations: Some prey do not camouflage themselves on bottoms, and some prey do not camouflage themselves at all.

Prey, such as cleaning shrimps that live on hosts like sponges, anemones, and fish have garishly colored bodies that blend well with those of their hosts but contrast sharply with other surroundings when they are loosened and tumbled free by currents or storms. Similarly, many burrowing worm, as well as some crab, shrimp, and even clam species bear gay exteriors that give them away when they are unearthed by feeding fish. This is why a bright-colored fly thrown into mud often appears "natural" to fish. The easy detection of such dislodged creatures—whether burrowing or hosted species—triggers vigorous feeding in bonefish, so include at least a few bright colors in your box along with all the whites, tans, olives, and ochers.

Selecting Bonefish Patterns for Different Conditions

Water depth, wind intensity, light level, and bottom structure each affect fly selection. Of all of these, getting your fly to fish level accounts for the most hook-ups. I consider this variable—water depth—so important that I carry my flies in three boxes arranged by sink rate—light, medium, and heavy. Then, using whichever box matches the depth I'm fishing, I select patterns to accommodate the other variables I encounter.

Water Depth and Fly Selection

The height of the water column and the depth at which fish feed, determine how far—and how fast—you must sink your fly. If fish are mudding on the bottom or cruising deep in four feet of water, only high-density fast sinkers will get down to them quickly enough to be seen. This is a perfect time for Saul Greenspan's See-Bone or Rick Ruoff's Deep Flea. When fish tail, however, feeding in water so shallow their caudal fins protrude, you need flies that not only sink to fish level, but also land softly and project enough bulk to be detected through feeding debris. You might try Len's Hackle Shrimp or Harry Spear's MOE, for example, or John Goddard's bright-colored Tropical Shrimp.

The ingenious rubber-band weight holder on Will Myers's Fur Charles and Buster Crab patterns allows anglers to switch eyes, altering sink rate to accomodate different water depths.

When fish tail or when they feed at middle depths, slower-sinking flies such as Page Roger's Shimmering Shrimp (top) and Jeffrey Cardenas' Palmered Crab (bottom) will stay at fish level long enough to be noticed.

For fish swimming at middle depths, where they can scan the waters for vulnerable prey, you should select a fly with a slower sink rate, putting it at the level where the fish are swimming and keeping it there long enough to be noticed. Neutral buoyancy patterns, such as a lightly weighted Borski Bristle Worm or Ben's Epoxy Bonefish Fly, might work well.

In the thinnest of depths, where fish of necessity feed millimeters below the surface, quiet, slow-sinking flies do well. There are also times when you find bonefish porpoising on the surface—usually during spawning. Either of these "shallow" situations calls for a slow sinker such as a Pflueger's HOY or a Lefty's Shallow H_2O Fly dressed with floatant. Even a floating fly may be effective.

Whether you fish many flies or only a few, you should carry them in enough different sink rates to cover the water depths you'll encounter. Table 3.7 illustrates a typical selection that covers common flats depths. Also, see Will Myers' Buster Crab (page 53) and his Fur Charles (page 81) for one especially inventive solution to matching sink rate to conditions. Their rubber-band weight-holder design allows you to change sink rate on-site

Water depth not only affects sink rate, it also influences choice of color and shininess. Patterns separated from sunlight by several feet of water—especially water containing sediment—appear darker and therefore less enticing to fish. Brighter flies or patterns with flashy elements attract better at these depths. Good choices are Andy Burk's orange Deepwater Bonefish Fly, Phil Taylor's Dr. Taylor Special, John Goddard's Tropical Shrimp, and Saul Greenspan's See-Bone in chartreuse.

Wind and Fly Selection

Wind complicates fly selection too. It challenges your casting by pushing flies off course. It also roils the water column below the surface, demanding more noticeable patterns to attract attention.

TABLE 3.7

WEIGHTING AND SINK RATE

TYPES	WEIGHT	TYPICAL PATTERNS
Deep sinkers	Split shot Lead barbell Lead keel strips	Clouser Deep Minnow Deep Flea Deepwater Bonefish Fly Del Brown Bonefish Fly Ference's Goby (lead) Foxy Lady Crab Golden Shrimp Magic Mantis Marabou Shrimp See-Bone
Middle Depth Flies	Bead chain Epoxy body Oversized hook Bend-back Glass eyes Sparse dressing	Bonefish Crab Charlies Clouser Deep Minnow (head) Gotcha Jim's Golden Eye Manjack Cay Charlie MOEs Nasty Gilbert Slinky Turd Fly Turneffe Crab
Shallow Flies	Hook only Smallest metal eyes Lead paste Plastic eyes	Bonefish Explorer Jim's Bonefish Puff Grassy Wonder Hare Trigger Intruder Ouch Pflueger HOY Spot Shallow H_2O Fly Victor's Candy

Tight, aerodynamic fly profiles will overcome the first of these problems. My favorite flies for penetrating wind are clean-profile, bead-chain-weighted patterns such as Gotchas, Charlies, sparse Clousers (with bead chain), and any pattern with a weighted epoxy body. These all seem to have the best balance of weight and streamlining to cast well in gusts, and I can control them much better than broad-profile patterns such as crabs or urchins. Heavier lead-weighted patterns sometimes perform well in wind too. I find lead-eye Clousers and other metal dumbbell patterns cast acceptably in wind as long as I drive them hard enough to keep their weight under control.

To overcome wind's second challenge—that of attracting notice in turbid waters—I often select brighter colors, flashier flies, and larger profiles. While a bigger fly might seem a poor choice in breezy conditions, some bulkier flies cast better in wind than you might at first think. Designs such as Baird's Stealth Crab and Orthwein's Jim's Bonefish Puff slice through air or contract into thin profiles when they are cast, then blossom back to full shape when they land. Table 3.8 shows some examples of flies that cast well in wind, both thin- and larger-profile patterns.

TABLE 3.8

WIND-CUTTING FLIES

THIN PROFILE	LARGE PROFILE
Ben's Copper	Hoochy Caucci Fly
Brewer's Amber	Jim's Bonefish Puff
Clousers	Marabou Shrimp
Ed's Sassy Shrimp	Missing Link
Gorell's Hackle Shrimp	Pearl Flash
Gotcha	Pop Hill Special
Harbour Island Clouser	Ralph's Hackled Epoxy Bonefish Fly
Intruder	Sneaky Snake
Nacho	Standard MOE (Brewer's)
Nasty Gilbert	Stealth Crab

Calm Water and Fly Selection

Calm, flat water demands the most delicate of landings to avoid spooking fish, while choppy water reduces the impact of splashdown.

Light-impact patterns are the most effective choice for such quiet conditions—the kind when even the tiny plip of a size 8 hook or a pair of 3/32" bead-chain eyes can be detected by fish from many yards away. Looks can deceive, however. When judging flies for impact, size may be less of a factor than density. Some small-profile flies with high densities, such as Charlies and Gotchas, unnerve fish more than large, airy patterns like Phil Chapman's Bone-Zai Crab tied of soft wool. One of the noisiest designs is the weighted, flat profile found in some of the earliest deer hair crabs. The buoyancy of their large bodies required a hefty pancake of lead that belly-flopped with a splat on impact.

Even eyeless or "blind" patterns—tied specifically for spooky conditions—sometimes cause schools to blow up. Blind Charlies and Gotchas possess bodies dense enough to make fish-spooking plips even with no eyes at all. Soft-element, eyeless patterns, however, such as Winston Moore's Agent Orange or the Pflueger HOY, land as quietly as a whisper.

I like to use flies with as little weight as possible for the spookiest of conditions (some typical choices appear in the left column of Table 3.9). But for times when I need to get something more substantial in front of fish—because of turbid water, or because I need

Small changes in the ratio of a fly's density to its cushioning can greatly alter splash impact. The exposed metal eyes on the Clouser Deep Minnow and the Crazy Charlie (far left and middle left) make noisier, splashier landings than the dampened orbs on the Tabory Bonefish Fly and the Nasty Gilbert (middle right and far right).

heavier weight to get down to fish level faster—I pick flies with bulkier yet heavier profiles, big flies that have been designed specifically to maintain stealth. Clever patterns such as Ellen Reed's Honey Lamb and Tim Merrihew's Nasty Gilbert contain dubbing shrouds that cushion the impact of their metal eyes. Lou Tabory's ingenious little deer hair pillow under the eyes of his Tabory's Bonefish Fly serves the same function. So do the deer hair heads on most of Tim Borski's designs. Other flies, such as Gorell's Hackle Shrimp, Jim's Golden Eye, the Spot, and the Bobby, employ hackle—either palmered around bodies or wound as collars—to deaden impact.

TABLE 3.9	
SPLASHDOWN IMPACT	
LIGHT-IMPACT FLIES	**HEAVIER FLIES MODEST IMPACT**
Bonefish Explorer	Beady Crab
Branham's Swimming Crab	Bonefish Joe
Grassy Wonder	Deer Hair Critter
Hare Trigger	Harbour Island Clouser
Intruder	J T Special
Jim's Bonefish Puff	Len's Hackle Merkin
Ouch	Len's Hackle Shrimp
Pflueger HOY	Magic Mantis
Pop Hill Special	Sir Mantis
Shallow H2O Fly	Sneaky Snake
Spot	Woolly Crab
Victor's Candy	

Light Level and Fly Selection

Sunlight affects fly selection because many patterns—especially the reflective ones—change dramatically as the intense sun of the subtropics rises and falls. Flies that readily attracted quarry in the low light of early morning may abruptly begin spooking fish as their tinsel, Mylar, and Flashabou elements glare in the intense rays of midday. Conversely, duller flies that performed well under yesterday's bright sun may attract no interest at all today, when cloud cover or muddy water deadens their appearance.

The first time I stumbled onto the importance of glare in flies, I had been taking fish all morning on a productive Bahamian flat off North Eleuthera's Nurse Creek on one of Bill Hunter's Apricot Charlies. Then about 10:30 A.M., as the sun intensified overhead, the fish began spooking at the same fly presented in the same fashion. At first I switched to a smaller size of the same pattern, but the fish continued to explode. Next I changed to another color, but to no avail. Then I switched to a wool-bodied pattern with the same gold-orange colors as the Apricot Charlie. Immediately the fish renewed their aggressive attack, streaking after the fly even when it landed yards away.

I've experienced enough similar situations since that I now regularly switch back and forth between dull and reflective flies as light level and fish behavior change. Sometimes I even rank flies for dark, average, and bright conditions.

While fly glare is not the most important variable to me, adjusting it *has* turned around several poor flats situations and accounted for a couple of my best bonanzas.

TABLE 3.10

FLIES FOR DIFFERENT LEVELS

LOW LIGHT	BRIGHT LIGHT
Ben's Copper	Bobby
Christmas Island Special	Bone Bug
Clousers	Flint's Rubber Ducky
Dr. Taylor Special	Harbour Island Clouser
Ed's Sassy Shrimp	Honey Lamb
Gorell's Hackle Shrimp	Missing Link
Gotcha	Pipe Cleaner Fly
Intruder	Sea Flea
Nasty Gilbert	Shallow H$_2$O Fly
Paris Flat Special	Turd Fly
Shroyer's Yellow Charlie	Vernille Sparkle Worm
Squimp	

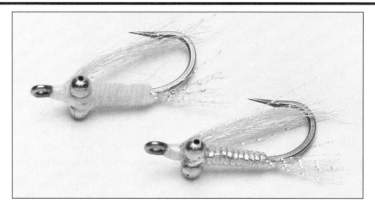

When the sun climbs high above the flats and flashy flies start to glint unnaturally, switching to duller versions of the same size and color, such as Bill Hunter's non-reflective variation of his Flats Fodder pattern (left), can keep the action going.

Snag-Proofing and Fly Selection

If you peer into the box of a Keys-bound angler, you'll see weed guards on almost every fly. But look into the fly box of an angler headed for Christmas Island or Andros, and you may not see a single mono spike or loop. The Keys require snag-proof flies because their abundant grass beds, which offer food to fish, also eat bare-hooked flies. Consequently, tiers of Keys flies (or patterns to be fished in grass elsewhere—like Belize) have found many ways to snag-proof them: mono spikes, mono loops, wire guards, inverted wings, hair guards, hackle guards, and others. Table 3.11 compares the trade-offs of these approaches, and Table 3.12 shows habitats where guards are most important.

SELECTING PATTERNS FOR DIFFERENCES IN BONEFISH DISPOSITION

Bonefish, like most creatures, do different things at different times. And because their dispositions change—depending on whether they are hunting, eating, resting, or fleeing from attackers—they require different approaches *and different fly patterns* at different times. These requirements are shown in Table 3.13.

TABLE 3.11

TYPES OF WEED GUARD

WEED GUARD	ADVANTAGES	DISADVANTAGES
Wire	Strong protection	Fish may feel and reject fly; may discolor
Mono Loop	Strong protection	Fish may feel and reject fly
Mono Spike	Moderate protection	Fish may feel and reject fly
Inverted Hair Wing	Fish won't feel; aids in flipping over fly	Moderate protection
Flared Hair Guard	Fish won't feel; aids in flipping over fly	Light protection
Hackle Guard	Fish won't feel; doubles as legs	Light protection

TABLE 3.12

HABITAT AND SNAG-PROOFING

GRASS	SAND	MANGROVE	CORAL HEADS	REEFS
Weed Guard	Plain Hook	Optional	Weed Guard	Optional

TABLE 3.13

PATTERN AND PRESENTATION CHOICES VERSUS FISH DEMEANOR

FISH DEMEANOR	FLY TRAITS	FLY APPROACH
Cruising Fish	Get down fast; good unaided action from wiggling elements	Cast ahead of fish; twitch when fish approach
Tailing Fish	Land softly; good visibility but small profile	Cast to "eye" side of fish; twitch to attract attention
Mudding Fish	Get down fast; bulky; highly noticeable profile, color, or vibration	Drift "downstream" into edge of mud
Resting Fish	Visible in deep water; pass scrutiny as natural	Cast well upcurrent and drift or "walk" fly naturally
Ambushing Fish	Bulky profile that drifts naturally with flow; opportunistic "big prey" pattern	Drift on current toward fish's lair

SELECTING BONEFISH PATTERNS FOR DIFFERENT HABITATS AND PREY

While different habitats demand flies with different functional characteristics, they also require flies with different profiles. Grass, mangrove, and coral habitats harbor different prey with different colors, shapes, and actions.

If you primarily fish grass beds, then the fish you encounter will be accustomed to seeing the small shrimp and crab species that thrive in grass habitats. If you drift the outer margins along reefs and oceanside cays, fish will more readily accept a big mantis shrimp, snapping shrimp, or swimming crab as belonging.

Table 3.14 shows typical bonefish habitats and the prey normally found in them.

Bonefish eat opportunistically and will likely chase any fly that looks appetizing. But sophisticated fish or stressed fish may be much more selective. At such times, choosing flies that mimic prey normally seen in the habitat you're fishing improves your odds. Table 3.15 lists major prey types and a few of the flies that suggest them. The fly profiles in chapter 2 give prey possibilities for most patterns.

TABLE 3.14
PREY MOST COMMONLY FOUND IN DIFFERENT BONEFISH FEEDING AREAS

FLATS AREAS		SHORELINE AREAS			REEFS
GRASS FLAT	SAND FLAT	MANGROVE STAND	SANDY SHORE	ROCKY SHORE	ALL
	Clams	Clams	Clams		
Common shrimps	Common shrimps	Common shrimps			Common shrimps
Mantis shrimps (spearers)	Mantis shrimps (spearers)			Mantis shrimps (smashers)	Mantis shrimps (smashers)
Snapping shrimps		Snapping shrimps		Snapping shrimps	Snapping shrimps
Small shrimps				Small shrimps	Small shrimps
Swimming crabs	Swimming crabs		Swimming crabs	Swimming crabs	Swimming crabs
Spider crabs		Spider crabs		Spider crabs	Spider crabs
	Mud crabs	Mud crabs			
Gobies; Toadfish		Gobies; Toadfish		Gobies; Toadfish	Gobies; Toadfish
Fish	Fish	Fish	Fish	Fish	Fish
Worms	Worms	Worms	Worms	Worms	Worms
	Urchins			Urchins	

This juvenile blue crab lives on the protected inside rocky shore of an outer cay in the northeastern Bahamas. Anglers who fish there with small white or pale green patterns will be showing the fish something that belongs there.

DOES FLY PATTERN MATTER?

Fly-fishing anglers often disagree—sometimes heatedly—over how much fly *selection* versus fly *presentation* compels a fish to strike. Some feel pattern selection to be the most critical of all fishing variables. They spend a lot of time analyzing the prey species their quarry eats and selecting flies to suggest them.

Others feel—just as strongly—that how a fly is delivered to a fish is far more important than what it depicts. Some of these "presentationists" distrust fly selection so thoroughly that they fish only one pattern, trusting their delivery skills to make their offering appeal-

Some big-fish flies. (Top to bottom, left to right) Craig Mathews' Pop's Bonefish Bitters, Craig Roger's Brain Teaser, Dick Berry's Pipe Cleaner Fly, Jim Orthwein's Golden Eye, Brian O'Keefe's Missing Link, and Jim Orthwein's Bonefish Puff. These are but six of the patterns appearing in this book that have taken double-digit bonefish. Look at the profiles closely—there are over two dozen big-fish patterns listed.

ing enough for the fish to eat. And some of them have developed such accomplished presentation skills that this exclusive strategy works. But these same anglers could probably also get a bonefish to eat a cigarette butt if they cast it to one.

In my mind, however, such purism is irrelevant to most bonefishing anglers. *Both* presentation and pattern selection are essential on the flats, and both should be mastered by serious bonefishing anglers.

TABLE 3.15

PREY AND SOME FLIES THAT SUGGEST THEM

PREY	FLIES THAT SUGGEST
Smaller Shrimps	Bird's Bonefish Fly, Bobby, Bone Bug, Christmas Island Special, Ed's Sassy Shrimp, Glass-Eyed Shrimp, Grassy Wonder, Greg's Tiny Shiny Shrimp, Harbour Island Charlie, Morning Hatch Shrimp, Perdi Shrimp, Sea Flea, Turd Fly, Victor's Candy
Large Shrimps	Ben's Copper, Ben's Epoxy Bonefish Fly, Boyle Bonefish Shrimp, Branham's Epoxy Shrimp, Brewer's Amber, Dave's (Whitlock) Shrimp, Dr. Taylor Special, Epoxy Shrimp (Borski), Eric's Standing Shrimp, Flint's Rubber Ducky, Greg's Flats Fly, Hallucination, Hare Trigger, Honey Lamb, Hoochy Caucci Fly, Jim's Golden Eye, Joe-to-Go, Len's Hackle Shrimp, MOE Shrimp (Spear), Myers' Shrimp, Paris Flat Special, Ron's MOE, Salsa Shrimp, Shimmering Shrimp, Silly Legs Bonefish Fly, Squimp, Standard MOE (Brewer's)
Mantis Shrimps	Bill's Mantis, Jim's Golden Eye, Magic Mantis, Magnum Mantis, Missing Link, Moxey Creek Shrimp, Rock Mantis, Shimmerskin Mantis, Super Shrimp
Swimming Crabs	Beady Crab, Bone-Zai Crab, Bonefish Crab (Moore), Branham's Swimming Crab, Camera's Crab, Capt. Crabby, Deer Hair Critter, Del Brown Bonefish Fly, Fleeing Crab, Flutterbug, Foxy Lady Crab, Hairy Legs Crab, Len's Hackle Merkin, Livebody Crab, McCrab, Woolly Crab
Reef, Spider, and Mud Crabs	Bugskin Crab, Crapoxy, Mini Crab Fly, Pop's Bonefish Bitters, Sand Bandit, Stealth Crab, Turneffe Crab
Toadfish and Gobies	Backcountry Bonefish Fly, Bonefish Explorer, Ference's Goby, Jim's Bonefish Puff, Missing Link, Ralph's Hackled Epoxy Bonefish Fly, Slinky, Tasty Toad
Errant Worms and Burrowing Worms	Bonefish Bunny, Brad's Tailbone, Deep Flea, Hoover, Jim's Rubber Band Worm, Kraft Fur Worm, Slinky, Vernille Sparkle Worm, Wiggle Worm
Other	Black Urchin, Clam Before the Storm, Lipstick Minnow, Ouch

Presentation *is* absolutely crucial in bonefishing—even a live crab poorly presented will spook fish. Yet pattern selection can be just as critical. On plenty of occasions bonefish have rejected all but one or two flies of the many I showed them, no matter how well I presented the others.

I find it difficult, therefore, to believe that bonefish fly patterns are all equal and that fly choice is irrelevant. Such reasoning seems unnecessarily restrictive to me and it fails to explain why bonefish key to specific patterns on certain tides, or at certain light levels, or in certain habitats, or at certain locations—sometimes for days—and then switch off to another. Or why large fish will ignore "proven" flies, leaving them to their smaller neighbors, but then abandon all caution to chase one specific prey form. Or why most Florida guides would rather give you the keys to their 4x4s than show you the fly patterns they save for tournament competitions.

I guess all this makes me an eclectic in the fly theory business. But over the years I've found I do better in bonefishing when I deliver the best presentation I can to the fish—*and* show them the best flies in my box.

And over those same years, the more I've learned about this omnivorous, yet wary, species, the more I've come to believe fly choice is crucial to its smartest members.

I find, therefore, that *both* pattern and presentation play critical roles in stalking *Albula vulpes*. In fact, the two are so intertwined in my fishing for this wary quarry that I find it impossible to separate them. How close I put a fly to a fish, how fast I want it to sink, and what action I give it (all *presentation* variables) depend—at least in part—on what prey my fly pattern suggests. On the other hand, sink rate, entry impact, and snag-proofing—all aspects of pattern *selection*—also depend on how and where I present the fly.

So I believe fly choice not only makes a difference in bonefishing but is an essential ingredient in the pursuit of this species. I've concluded I must integrate it into my approach along with all the other factors that play a role in bringing a silver phantom to the end of my fly line. It's not the *only* factor, but it is one of the critical factors I must attend to when I am serious about my fishing.

4

TYING SEQUENCES

◆ ◆ ◆

Mastering These Step-By-Step Instructions Will Teach You to Tie Most Bonefish Flies

Most flies developed for pursuing a single species share traits that set them apart from patterns designed for other fish. Deer hair bodies and mono weed guards typify bass flies. Married-feather wings and lavishly colored bodies distinguish salmon patterns. And long-nosed profiles with splayed tails define tarpon flies.

Bonefish flies bear unique traits too. Bulbous metal eyes, inverted wings, plastic-coated bodies, and epoxy heads are but a few of the unusual features that betray them.

Most of these elements present no special challenge to fly tiers. Yet, as is always the case in tying, those who specialize in one type of pattern learn skills and tricks that make construction better and easier.

The pattern instructions that appear in this chapter will help you master some of those skills—enough, at least, so you can begin tying most flats patterns on your own. As an added benefit, while you practice your tying, you will be filling your fly box with some of the most effective patterns in use on the flats today.

TYING THE GOTCHA

SKILLS
Bead-chain eyes and the quintessential bonefish fly "shrimp" shape.

RECIPE
Hook: Mustad 34007; sizes 2, 4
Thread: Fluorescent or Gotcha Pink Danville Flat Waxed Nylon
Eyes: 1/8" bead chain on size 4, or 5/32" bead chain on size 2; use 1/50 oz. or 5/32 " lead barbells for fast-sink situations
Tail: Pearl Mylar tubing
Body: Pearl Diamond Braid
Wing: Yellow Krystal Flash over blond craft fur

TYING STEPS
Step 1: Position the eyes on the shank to allow enough room for the oversized pink nose. On a size 4 hook, I put them 3/16" to 1/4" behind the hook eye. Tie in the eyes, securing them to the shank by wrapping the thread in a figure-eight path around both the bead chain and the shank.

   Then wrap a "donut" in a horizontal plane underneath the bead-chain eyes, binding all wraps tight. Super Glue them if you're compulsive.

Step 2:   Behind the eyes, attach a flattened piece of pearlescent Mylar tubing onto the top of the shank, forming an underbody. The tubing should extend one full shank length beyond the bend to form the tail. Brush out the frayed ends of the Mylar fibers.

Step 3:   Tie in pearlescent Diamond Braid on top of the Mylar tubing, binding it along the shank as a second underbody. Then wind pink thread heavily over the underbody, so that a pink hue will show through after the body is wrapped. Next, wind the Diamond Braid forward to the eyes to form the body. Figure-eight wrap at the eyes and trim off.

Step 4:   Inverting the fly, tie in a craft fur wing. In length, it should extend to the end of tail.

Step 5:   Tie in a dozen Krystal Flash fibers to match the length of the wing. Invert. Build up the head with pink thread and whip-finish.

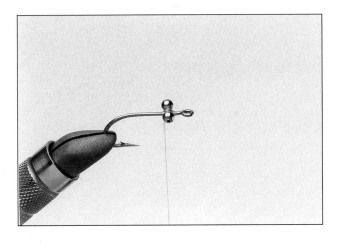

Gotcha Step 1: Tying in the Gotcha's eyes.

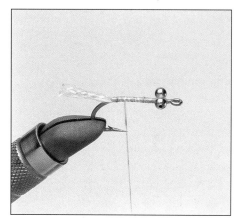

Gotcha Step 2:Attaching the tail.

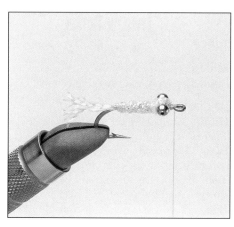

Gotcha Step 3:Winding on the body.

Gotcha Step 4:Winging the fly.

Gotcha Step 5:Building up the head.

Tying the Jim's Golden Eye

Skills
Plastic bodywrap, palmered legs, off-center tail, and reverse-position eyes.

Recipe
Hook: Mustad 9674 or 38941; sizes 2, 4
Thread: Beige Monocord 3/0
Antennae: Peccary (or moose mane)
Eyes: Medium (1/8") gold bead chain
Head/Face: Nugget Gold FisHair and gold Mylar tubing fibers, brushed out
Body: Clear Swannundaze or V-Rib over gold Mylar tubing
Legs: Brown saddle hackle, palmered in crevices of V-Rib and clipped on back and sides

Carapace/Tail: Nugget Gold FisHair twisted into rope and pulled over back, then doubled back alongside itself and lashed to one side as an off-center tail or telson; coat heavily with Hard As Nails

TYING STEPS

Step 1: Tie in the thread midshank and wind it to the hook bend. For the face, tie in a bunch (about one-half the diameter of a wooden matchstick) of FisHair at the bend and wind it 1/8" down the bend to cant the hair downward.

Step 2: Attach the peccary (or moose mane hair) antennae at the bend on top of the Fishair; trim all the butts and bind them down tightly onto the shank.

Step 3: Remove the core strings from the gold Mylar tubing. Fray the end of the tubing about 1/4" and slip it over the shank (the hook shank goes inside the Mylar tubing). Push the tubing along the shank until its frayed fibers all but overlap the Fishair ends. Bind in place.

Step 4: Tie in the bead-chain eyes with figure-eight wraps. Behind the eyes, tie in a second bunch of Fishair twice the diameter of the first (matchstick diameter). The butt end of the Fishair should point toward the hook eye, and the running end should lie across the bead chain and face (it will later double over onto itself, forming the carapace).

Step 5: Tie in the butt end of a long, narrow saddle hackle. Then tie in the Swannundaze (or other plastic bodywrap) on the underside of the shank; wind the thread over both it and the Mylar tubing underbody as a rib, spiraling it to the hook eye.

Step 6: Wrap the plastic bodywrap to the hook eye so its edges barely abut. Then wind the hackle to the hook eye, tugging its quill into the crevices in the plastic wrap. Clip the hackle on the top and sides, leaving the swimming legs.

Step 7: Twist the FisHair into a tight rope and pull it over the spine of the shrimp to form the carapace. Wind the thread about ten turns toward the hook eye to secure it. Wind the thread back toward the head of the shrimp (over the turns you just made), then bend the FisHair back on itself, forming an off-center tail or deflector. Then wind the thread over *both* the body and the deflector-tail, to bind them together. Whip-finish, and clip the FisHair tail perpendicular to its length, leaving a blunt, stubby end.

Step 8: Lacquer the back heavily, saturating the FisHair strands. Once dry, bend the spine of the hook to hump the shrimp, thus adhering the carapace tightly to the body.

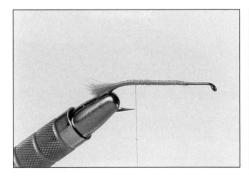

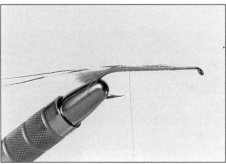

Jim's Golden Eye Step 1: Attaching the face.   *Jim's Golden Eye Step 2: Adding antennae.*

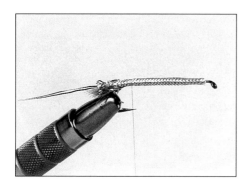

Jim's Golden Eye Step 3:Applying the underbody.

Jim's Golden Eye Step 4:Tying in the eyes and carapace.

Jim's Golden Eye Step 5:Attaching legs and bodywrap.

Jim's Golden Eye Step 6:Winding on the body and legs.

Jim's Golden Eye Step 7:Finishing the carapace and shaping the tail.

Jim's Golden Eye Step 8:Coating the carapace and shaping the back.

TYING THE NASTY CHARLIE (OR CRAZY CHARLIE)

SKILLS
Bead-chain eyes, hackle wing, plastic bodywrap, and the quintessential "Charlie" shrimp shape.

RECIPE
Hook: 34007 or 3407; sizes 1, 2, 4, 6, 8
Thread: White Monocord 3/0, or color to match body
Eyes: 1/8" silver bead chain
Tail: Ten or twelve strands silver tinsel
Body: 15-lb. Mason or other clear mono over flat silver tinsel (underbody later changed to silver or pearl Flashabou)
Wing: Two long white saddle hackles, convex sides facing to splay tips

TYING STEPS

Step 1: Position the eyes on the shank 3/16" to 1/4" behind the rear of the hook eye, to allow enough room to tie in the wing and finish the head. Secure the bead-chain eyes to the hook by wrapping in a figure-eight path around the eyes and shank. Then wrap a "donut" in a horizontal plane underneath the bead-chain eyes, binding all wraps tight. Super Glue.

Step 2: Behind the eyes, attach six or eight silver tinsel or pearlescent Flashabou fibers on top of the shank as an underbody, extending them one half-shank length beyond the bend to form the tail.

Step 3: Tie in 15-lb. Mason mono (or other clear bodywrap such as V-Rib, Larva Lace, or Swannundaze) along the bottom of the shank, and overwind with silver tinsel or pearlescent Flashabou (or pearlescent Mylar tinsel).

Step 4: Wind the mono or body material forward to the eyes to form the body.

Step 5: Inverting the fly, tie in two long white saddle hackles, convex sides facing each other to splay the tips. Invert again and build up the head with thread. Whip-finish.

Note: To tie the "Crazy" style of this fly, popularized by Orvis, use Flashabou fibers for the tail, clear V-Rib (or similar plastic wrap) over the Flashabou for the body, and calf tail for the wing.

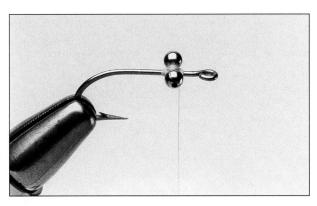

Nasty Charlie Step 1: Tying in the eyes.

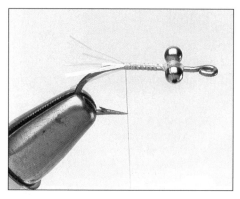

Nasty Charlie Step 2:Adding the tail.

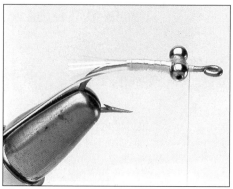

Nasty Charlie Step 3:Winding the underbody.

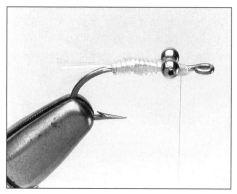

Nasty Charlie Step 4:Winding the outer body.

Nasty Charlie Step 5:Winging the fly.

TYING THE DEL BROWN BONEFISH FLY (DEL'S MERKIN)

SKILLS
Splayed-tail claws, figure-eighted yarn body, and dumbbell body weight.

RECIPE
Hook: 34007; size 2 (or 1/0 for permit)
Thread: Chartreuse Danville Flat Waxed Nylon
Eyes: Medium chrome-plated lead
Hackle/Feelers/Claws: Five or six strands pearlescent Flashabou, body length; then three natural variant or cree neck hackles on each side of bend, splayed apart, one-and-one-half times body length
Body: Alternating strands tan and brown Sport Yarn, Aunt Lydia's Rug Yarn, or other small-diameter yarn, figure-eighted tightly onto shank
Legs: Three or four strands white rubber hackle; on the samples Del sent, the permit version had four sets of legs, the smaller bonefish version had three

TYING STEPS

Step 1: Figure-eight the lead dumbbell eyes to the spine (back) of the hook just behind the hook eye. Wind the thread to the hook bend, and tie in five or six strands of pearlescent Flashabou about as long as the body. Next, straddling the Flashabou, tie in two sets (three each) of variant hackles, with their convex sides facing inward so the tips of the two sets are splayed away from each other.

Step 2: Tie in about a 2" strand of yarn, figure-eighted at its middle to the spine (backside) of the shank.

Step 3: Continue figure-eighting yarn strands, alternating light- and dark-colored pieces, until the hook is covered with strands (a size 4 should take about ten) sticking out perpendicular to the shank.

Step 4: Trim the ends of the yarn into a rounded oval disk about 1/2" in diameter, being careful not to cut off the tail assembly.

Step 5: Invert the hook in the vise into the hook-point-up position, and tie in four precut rubber strands for legs. Space them equally along the shank, working them in between the yarn strands and securing them with square knots (most other knots will prevent them from lying straight). Trim the legs (you should now have eight of them) so they extend about 3/8" beyond the body, tie off, and Super Glue the thread on both the top and the bottom. Tip the legs with a red permanent marker.

Del Brown Bonefish Fly (Merkin) Step 1: Attaching the lead weight and tail.

Del Brown Bonefish Fly (Merkin) Step 2: Starting the yarn body.

Del Brown Bonefish Fly (Merkin) Step 3: Completing the body and shaping it.

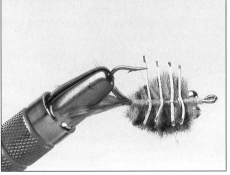

Del Brown Bonefish Fly (Merkin) Step 4: Attaching the legs.

Tying the MOE Shrimp

(Harry Spear's original MOE, grizzly version. For the furnace-and-tan version, see the profiles, page 123.)

Skills
Epoxy body, mono eyes, mono weed guard, and rooster tail.

Recipe
Hook: 34007; sizes 2, 4
Thread: Chartreuse Monocord, or Flat Waxed Nylon 3/0
Tail/Claws/Legs: White marabou, then olive marabou, then a pair of grizzly hackles, flanking marabou and flared out
Eyes: Burnt 60-lb. or 80-lb. Ande prestretched mono, figure-eighted to shank
Body: Fasco or similar tub epoxy, forming flat diamond shape over mono eyes
Weed Guard: Pair clear mono spikes (15-lb. hard Mason for size 2 hook; 12-lb. for size 4 hook)

Tying Steps

Step 1: Pull the fibers off one side of the quill of a white marabou blood feather and tie them in at the bend. Next tie in an equal amount of fibers pulled from one side of an olive marabou blood.

Step 2: Flank the stacked marabou with a matched pair of grizzly neck or saddle hackles, convex sides facing each other so they flare out from the hook. Pull one turn of thread under the tail assembly to lift it into a high-tail "rooster" style, and resume the wraps to the front of the hook.

Step 3: Tie in a 7/16" length of 80-lb. mono that you've heated on its ends with a sooty candle to form two dark eyes.

Step 4: Mix a small amount of Fasco or similar tub epoxy. Carefully measure two equal parts and mix them thoroughly by stirring them for at least a full minute (if you don't mix the epoxy thoroughly it comes out tacky and won't harden). Avoid letting the mix set before you apply it or it will develop memory and will not retain shaping.

Apply the epoxy mix with a toothpick or dental tool to form a flat diamond shape over the "cross" formed by the mono eye shaft and the shank. Thin the body as you work to the outer edges, and shape the edges into a crescent-shaped, concave curve between each point on the body's outline. Try to keep the body thin—fish do not seem to like fat bodies as much as thin ones.

Step 5: Attach a pair of clear mono spikes (15-lb. hard Mason for size 2 hooks; 12-lb. for size 4 hooks) to the underside of the body. Prepare them first by passing their butt ends next to a flame to slightly fatten them. Once they're hard, sink these "anchors" into the epoxy body.

Step 6: Then, place the fly, in a fishing orientation (body up, hook down), into an oven preheated to 140°F *with the heat turned off*. Leave it in the oven for about fifteen minutes to remove moisture and set the epoxy.

Notes: Prepare the mono eyes by holding the mono in a forceps and putting one end into a sooty candle flame until it melts and blackens. Then hold the mono vertically to allow a round eye to form as a droplet. Repeat for the other side. You should have an eye shaft about 7/16" to 9/16" long when you're finished.

MOE Shrimp (Harry Spear) Step 1: Tying in the marabou tail.

MOE Shrimp (Harry Spear) Step 2: Flanking and lifting the tail.

MOE Shrimp (Harry Spear) Step 3: Adding the eyes.

MOE Shrimp (Harry Spear) Step 4: Preparing and applying the body material.

MOE Shrimp (Harry Spear) Steps 5 and 6: Add weed guards and cure.

Tying the Standard MOE (Brewer's)

Skills

Hot glue over bead chain for bodies and heads.

Recipe

Hook: 3407; sizes 2, 4, 6, 8
Thread: Pink Danville Plus
Eyes: Medium (1/8") silver bead chain
Tail: Five or six strands Krystal Flash; then two strands pink rubber hackle; then shrimp pink marabou
Head: Coral "Hot Head" glue stick

Tying Steps

Step 1: Tie in the eyes, then the rubber hackle, and then the marabou. Bring the glue-gun nozzle to base of the tail and start laying in the head of the fly by bringing a bead of Hot Head glue forward to the eye.

Step 2: Continue the bead of Hot Head glue forward to just behind the hook eye.

Step 3: Repeat steps one and two on the opposite side, again working from back to front with the Hot Head glue.

Step 4: Turn the fly over (hook-point up) and fill in the top half (the upper half that is now facing you) of the head with glue.

Step 5: Turn the fly over again (hook-point down) and fill in the remaining half of the head (the side now facing up).

Step 6: Invert the hook once more (point up) for a count of six to ten; then invert it again (point down) and paint the eyes black (optional).

Notes: Doug uses a heated glue material he calls "Hot Head," which he finds more buoyant than epoxy so it doesn't smack the water as hard. He also finds it easier to work with than most epoxies and other glue materials—even for new users. The glue gun and glue sticks are available through dealers. (You can contact his company for names—see chapter 7.)

The fly can be tied in other colors: Change the pink marabou to tan, shrimp orange, sunrise, grizzly (dyed pink, amber, yellow, or olive). Change the Hot Head glue and rubber hackle to match.

Standard MOE (Doug Brewer) Step 1: Attach eyes and tail and begin applying hot glue.

Standard MOE (Doug Brewer) Step 2: Complete first side.

Standard MOE (Doug Brewer) Step 3: Form second side.

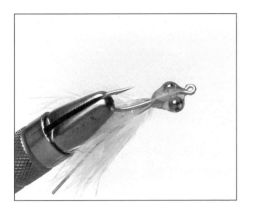

Standard MOE (Doug Brewer) Step 4: Fill in the upper half of head.

Standard MOE (Doug Brewer) Step 5: Fill in the bottom half of head.

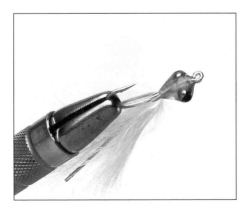

Standard MOE (Doug Brewer) Step 6: Shape, set, and add eyes.

TYING BEN'S EPOXY BONEFISH FLY

SKILLS
5-Minute Epoxy body with wound-in hackle; and tinsel underbody

RECIPE
Hook: Mustad 3407; sizes 1, 2, 4, 6, 8
Thread: White or tan 6/0 or 2-lb. mono
Tail: Two cree or grizzly (or furnace or badger) saddle hackles, flared outward, over dyed Arctic fox, over two to four sprigs Krystal Flash (or Lite Brite) and two to four strands Flashabou
Eyes: Bead chain, lead barbells, or Styrofoam, blackened (Ben sometimes uses Witchcraft prismatic decal eyes over ends of dumbbells)
Body: Devcon 5-Minute Epoxy over Mylar Christmas tree tinsel (Saltwater Flashabou is a good substitute)
Hackle: Cree, grizzly, furnace, or badger, palmered forward
Weed Guard: 12-lb. or 15-lb. Mason hard mono "spikes"

TYING STEPS

Step 1: Tie in the bead-chain eyes. Tie in two to four strands of Flashabou at the bend, then two to four strands of Krystal Flash, then a shank of Arctic fox tail hair. Take a wind or two of thread under the tail to lift it.

Step 2: Tie in two splayed cree hackles (convex sides facing each other).

Step 3: Tie in a grizzly hackle (which will later be wound forward for the legs) and pull it over the tail so it's out of the way. Blacken the eyes with a permanent marker. Tie in the underbody material (Saltwater Flashabou, Christmas tinsel, or other).

Step 4: Wrap a tapered body to the eyes, and figure-eight the bodywrap around the eyes, filling the gap between them.

Step 5: Mix Devcon 5-Minute Epoxy, carefully measuring two equal amounts and stirring them completely. Apply to the body, retaining the taper and turning the body to keep the epoxy from drooping. Wind the hackle through the epoxy to the head, and tie off. Push two 15-lb. mono weed guard spikes into the Devcon before it's dry (mono will anchor better if it's slightly melted at base end). Trim off the hackle on the sides and bottom.

Notes: Ben varies the color of tail and body: tan, pink, and lime. You can use craft fur or calf tail instead of fox.

Ben's Epoxy Step 1: Tie in eyes and tail.

Ben's Epoxy Step 2: Flank tail.

Ben's Epoxy Step 3: Attach legs and underbody.

Ben's Epoxy Step 4: Wind and shape underbody.

Ben's Epoxy Step 5: Apply and shape outer body.

Tying the Vernille Sparkle Worm

SKILLS
Extended body for a seaworm (polychaete) shape.

RECIPE
Hook: 3407 or 34007; sizes 2, 4
Thread: White Monocord 3/0, or clear 2-lb. mono
Weight/Eyes: Lead wire wrapped on shank, or medium (1/8") chrome bead chain
Undertail: Four to six short sprigs Krystal Flash
Tail: Vernille, tipped with four to six short sprigs Krystal Flash

Body/Head: Arizona sparkle yarn or vernille; optional head of Kreinik Micro Ice Chenille

Weed Guard: 12-lb. Mason

TYING STEPS

Step 1: Figure-eight the small bead-chain eyes to the spine of the hook just behind the hook eye. Spiral the thread to the bend and tie in four to six short fibers of Krystal Flash, flared down the bend.

Step 2: Tie a length of vernille on top of the Krystal Flash at the same point so it extends 1-1/4" to 1-1/2" behind the hook as a tail. Tie in a second strand of vernille and wind it to the hook eye.

Step 3: Tie in the Micro Ice Chenille and form a head by figure-eighting it around the bead-chain eyes. Whip-finish and tie off.

Step 4: Using a needle, bodkin, pin vise, or bent-open paper clip as a tool, hold the end of the vernille against the tool and tie on your thread, lashing the vernille to the tool near its point.

Step 5: Tie four to six Krystal Flash fibers onto the end of the tail, whip-finish, slip out the bodkin, and tie off.

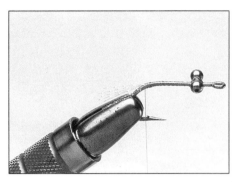

Vernille Sparkle Worm Step 1: Tie in eyes and flash.

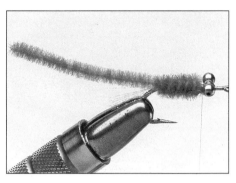

Vernille Sparkle Worm Step 2: Attach extended tail and body.

Vernille Sparkle Worm Step 3: Form head.

Vernille Sparkle Worm Step 4: Prepare tail for finishing.

Vernille Sparkle Worm Step 5: Top off tail with flash.

TYING THE BEADY CRAB

SKILLS
Bead-chain underbody, hackle claws, splayed rubber legs, and figure-eighting a chenille carapace.

RECIPE
Hook: 34007; sizes 2, 4, 6
Thread: Chartreuse Danville Flat Waxed Nylon 3/0
Underbody/Weight: Two strands 3/32" bead chain
Claws: Pair of cree hackle tips
Legs: Four strands Sili Legs
Body: Olive tan, or beige Danville Speckled Crystal Chenille, size 0 (or extra small)
Weed Guard (optional): 12-lb. Mason

TYING STEPS

Step 1: Figure-eight the midpoint of a strand of four beads of a very small (3/32") bead chain to the spine, at the hook bend. Figure-eight a second strand parallel to the first, just behind the hook eye. Bind both strands tightly. The four-bead strand is attached as you would normally attach a standard two-bead eye segment: Wind in a figure-eight fashion, then tighten with horizontal "donut" wraps underneath the bead chain.

Step 2: Bind together the two outermost beads of the two strands (those on the side closest to you), pulling them almost into a V; then angle your bobbin 90° and make additional wraps, perpendicular to the first, forming a "bow tie" in the center. This tightens the bead chain into a frame (as shown) and forms a thread platform for the claws and legs.

Step 3: Attach the two hackle claws (shiny-side down—they will be inverted in the fly's final orientation). Lay their butts along the hook spine and between the two strands of bead chain; bind the stubs to the thread platform (and shank).

Step 4: Pull the hackle claws into their approximate position—at a 90° angle from shank (and lying along the two strands of bead chain). *Gently* lock them into this orientation by making a couple of wraps in the corners at their base.

Step 5: Cut four 1-1/2" segments of Sili Legs and fold them over your tying thread. Pull them along the thread down onto the thread platform, and bind them down, splaying them *toward the hook-point side*. This will help invert the fly when it sinks.

Step 6: Tie in the chenille, and move the thread to the hook eye. Wind the chenille in large figure-eight wraps, separating the legs and filling in the body.

Step 7: Invert the fly. Then angle the chenille 90°, and wrap two or three perpendicular turns so the chenille lies in between the claws and eyes. This finishes filling the body profile and binds it together. Tie off and trim the legs.

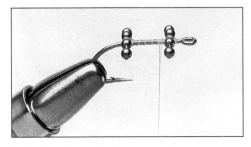

Beady Crab Step 1: Attach bead-chain frame.

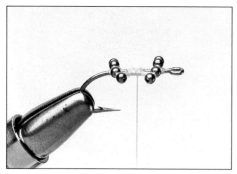

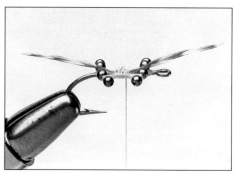

Beady Crab Step 2:Tighten frame and add leg platform.

Beady Crab Step 3:Attach claws.

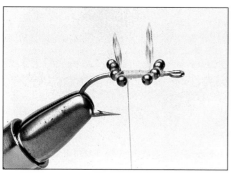

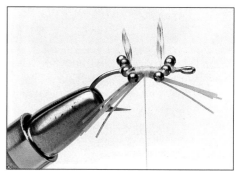

Beady Crab Step 4: Position claws.

Beady Crab Step 5:Add legs.

Beady Crab Step 6:Wind body.

Beady Crab Step 7: Lock in chenille with perpendicular turns.

5

DESIGN ALTERNATIVES AND TRENDS

◆ ◆ ◆

New Directions in Materials and Designs

This chapter—by its nature—offers more to fly tiers than non-tiers. Yet even bonefishing anglers who always buy their flies should find something useful here. They may discover, for instance, that they can select patterns much more wisely, and fish them more effectively, when armed with a better understanding of how fly tiers simulate prey, how they choose materials, and how they adapt a pattern's functional mechanics to cast to spooky, moving targets.

For those anglers who *do* tie flies, this chapter gives a brief snapshot of current bonefish fly pattern design. It summarizes how tiers are exploring new prey forms, employing new materials, and solving functional challenges inherent in bonefish patterns.

The techniques and trends described here embrace much of the innovative work occurring in flats fly construction today. But the few dozen examples I cover hardly exhaust the invigorating creativity now burgeoning throughout bonefish fly design. At most, these illustrations tug at the edges of the enormously rich fabric of saltwater pattern innovation that is underway in this sport—an explosion in fly tying that promises as much excitement at the vise as on the casting deck.

PREY SHAPE

For the first nine decades of bonefish fly design, any prey shape you chose to tie was fine as long as it was a shrimp. But things have long since changed. As scientific studies of bonefish eating habits and bonefish prey have become more accessible, anglers have begun examining flats habitats and the prey species that live in them much more closely ...and that has profoundly affected their flies.

Crabs

In every habitat where they hunt, bonefish thrive on crabs of all kinds. Spider crabs and swimming crabs live in reefs and among coral heads. Mud crabs and hermit crabs scurry along shorelines. And a mixture of all of these inhabits the shallow sand and grass fields we call the flats.

Some crab families have uniform legs. Others have dominant foreclaws. And still others have paddle-like swimming legs. Most crabs also display prominent eyes, either embedded under shells or extended on long stalks. But by far the most noticeable aspect of this tantalizing prey's anatomy is the fat, meaty body that comes in shapes varying from oval to square to triangular to round. And it is depicting these flat, wide shapes that most challenges fly tiers—because of the difficulty of making crab imitations which can land quietly and sink fast.

Fortunately, however, tiers have responded to such hurdles with great ingenuity. Bob Veverka, for example, in his Capt. Crabby, has created a light, natural-looking carapace of epoxy on a webbed frame of Corsair that lands softly and sinks well. In another of his designs, the Foxy Lady Crab, Bob has captured the crab body's breadth through a soft-hair carapace and a set of rubber legs, creating a fly that lands even more quietly. Jack Gartside's Flutterbug carries this flattened- or splayed-hair technique even further with a flared (and cushioning) carapace of raccoon tail fur.

Bob Veverka's Capt. Crabby combines a new material—Corsair tubing—with such conventional building blocks as epoxy, hackle, and rubber legs to achieve a novel design that's lighter and quieter than most other hard-bodied crab patterns, capturing the look of a natural.

Nothing has affected bonefish fly design more profoundly than the growing awareness of prey diversity in the bonefish's diet. Anglers have discovered a wealth of shapes, colors, and actions to portray, and they are finding fly selection demands more than just choosing colors and sink-rates. Shown clockwise from the top are: mud crabs, snapping shrimp, gobies, mantis shrimp, fan worm, swimming crab, and common shrimp.

Terry Baird's Stealth Crab adopts a totally different approach. Using delicate Guinea-fowl hackle to mimic breadth, it has no real weight to create splash. And in another design, his sparse Sand Bandit pattern, Terry has suggested a crab without using a carapace at all.

Tiers using wool, yarn, and synthetic fibers have brought much innovation to this aspect of fly design. The Del Brown Bonefish Fly, Phil Chapman's Bone-Zai Crab, Tim Borski's Deer Hair Critter, and Joe Branham's Swimming Crab are among the lightest of crab patterns ever. Another wool pattern, one ingeniously weighted with lead from a wine bottle's neck wrapper, is Bill Tapply and Andy Gill's Woolly Crab—it has some of the most realistic sinking and swimming movements I've seen. And Winston Moore, in his simple little Bonefish Crab, has combined wool and plain old contact cement into a pattern that—because it is hard but slightly porous—has excellent landing and sinking profiles. It will become a standard for future designs.

And these are but a sampling of crab innovation. Carl Richards' supple latex patterns—see his Blue Crab—land softly and mimic crab color, shape, and texture almost perfectly. Craig Mathews' cleanly designed Pop's Bonefish Bitters pattern lands and sinks better than many non-crab patterns, yet projects a realistic profile (study also his Hermit Crab Bitters). Another of Craig's designs, his Turneffe Crab, employs the novel synthetic material Furry Foam. Similarly, one of Ben Estes's experiments uses Livebody Foam. Both combine appetizing profiles with judicious weighting.

George Anderson's McCrab, a pioneer of crab-fly design, was one of the first flies ever to capture the crab look with sculptured deer hair. Chenille can also portray shape well; see patterns such as Charlie Gowen's Mini Crab Fly, or the Beady Crab. One other material, Big Fly Fiber, has, when combined with the adhesive Marine Goop, resulted in perhaps the best "crabby" look of all—Will Myers's Buster Crab.

Another innovation in crab fly design—the use of lively legs—also promises to further prey profile. Rubber bands, Sili Legs, rubber hackle, Lumaflex, Larva Lace tubing, and other materials have added much more accurate simulation to newer patterns.

Shrimps

Tiers have taken many of the design innovations and new materials applied to crab flies (as well as the same appreciation for prey anatomy) and applied them to imitating the many shrimp species bonefish eat. The result is a revolutionary look at the shrimp shape that goes way beyond the classic Crazy Charlie, Horror, and other early interpretations.

Various combinations of synthetic hair and adhesives are giving better looking profiles to such patterns as the Ultra Shrimp, Eric's Standing Shrimp, Branham's Epoxy Shrimp, and Myers' Shrimp. Reversing leg orientation, in patterns such as Ed's Sassy Shrimp, the Squimp, and Barry and Cathy Beck's Silly Legs Bonefish Fly, has provided more realistic upper-body and leg-action profiles.

Epoxies, hot glue, and many other synthetics have increased shrimp-pattern translucency, pushing flies far beyond the opaque bodies of chenille and wool seen in the early Keys flies. Doug Brewer's Hot Head glue patterns—his Perdi Shrimp, for example—look good and sink well. Florida Keys anglers and guides have experimented with making prey shapes of epoxy for years. Tim Borski and Harry Spear have created some of the best of these. Tim's critical eyes and artistic hands have produced such attractive patterns as the Epoxy Shrimp and the Kraft Fur Worm. Harry, who uses a slow-drying, creamy-translucent epoxy that he shapes with a dental tool or toothpick, creates the most delicate epoxies I have ever encountered. His MOE, the original epoxy pattern that defined this type, is one of the best looking and functioning shrimps you can fish.

Tim Merrihew and Ellen Reed have given us one other shrimp profile innovation that is proving effective. As seen in the Nasty Gilbert and the Honey Lamb, they have dubbed

By weighting the tail and then locating a forked weed guard in the foreleg position (which doubles as a prop for the upper body), Eric Peterson has captured the vertical posture that shrimp assume when attacked or retreating.

the upper body (or cephalothorax), producing a natural profile in a quiet-landing design. Another novel approach, the use of vinyl tubing as a carapace, appears in Scott Sanchez's very fetching Scott's Tube Shrimp.

The search for better eyes has resulted in still more creativity. Melted mono dipped in epoxy and allowed to form teardrop orbs (as in Phil Chapman's designs) makes very attractive eyes. Ben Estes and Bob Veverka both press stick-on prismatic eyes onto lead barbells and coat them with epoxy for arrestingly realistic looks. Scott Sanchez sent me patterns adorned with plastic hair-brush bristles that portray shrimps' extended eyestalks better than anything I've seen.

Mantis Shrimps

Increased awareness of the role of the mantis species in the bonefish diet has yielded such exciting and productive new patterns as the Moxey Creek Shrimp, Sir Mantis, Super Shrimp, Magic Mantis, Shimmerskin Mantis, and Magnum Mantis. These larger diameter, longer bodied patterns with huge, extended eyes give anglers tantalizing new offerings for rocky shoreline habitats where the naturals they imitate live. Other "big-shrimp" profiles may suggest the large mantis prey shape as well, including the Jim's Golden Eye, Squimp, and Silly Legs Bonefish Fly.

Worms

Polychaetes, like mantises, represent another of the rich new prey categories for tiers to imitate. These prey come in a seemingly endless variety of types—from free-swimming to tube-dwelling to burrowing—and they display many colors and shapes.

Worm pattern creation has attracted such innovative tiers as Rick Ruoff, Ben Estes, Brad Kistler, and Bill Sullivan. Rick's Deep Flea sits on the bottom wiggling its feathery shape, mimicking the burrowing worms that project their tentacles from the bottom to feed on nutrients in the incoming tides. Brad Kistler's innovative Tailbone suggests much the same profile by using peacock herl tips. Ben's Vernille Sparkle Worm can be crawled across flats to mimic an errant threadworm, as can the Slinky and Bill Sullivan's Wiggle Worm, emulating both the shape and the action of swimming polychaetes.

Watching prey movement has led tiers to explore new profiles and actions in patterns. The Wiggle Worm's rubber tail (right) coils and ripples when retrieved, and Rick Ruoff's innovative Deep Flea (left) stands vertically on the bottom, so even at rest it wiggles like the outstretched tentacles of burrowed polychaete worms.

Fish

Sculpin-like gobies and toadfish comprise one of the newest prey shapes tiers have begun to imitate with everything from chenille to deer hair to Plushille. Rick Ruoff's Backcountry Bonefish Fly, Brian O'Keefe's Missing Link, Jack Gartside's Explorer, Harry Spear's Tasty Toad, and Tom Ference's Ference's Goby suggest these fat-headed, nourishing creatures, which a recent eating habit study in the Florida Keys found to be a much more important constituent of bonefish diet than was previously believed.

The recent discovery by Florida fisheries researchers of the importance of toadfish and gobies in bonefish diet is spawning new prey shapes to suggest these sculpin-shaped fish species. Shown here are Spear's Tasty Toad and Ference's Goby.

Locating eyes in different orientations lets tiers achieve a variety of fly actions, as well as different splash characteristics and prey profiles.

PREY ACTION

Building natural action into flies has advanced as we have gained a better understanding of food species and how they move. It has also evolved in tandem with innovative approaches to fly weighting and movement.

Crabs, the helicopters of the underwater world, move sideways and up and down, and crab patterns have begun reflecting this with different forward-, rear-, and side-facing orientations on the hook. Off-center weighting also contributes to realistic shrimp and crab fly action by angling descents, and creating up-and-down swimming patterns. Mantises, in contrast, move on the bottom. They scurry like centipedes, they face attackers with armorplated tails and feisty claws, and they provide tiers with a whole new category of rear-facing profiles to imitate. Worms seem to move in every possible way. Some crawl, some project tentacles from burrows, and others swim, creating opportunities for tiers to reflect this diversity with many different materials and designs: Examine the vertical pulsations of the Deep Flea and Brad's Tailbone, and the horizontal crawling action of the Vernille Sparkle Worm and Wiggle Worm. Even clams and snails move when blown out of their burrows by schools of excavating bonefish.

Flies with new action, such as Bill Sullivan's Wiggle Worm, Rick Ruoff's Deep Flea, Jim's Golden Eye, Bob Veverka's Capt. Crabby, and Jeffrey Cardenas' Palmered Crab, all explore angles of this new frontier of bonefish fly design.

PREY COLOR

Pendulums swing in all aspects of fishing. Fly color is no exception. Bonefish flies have taken on a distinct earth-tone look over the last decade. Anglers and tiers have accurately perceived that, for survival, many flats prey are colored to match the bottoms on which they live, and fly boxes have changed to accommodate this observation. So far, so good—the majority of flies in this handbook are in accord with this perception.

Bonefish, however, eat many garishly colored worms that burrow, and many fluorescent-hued shrimps and crabs that live on brightly colored sponges and anemones. Moreover, many of the shrimps and crabs sport intensely colored egg sacs during spawning that seem to trigger bonefish. As Tables 3.1 to 3.6 in chapter 3 show, tan, white, and olive are good colors for catching fish, but they are not the only ones. (See chapter 3 for some further thoughts on prey color as it relates to flies.)

MATERIALS TRENDS

Looking back across the last few decades of bonefish fly design, it is difficult to overstate the role new materials have played in pattern development trends. Try to imagine today's bonefish flies without metal barbells, vinyl bodywrap, chenille, synthetic hair, Krystal Flash, or either Mylar tinsel or Mylar tubing—none of which existed when Joe Brooks, Jimmie Albright, and Pete Perinchief were pioneering the sport.

A list of today's most important materials, whether judged by their frequency of use in all patterns, or by their appearance in only the most popular patterns, would clearly include all of the above elements. Other prominent components would be Antron, Mylar in all its many forms, polypropylene yarn, body foams, craft fur, 5-Minute Epoxy, deer hair, and, of course, saddle, breast, and neck hackle from fowl and game birds.

If, however, you focus on only the *newest* patterns and their most common constituents, a few additional important materials surface. Liquid latex, Zelon, Corsair, Plushille, epoxy paste (Fasco), and hot glue, for example, have all become important new tools for tiers building broader, three-dimensional shapes to portray new prey species. Designers such as

Inventive Austrian tier and angler Roman Moser, who brought anglers the ingenious long-fibered body material "Plushille," uses it to create many provocative new prey patterns.

Carl Richards and Craig Mathews are adding whole categories of prey to our repertoire with such new elements.

On another front, subtly reflective materials from companies such as Kreinik, Spirit River, Umpqua, Wapsi, and Oregon Upstream are helping designers add just the right amount of flash and sparkle to newer designs. And rubber bands, rubber hackle, and rubber leg material are rapidly becoming some of the most common elements in use for making lively appendages in new flies.

All this said, materials—no matter how novel or effective—are but facilitators for tier creativity. Bob Clouser, Rick Ruoff, Lefty Kreh, and Dave Whitlock, for example, have all created exceptionally productive flies out of traditional materials. And almost all tiers blend old elements with new, choosing contemporary materials when they solve problems and not just for their novelty.

But still, a new discovery in the right hands begs for inventive application . . . . Dave Whitlock tells me he has been experimenting with the new water-absorbing, three-dimensional material, Sponj-Skin. He has already developed a whole new line of flies out of this innovative substance!

FUNCTIONAL TRENDS

Nothing more drives change in bonefish flies than the functional hurdles they must overcome. It was the need for fast-sinking flies to reach moving fish that led tiers to discover metal eyes. And it was the desire to avoid hangups in turtle grass and coral heads that led to the use of inverted hooks and a parade of snag-proofing techniques. Overcoming wind and avoiding noisy landings have sent tiers on similar quests.

Sink Rate

Tiers who bonefish a lot elevate sink rate to a science. Their fly boxes contain many versions of their favorite patterns, all carefully concocted in different sink rates so one or another can be thrown in any depth of water at fish that are traveling at any rate of speed. The following are a few of the many sink-control methods such tiers employ.

Ben Estes has been tying his Ben's Epoxy Bonefish Flies for many years, and he can tie them in an incredible range of sizes and sink rates to handle any nuance of depth, water speed, or fish speed. Ben adjusts the density of the fly by altering the ratio of eye weight to body bulk, tying it with lead, bead-chain, glass bead, and Styrofoam bead eyes in many different sizes.

Harry Spear achieves much the same control with epoxy. He gently sculpts the shape and mass of the epoxy in each of his MOE flies to achieve a delicate balance between a soft landing and a fast descent. Another Keys tier, Tim Borski, has pioneered the judicious weighting of epoxy and deer hair to create large, meaty profiles such as those of his Deer Hair Critter and Kraft Fur Worm. He varies both body bulk and weight to achieve whatever sink profile he needs.

Jim Orthwein's newest fly, Jim's Bonefish Puff, illustrates this balancing act too, but it uses softer, water-absorbing marabou. The carefully calculated Puff rides in its normal hook-up position when weighted with metal eyes, and in the hook-down position when fished eyeless for shallow, spooky conditions. In the hook-down position, Jim reverses the order of wing colors to maintain proper orientation of the white belly color on the fly's bottom.

Nowhere does sink rate become more challenging or more obvious in importance than in crab patterns. George Anderson, who developed one of the earliest and best known

Will Myers' unique variable-weight Buster Crab pattern offers anglers a new way to adjust sink rate on site.

among them—the McCrab—has constantly fine-tuned the balance of size, weight, and density of his pattern to make it land quietly yet sink fast. He has arrived at a combination of weights—a lead barbell and a dense belly plate of Orvis Heavy Metal coated with Plasti-dip—to overcome the natural buoyancy of deer hair.

At the other extreme, Winston Moore's Bonefish Crab, which he constructs of very light wool hardened with contact cement (not Super Glue), may be the lightest of all crabs. It takes very little weight to drop it quickly and quietly. Will Myers' ingenious variable-weight Buster Crab offers another approach: a light, synthetic hair body with a rubber-band weight holder that allows anglers to switch the amount of weight on the fly, varying it on-site to match conditions! And the Woolly Crab—a joint venture of Bill Tapply and Andy Gill—combines bead chain with belly lead cut from the wrapper of a wine bottle to yield one of the best sink rates and descent profiles I've seen. In one other case, Montana tier Craig Mathews developed his foam-bodied Turneffe Crab, weighted with very small bead chain, to be effective on Belize's big, spooky fish on thin, threatening flats.

Snag-Proofing

Snag-proofing with stiff weed guards preoccupies a lot of anglers who stalk the grass bottom flats of the Florida Keys and some Bahamas locations. Weed and coral shields may seem a boring design element, but when needed, they must be properly designed or they will become "fish guards" as well as weed guards. Furthermore, in the hands of some tiers, weed guards have evolved into dual-purpose devices that enhance the fly in other ways.

To fulfill the basic weed guard function of preventing snags, those who use them most (the guides and anglers of the Florida Keys) clearly prefer hard mono in the 10-lb. to 20-lb. range. Steve Bailey uses 15-lb. (.019" dia.) to 20-lb. (.022" dia.) Mason on his Bonefish Bunny. Harry Spear, in tying his original MOE, uses 16-lb. (.020" diam) Mason for size 1 hooks, 15-lb. (.019" dia.) Mason for size 2 hooks, and 12-lb. (.017" dia.) Mason for size 4 hooks. Rick Ruoff uses 20-lb. Ande on his Absolute Flea, Will Myers uses 12-lb. Mason on his Myers' Shrimp, and Ben Estes uses 12-lb. to 15-lb. Mason on the Ben's Epoxy Bonefish Fly.

Novel designs can turn necessary attributes such as weed guards into design elements that enhance profile. Les Fulcher's mono spikes resist snags and serve as extended eyes or antennae.

A number of shrimp patterns illustrate the dual-purpose approach in weed guard design. Joe Branham's Epoxy Shrimp and Eric Peterson's Eric's Standing Shrimp, for example, use forked guards on the upper body (the cephalothorax) to help the flies stand in lifelike, near-vertical positions when they sink onto their weighted tails. Will Myers uses a looped weed guard on his Myers' Shrimp; it doubles as a weight holder to which he adds Orvis' high-density putty. Les Fulcher's Bonefish Joe may be the best example of all of integrating a hook shield into a fly's profile. His two upright mono spikes double as elevated eyestalks or antennae in this intriguing pattern.

Another strategy for tying snag-proof flies—one that Craig Mathews has heavily explored—employs stiff materials such as deer hair to flare around the hook point, deflecting it from penetrating grass and preventing it from catching on coral structure. His Turneffe Crab, Pop's Bonefish Bitters, and Hermit Crab Bitters rely on this technique.

Splashdown Impact

How softly your fly lands sometimes makes the difference between a hooked fish and a spooked fish. Other times, however, the splat or plip of a fly splashing down *attracts* bonefish, and even triggers strikes. Either way, impact noise affects bonefish enough for anglers to want to control it: Some days you want a fly with whisper-quiet impact; other days, one that slaps its presence onto a calm flat will take more fish.

In general, the harder or denser a fly, the more noise it makes when it lands. Thus a fly with a soft chenille body like Bill Hunter's "soft" Flats Fodder makes less noise than Bill's all-but-identical "hard" Flats Fodder, which he ties with a denser, vinyl-covered body. Likewise, Zelon or wool carapaces are quieter than epoxy or glue carapaces.

Lengthening and separating the fibers of the cushioning material also softens landing impact, which makes Les Fulcher's Bonefish Joe, with its spiky deer hair, land more quietly than a densely packed deer hair crab or goby body. Palmered and folded hackle serves the same function in patterns such as Jim's Golden Eye, Brian O'Keefe's Turd Fly, George Warren's Super Shrimp, and many others. One of the most interesting of these is Len Wright's folded-hackle version of the Del Brown wool-carapace crab. Len's Hackle Merkin lands as delicately as the proverbial feathers it contains.

One further extension of this diffusive-element technique is seen in the meaty-looking profiles of patterns such a Bob Veverka's Foxy Lady Crab, Phil Chapman's Hallucination, and Jack Gartside's Flutterbug. With its "wings" made of bulky but airy materials, each fly looks hefty but lands as softly as a leaf.

Crab bodies present another landing-noise problem. A crab imitation's flat profile belly-flops on landing, and can slap the water with amazing impact. One of the first crab patterns I ever threw at a fish had a flat lead belly-plate glued to its bottom and it landed with the finesse of a turkey platter. But designers such as Winston Moore, Will Myers, and Tim Borski have pushed us way beyond those early, crude efforts. Winston's Bonefish Crab (a diminutive version of his Permit Crab) softens landings with a wool body, slightly hardened with model cement. Will Myers gave the Buster Crab a craggy undercarriage that breaks up this splatting effect. Borski uses roughly trimmed deer hair in a similar way on many of his patterns, as does Carl Richards with his latex bodies, and Craig Mathews with his spiky-legged Bitters series.

Of course for all rules, it seems exceptions always arise to make us scratch our heads. Harry Spear's MOE looks hard, flat, and dense, yet it lands fairly quietly and it takes many spooky Keys fish. But Harry is a genius who has put in many hours on the water and at the vise. His MOE patterns are purposely hand-molded to be thin, rough, and not really flat at all. He "feathers" the material to the edges when hand-molding the body, and he lets the fly dry with tiny moguls that dissipate impact. He reduces noise in another pattern, his Tasty Toad, by rubbing the edges with glue and pinching them imperfectly to create an irregularly edged profile.

As the sport of bonefishing develops further—and the art of bonefish fly tying along with it—more innovations will occur. But bonefishing will always be one of fly design's most exciting areas, because of the challenging demands put on patterns by the prey, by the fish, and by the unique demands of sight-fishing to moving targets.

FLY MATERIALS

◆ ◆ ◆

A Glossary of the Essential Bonefish Fly-Tying Materials

Most materials found in bonefish flies differ little from the basic elements that tiers employ in patterns for other gamefish. Indeed, many of the components of bonefish patterns are identical to those that constitute trout, bass, steelhead, and other flies, and they serve the same purposes. Hackle, hair, and synthetic winging materials suggest legs, tails, and other appendages. Dubbing, chenille, and tinsels form bodies. Mono and wire function as weed guards. And so on.

Some staple components of flats patterns, however, appear rarely in other flies. Few flies tied for other quarry consume such large quantities of metal eyes and vinyl body wrapping. Other items such as epoxy, Krystal Flash, rug wool, and craft fur also disappear rapidly from the benches of bonefish pattern makers. So if you are planning to tie some of the patterns found in chapter 2, you may need to add a few items to your materials inventory.

This chapter lists the basic tying components you need for the patterns in chapter 2. It describes each briefly, but with enough detail so you can identify what you need when you order material from suppliers. Difficult-to-find items are also listed in chapter 7, "Sources," after the names of retailers or wholesalers who supply them; this will help you track down local sources.

With the burgeoning availability of synthetic and natural tying materials, fly tiers have the tools to create anything they can imagine.

ANTRON A fine, lustrous, and translucent Dupont synthetic fiber. Comes in strands or shanks, and in dubbing form. Can be used for winging, wrapping bodies, and figure-eighting in strips to form carapaces.

ARCTIC FOX TAIL A fine, lustrous, long tail hair. Dyes with good translucency.

ARIZONA SPARKLE YARN Highly saturated colors and intense micro sparkle elements characterize this bodywrap material.

AUNT LYDIA'S CRAFT & RUG YARN Sparkling 100-percent polyester yarn in many colors for bodywrapping and (in short strands) for figure-eighting to shanks to form crab carapaces.

BEAD CHAIN Metal bead chain (once popular as a pull cord for lamp fixtures and still available by the foot in some hardware stores) is now common in fly shops and comes in silver or gold colors, and sometimes in stainless. Common diameter sizes: 3/32", 1/8", 5/32", 3/8".

BESTCO EYES Non-lead/nontoxic "painted" eyes with a barbell shape of a slightly longer profile than lead eyes; made of cast metal in five sizes, roughly comparable in diameter to lead barbells and bead chain. The eyes come with white, yellow, or red epoxy irises, and black pupils.

BIG FLY FIBER A lightweight, synthetic, hairy fiber for building bulky bodies without adding too much weight. Formerly called "Hairabou." Many colors.

BRITE EYES Brass eyes in shiny nickel plate or black; sizes small, medium, and large.

BUCKTAIL This versatile, hollow hair functions as everything from wings and carapaces to flared collars, weed guards, legs, and antennae. The finer and less hollow hair near the upper part of the tail has more action, less buoyancy, and a faster sink rate.

BUGSKIN A leather-like, open-cell, flexible synthetic material that absorbs water and comes alive when submerged. In saltwater designs, used primarily as a carapace.

CALF TAIL Fine tail hairs dyed in many good colors. Often used in inverted wings. Look for tails with the longest and straightest hair fibers.

CHENILLE, CLOTH One of the most commonly used body materials in bonefish flies, this cloth-like bodywrap material has thousands of short, nubby cotton or blended-synthetic fibers twisted onto a cord to form a fuzzy rope. It comes in many, many colors. Vernille and Ultra Chenille are finer, with tighter ribbing. Chenille is also made of other fibers (see Chenille, Mylar) or with other materials, such as nylon or Mylar flecks added for flash effect.

CHENILLE, MYLAR See Speckled Crystal Sparkle Chenille, Estaz, Flash Chenille, Ice Chenille, and Micro Ice Chenille.

CHENILLE, VARIEGATED Same as regular cloth chenille except multicolored; usually two colors, such as tan/yellow or olive/black.

CORSAIR A stiff nylon mesh tubing that comes in 1/2", 1/3", and 1/4" diameters. This material was pioneered by Jack Gartside for the bodies of striped bass patterns, which he describes in his *Flies for the 21st Century*. Corsair makes an excellent frame for epoxy bodies—see Bob Veverka's Capt. Crabby.

CRAFT FUR A synthetic hair for wings. Comes in many colors. Also called "doll's hair." Two related products sold specifically for fly tying are Mystic Bay Fly Fur and Gehrke's Fish Fuzz.

CRYSTAL HAIR Thread-thin, flat strands of Mylar fiber twisted to expose many tiny reflecting surfaces that twinkle. Used for wrapping, winging, forming appendages, and adding flash; a wide array of colors is available. Crystal Hair is similar to Krystal Flash and Flashabou Accent.

DAN BAILEY (SAAP) BODY FUR Lustrous, very long Antron-like fibers on a "rope" core that are twisted to form a dense, long-fibered rope for wrapping bodies and heads. It can be clipped and shaped like deer hair, but is softer and less buoyant. Similar to Plushille.

DAN BAILEY (SAAP) WING FIBER A high-sheen, translucent synthetic fiber with sparse, fine Mylar "threads" interspersed. Comes in shanks. Can be used for winging, wrapping bodies, and figure-eighting in strips to form carapaces. Similar to Zelon.

DAZL EYES Non-lead/nontoxic hour-glass-shaped eyes, in sizes 3/32", 1/8", 5/32", 3/16", and 7/32"; and in bronze, gold, and nickel.

DAZZLE LINK A rich-lustered, supple wing material used by Bob Veverka in his Foxy Lady patterns.

DEER BODY HAIR Can be packed, spun, and clipped to many shapes to form bodies, heads, and carapaces.

DIAMOND BRAID A braided Mylar material. Similar to Poly Flash and Poly Flash Yarn.

EAGLE CLAW HOOKS Model D67 (sizes 1 to 6) is used in many bonefish patterns.

EPOXY, 2-TON (DEVCON) Cures very clear. Stronger than 5-Minute Epoxy, 2-Ton takes longer to set up and is therefore preferred by many commercial tiers.

EPOXY, 5-MINUTE A viscous, liquid epoxy glue that comes in two separate containers. It sometimes dries slightly yellow or amber. The Devcon brand comes in a handy two-in-one plunger for easy dispensing. The Z-Poxy brand is also very good.

EPOXY, CRYSTAL CLEAR Rod-builders' liquid finishing epoxy, used by many Keys guides and tiers to coat and strengthen underbodies, and to protect eyes and heads.

EPOXY, FASCO NO. 110 A paste-like, two-part epoxy compound that comes in tubes, tubs, quarts, and gallons; it has the consistency of Vaseline. This is the epoxy Harry Spear uses in his original MOE.

ESTAZ Reflective nylon chenille roping for bodies. Similar to Ice Chenille, Flash Chenille, and other Mylar chenilles. Many vibrant colors.

EYES, PRISMATIC Stick-on disks in silver, gold, pearl, red, yellow, and green, with a prism-like layer that refracts light.

FASCO EPOXY NO. 110 See Epoxy, Fasco No. 110.

FIRE FLY TYE Embossed tinsel for wrapping and winging. Wide array of colors.

FISH FUZZ A premium synthetic hair material with very good sheen and color saturation. A wide array of very fishy colors is available. Excellent action.

FISH SCALE A synthetic cord with fine flash elements. Similar to Poly Flash and Mylar tubing.

FISHAIR A long, strong synthetic hair that comes in three different grades of fineness—24, 50, and 70 (heaviest) denier. One of the widest arrays of color available in human-made fibers.

FLASH CHENILLE, LONG Mylar chenille with lots of flash and fibers long enough to form a 1/2" diameter roping for wrapping bodies and heads. A wide array of colors is available.

FLASH CHENILLE, SHORT Chenille made of flashy Mylar fibers forming a 1/4" roping for wrapping bodies and heads. A wide array of colors is available.

FLASHABOU Flat Mylar in very thin strips for wrapping and adding flash to wings. A wide array of colors is available.

FLASHABOU ACCENT Thread-thin, flat strands of Mylar fiber twisted to expose many tiny reflecting facets. Used for adding flash to patterns and for wrapping, winging, or forming tails, antennae, claws, or legs. A wide array of colors is available. Very similar to Krystal Flash.

FLASHABOU DUBBING A dubbing mix that contains extremely fine Flashabou filaments. Several colors.

FLAT WAXED NYLON THREAD Strong (3/0). Lies very flat. Comes in a wide range of colors.

FLY FUR A premium synthetic hair material for winging. Excellent sheen. A wide array of coded colors is available.

FLYMASTER THREAD A light-profile thread, but very strong (6/0). Comes in more colors than any other thread. It's good for small patterns and for avoiding buildup in patterns with many layers.

FURRY FOAM A flocked synthetic foam in a felt-like material that's good for making bulky shapes such as crab bodies.

FUZZY LEECH YARN A small-diameter shaggy yarn with long, lustrous fibers that look and act like dubbing.

GAMAKATSU HOOKS The Salt Water O'Shaughnessy model (sizes 1 to 8) is appropriate for bonefish flies.

GHOST FIBER A lustrous and translucent synthetic fiber from Roman Moser. Comes in shanks. Can be used to form wings, wrap bodies, and figure-eight strips onto hook shanks to form carapaces. You can also chop it up and use as dubbing. Comes in many good earth-tone colors.

GLIMMER Fine, shredded metallic Mylar in several colors. Ties well as dubbing or in wings.

GLIMMER FLASH CHENILLE Mylar chenille roping for wrapping bodies and heads. A wide array of colors is available.

GLO-BRITE CHENILLE A vibrantly colored, medium-sized chenille with strands of both Mylar and cloth mixed in—a kind of halfway step between the Mylar chenilles and conventional cloth chenilles. It makes a very nice medium-bright body.

HACKLE See Neck and Breast Hackles and Saddle Hackles.

HOLOGRAPHIC FLASH Supple Mylar strands with multicolored, prismatic flash, for wings, tails, bodywrap, and just adding flash.

HOT HEAD GLUE A line of glue sticks for glue-gun flies that comes in an especially wide range of colors. A Doug Brewer product, used in his Standard MOE fly. Easy to apply, and has excellent translucency.

ICE CHENILLE Similar to other Mylar chenilles such as Flash Chenille, Estaz, Cactus Chenille, and so on, but comes in extremely bright, saturated colors.

KREINIK TYER'S RIBBON A flat, small-faceted bodywrap material that's a bit like pressed Diamond Braid or Poly Flash. It produces bodies with smaller profiles than the larger braided material. Excellent colors. Can be hard to find.

KRYSTAL FLASH Thread-thin, flat strands of Mylar fiber twisted to expose many tiny reflecting facets. Good for adding flash to patterns, and for wrapping, winging, or forming tails, antennae, claws, or legs. A wide array of colors is available. Similar to Crystal Hair and Flashabou Accent.

LARVA LACE BODY MATERIAL (OR TUBING) A hollow vinyl compound piping used for ribbing, bodywrapping, antennae, legs, and so on. You can insert Krystal Flash or other fine-diameter material inside it to simulate skeletons under translucent skin.

LARVA LACE RIBBING Vinyl-plastic ribbing or bodywrap with a D-shaped cross section. Comes in many colors and two sizes—Midge Lace (small) and Nymph Rib (medium). Similar to V-Rib and Swannundaze, but softer and more pliable.

LEAD EYES Barbell-shaped eyes cast from lead in sizes 3/32", 1/8", 5/32", and 3/8", or 1/100 oz., 1/50 oz., 1/36 oz., and 1/24 oz. Plain and nickel plated.

LITE-BRITE Very fine Mylar filaments in a dubbing mix.

LURE TAPE A body tape in silver, gold, and pearl, with a prism-like layer that refracts light.

LUREFLASH (TWINKLE) Similar to Flashabou Accent, Crystal Hair, and Krystal Flash. Many colors.

MARABOU Extremely fine fibered, soft, turkey flank feathers. One of the liveliest tailing and winging materials in bonefishing. Comes dyed in every color imaginable. The best—blood marabou—is worth the price for its fine fibers.

MICRO ICE CHENILLE (KREINIK) Very fine Mylar or Flash Chenille. Good for smaller patterns or for the fine heads and bodies on larger patterns. Excellent colors.

MODGE PODGE A paste found in crafts shops and used by some tiers as an underbody for epoxy (see Eric Peterson's patterns).

MONOCORD THREAD Strong 3/0 thread. Somewhat bulky, but very common in bonefish flies tied in sizes 4 and up, and those in which thread buildup is not only acceptable but often preferred, to enhance profiles. Many good colors.

MUSTAD HOOKS Long the standard for bonefish flies. Available in 34007 stainless (sizes 1 to 8) or 3407 plated carbon steel (sizes 1 to 12); also in 34011 long-shanked stainless (sizes 1/0 to 6), for lengthier profiles.

MYLAR PIPING A woven mesh tubing of flashy Mylar filaments. Comes with a removable, string-like core. Common in gold, silver, and pearl, and now dyed in many pearlescent and fluorescent colors.

MYLAR TINSEL Flat single-strand wrapping or ribbing, often gold on one side and silver on the other. It also comes in pearlescent. Many widths.

NECK AND BREAST HACKLES, COCK AND HEN Often used in matched pairs to flank tails or wings, or—when flared apart—to suggest claws. Grizzly, furnace, badger, and cree are among the most popular in shrimp and crab patterns.

NECK AND BREAST HACKLES, PHEASANT Often used alone or in matched pairs to form carapaces on crabs and shrimps, and sometimes to suggest claws. Ring-necked pheasant and golden-pheasant plumage provide some naturally mottled looking patterns and are among the most popular in shrimp and crab patterns.

OPAL ESSENCE A bodywrap similar to Mylar tubing, but with intense pearlescent sparkle.

PARTRIDGE HOOKS Model CS52 Sea Prince, sizes 1 to 4; long-shanked CS29GRS, sizes 2 to 8; and CS11GRS, sizes 2 to 10. This respected maker of premium hooks makes an excellent and strong stainless saltwater model for bonefish, the Sea Prince, which it has been bringing down into the smaller sizes consistent with tying trends. Partridge also offers a satin-finish Gray Shadow coating on some models (its "Niflor" process embeds nickel and phosphorous in the hook surface, making it both dull and corrosion-resistant). This finish reduces reflection, which may be advantageous to anglers in bright light conditions.

PECCARY A quill-like hair from Southwestern boar that makes for excellent barred and mottled antennae. Moose mane and Chinese boar are possible substitutes.

PHEASANT BREAST FEATHERS See Neck and Breast Hackles, Pheasant.

PLUSHILLE Lustrous, very long synthetic (Antron-like) fibers on a "cord" core that are twisted to form a dense, long-fibered, chenille-like rope for wrapping bodies and heads. It can be clipped and shaped like deer hair, but is softer and less buoyant. Also see Don Bailey (SAAP) Body Fur.

POLAR AIRE A synthetic hair developed as a substitute for polar bear. Shiny, translucent, with vibrant saturated colors.

POLY FLASH YARN   A braided Mylar roping material. Similar to Diamond Braid.

POLY PRO YARN   A polypropylene fiber that comes in shanks and substitutes for wool and synthetic yarns. Used for winging or for winding as body material. You can also figure-eight short strands of it onto the hook shank to form a flat carapace.

RABBIT   A supple and lively hair; it comes in hides or cut into strips. Use cross-cut for palmering bodies (as on the Hare Trigger), or Zonker-style for strapping to the length of the hook (as on Brian O'Keefe's Hoover).

REFLECTIONS   A highly reflective, multicolored winging material made by twisting together three strands of colored nylon. A cross between Krystal Flash and Flashabou. Good also for ribbing, and very reflective as an epoxy underbody.

RUBBER HACKLE OR RUBBER LEGS   Finely scored latex sheets that pull apart into thread-thin strips for legging material. Comes in many colors. Takes marking pens well for tipping and mottling.

SAAP BODY FUR   See Dan Bailey (SAAP) Body Fur.

SAAP WING FIBER   See Dan Bailey (SAAP) Wing Fiber.

SADDLE HACKLES   One of the most important elements in creating legs and swim-merets (by palmering) or claws and forelegs (by tying as flanked and splayed pairs). Also used to give fly wings and body movement (this is especially true of grizzly hackles). Grizzly, furnace, badger, and cree are among the most popular.

SALMO WEB   A coarse, shaggy Antron-type dubbing blend that is often used in trout, steelhead, and salmon patterns. Comes in many good flats colors.

SCUD BACK   A translucent, latex-like elastic ribbon in insect and earth-tone colors that makes good carapace shells for shrimps and crabs.

SEA PRINCE HOOKS   See Partridge Hooks.

SILI LEGS   A thin rubber material (pencil-lead-sized), often containing flakes of contrasting colors, that is used for legs and antennae.

SILI TAILS   A thin, *flat,* crescent-shaped rubber material, often containing flakes of contrasting colors, that is used for tailing. Two sizes.

SINGLE-STRAND FLOSS   A nylon, one-strand floss used for tags and bodywrap in many freshwater patterns. It's also used by some tiers as a tying thread.

SLF HANKS AND DUBBING   A premium high-luster, translucent, synthetic hair-like fiber. Comes in hanks and in dubbing form. Can be used for winging, wrapping bodies, and figure-eighting in strips to form carapaces. Many very intense colors. Developed for salmon patterns.

SPARKLEFLASH   A highly reflective flash winging material in which each two or three spirally twisted nylon strands wraps around each individual strip of synthetic flash material, twisting it at an angle, to make it sparkle like Krystal Flash. Good for winging and ribbing, and also as an epoxy underbody.

SPECKLED CRYSTAL SPARKLE CHENILLE   A Danville combination of cloth and Mylar tinsel chenille in three sizes and many excellent colors. It has the flash attraction of Mylar and the water absorption of cloth fiber.

SPONJ-SKIN   A novel, porous synthetic material that blossoms into a three-dimensional shape when wet. Dave Whitlock is designing a series of new flies using this innovative material and Bill Catherwood has been experimenting with it for crab bodies.

SUPER HAIR Currently the finest and supplest crimped nylon hair. Comes in many excellent colors for suggesting bonefish prey.

SWANNUNDAZE Plastic vinyl bodywrap. Comes in many colors, standardized by code numbers.

TIEMCO HOOKS Model 800S (sizes 1 to 8) is used in many bonefish patterns.

ULTRA CHENILLE Similar to vernille, but with even finer and tighter fibers. It has a moderately stiff core.

ULTRA HAIR A very fine diameter, crimped nylon hair that comes in many colors. Coarser than Super Hair.

UNI-THREAD Spun polyester thread, very strong (for a thin profile) and now available in many colors. Comes in 6/0 and 8/0.

V-RIB A D-shaped plastic vinyl bodywrap or ribbing. Comes in many colors. Similar to Larva Lace and Swannundaze.

VERNILLE Similar to chenille but with finer and tighter fibers, and a somewhat stiffer core.

WOOL This natural fiber (on hide or in shanks) can be packed and spun like deer hair, or figure-eighted to the shank in strands to form a flat carapace. See Phil Chapman's Bone-Zai Crab or Joe Branham's Swimming Crab. It comes dyed in many colors and also takes marking pens well.

ZELON A premium high-luster, translucent synthetic fiber. Comes in crinkled strands and in dubbing form. Can be used for winging, wrapping bodies, figure-eighting in strips to form carapaces, and lots of other things.

SOURCES

♦ ♦ ♦

Where to Find Flies, Custom Tiers, and Materials

The following list of tackle shops, custom tiers, and materials suppliers can help you find the flies and fly-tying materials you need to fill your boxes for a bonefish trip. Whether you're looking for off-the-shelf flies, or a custom tier who will produce specific patterns to order, you should find help among the names listed here.

For anglers who construct their own flies, the names of distributors and manufacturers of tying material also appear in the list. Some of these are retailers who sell to you directly. Others are wholesalers or product manufacturers—they may prove useful if you are trying to track down a particular item, color, or size, and you need the name of a local dealer who carries it.

The listing is alphabetical by name of business or name of individual. Each entry is coded: O = Off-the-shelf fly patterns; C = Custom-tied fly patterns; T = Tying materials; W/M = Wholesaler or Manufacturer.

American Angling Supply, 23 Main Street, Salem, NH 03070. Phone 800-264-5378. Dave Beshara or Al Bovyn. (O,T)

Austin Angler, 312-1/2 Congress Avenue, Austin, TX 78701. Phone 512-472-4553. Larry Sunderland. (O,T)

Baily, Steve, 865 Bethany Court, Fort Myers, FL 33909. Phone 813-489-1379. (C)

Baird, Terry, 11158 N.W. Kathleen Drive, Portland, OR 97229. Phone 503-644-8607. (C)

Bay, Ken, 145 N. Halifax Avenue, Apt. 106, Daytona Beach, FL 32118. Phone 904-239-7164. (C)

Bestco (nontoxic painted eyes), 56 Elmwood Drive, North Kingston, RI 02852. Phone 401-884-3862. Stu Dickens. (W/M)

Bestway Outdoor Inc.(Super Hair), 1649 Romain Drive, Columbia, SC 29210. (M)

Bill's Fly Shop (peccary, Nugget Gold FisHair, Glo-Brite Chenille), 85 Gardner Road, Hubbardston, MA 01452. Phone 508-928-5638. Bill Wilbur. (O, C, T)

Blue Ribbon Flies (Zelon, Glo-Brite Chenille), Box 1037, West Yellowstone, MT 59758. Phone 406-646-7642 or 406-646-9365. Craig and Jackie Mathews. (O, C, T)

Bob Marriott's Fly Fishing Store, 2700 W. Orangethorpe Avenue, Fullerton, CA 92633. Phone 800-535-8633. (O,T)

Borski, Tim, P.O. Box 122, Islamorada, FL 33036. Phone 305-664-9367. (C)

Branham, Joe, 3903 South Bend Drive, Valdosta, GA 31602. Phone 912-253-0457. (C)

Brewer, Doug (Hot Head Glue), P.O. Box 699, Florence, MT 59833. Phone 406-777-5485. (C, T, W/M)

Brown & Wright, 120 Still River Road, Harvard, MA 01451. Phone 508-456-8714. Dick Brown. (C)

Cabela's, 812 13th Avenue, Sidney, NE 69160. Phone 800-237-4444. (O, C, M)

Cascade Crest, 13290 Table Rock Road, Central Point, OR 97502. Phone 503-826-4030. Pat Dunlap. (W/M)

Catherwood, Bill, 399 Marshall Street, Tewksbury, MA 01876. Phone 508-851-3359. (C)

Clouser's Fly Shop, 101 Ulrich Street, Middletown, PA 17057. Phone 717-944-6541. Robert Clouser. (O, C, T)

Corsair Products (Corsair, Fire Fly Tye, polypropylene yarn, Glimmer), 33 Carroll Road, Woburn, MA 01801. Phone 617-932-0558. Kate Lavelle. (T)

Dan Bailey's Fly Shop (SAAP Body Fur, SAAP Wing Fiber, Long Flash Chenille, peccary), P.O. Box 1019, Livingston, MT 59047. Phone 800-356-4052. John Bailey. (O, C, T, W/M)

Eagle Claw, Wright & McGill, 4245 E. 46th Avenue, Denver, CO 80216. Phone 303-321-1481. (T, W/M)

F.A. Johnston (Swannundaze), NJ. Phone 201-933-4887. (T, W/M)

Fairfield Fly Shop, The, 917 Post Road, Fairfield, CT 06430. Phone 203-255-2896. Eric Peterson. (O, C, T)

Fasco, 7735 W. 20th Avenue, Hialeah, FL 33014. Phone 305-821-9441. (T, W/M)

FisHair Enterprises, 1484 W. County Road C, St. Paul, MN 55113. Phone 612-636-3083. (W/M)

Flint, Dave, 77 Cherry Street, Spencer, MA 01562. Phone 508-885-7041. (C, T)

Fly Shop, The, 4140 Churn Creek Road, Redding, CA 96002. Phone 800-669-FISH. Mike Michalak or Andy Burk. (O, C, T)

Gamakatsu, P.O. Box 1797, Tacoma, WA 98401. Phone 206-922-8373. Bob Funk. (W/M)

Gartside, Jack, 10 Sachem Street, Boston, MA 02120. Phone 617-277-5831. (C, O)

Gehrke's Fish Fuzz, Snake River, Hell's Canyon, Asotin, WA 99402. Phone 509-243-4100. (T,W/M)

George Anderson's Yellowstone Angler, Hwy. 89 South, P.O. Box 660, Livingston, MT 59047. Phone 406-222-7130. (O,T)

Hareline (Krystal Flash), 24712 Territorial Road, Monroe, OR 97456. Phone 503-847-5310. Bob Borden. (T,W/M)

Hedron (Flashabou, Flashabou Dubbing, Fire Fly Tye, Flashabou Accent), 402 N. Main Street, Stillwater, MN 55082. Phone 612-430-9606. Don Mears. (W/M)

Heritage Textiles (craft fur), P.O. Box 18705, Philadelphia, PA 19133. Phone 215-425-0595. George Jefferson. (T,W/M)

Hobbs Feather Co. (Flash Chenille, Glimmer, Glimmer Flash Chenille), 202 W. 4th Street, West Liberty, IA 52776. Phone 319-627-4258. (T,W/M)

Hunter's Angling Supplies (Arctic Fox Tail, peccary, Nugget Gold FisHair, Danville Speckled Crystal Chenille), Central Square Box 300, New Boston, NH 03070. Phone 800-331-8558. Nick Wilder. (O,C,T)

Inter-Tac Inc. (Larva Lace), Box 6340, 110 W. Midland Avenue, Woodland Park, CO 80866. Phone 800-347-3432. Phil Camera. (W/M)

International Angler, 503 Freeport Road, Pittsburgh, PA 15215. Phone 800-782-4222. Tom Ference. (O,C,T)

International Fly Tyers Symposium, Seven Springs Mountain Resort, Champion, PA 15622. Phone 814-926-2676. Chuck Furimsky. (W/M)

K & K Flyfishers Supply, 8643 Grant, Overland Park, KS 66212. Phone 800-795-8118. (O,C,T)

Kaufmann's Streamborn, P.O. Box 230332, Portland, OR 97223. Phone 800-442-4359. Randall Kaufmann. (O,C,T)

Kreinik Manufacturing Co. (Tyer's Ribbon, Micro Ice Chenille), 3106 Timanus Lane, Suite 101, Baltimore, MD 21244. Phone 800-537-2166 or 410-581-5088. Al Hafner. (W/M)

L.L. Bean, Freeport, ME 04033. Phone 800-221-4221. (O,T)

Lower Forty Outfitters, 134 Madison Street, Worcester, MA 01610. Phone 508-752-4004. Jim Bender. (O,T)

McKenzie Flies, 1272 River Road, Eugene, OR 97404. Phone 503-689-8371. (W/M)

Menemsha Minnows, 60 Middle Haddam Road, P.O. Box 62, Middle Haddam, CT 06454. Phone 203-267-0287. Page Rogers. (C)

Miheve, Greg, 507 Dory Avenue, Fort Walton Beach, FL 32548. Phone 904-244-1602. (C)

Moffo, Capt. Lenny, Route 4, Box 1028, Summerland Key, FL 33042. Phone 305-743-6139. (C)

Mustad & Sons, 247-253 Grant Avenue, Auburn, NY 13021. Phone 315-253-2793. Klaus Kjelstrup. (W/M)

Mystic Bay Flies (Fly Fur), P.O. Box 602, Green's Farms, CT 06436. Phone 203-255-4310. Jeff Hahner. (O,W/M)

Oregon Upstream (Sparkleflash, Reflections, Lazer Light, Mara Wool, Coastal Deer Hair), P.O. Box 86701, Portland, OR 97268. Phone 503-557-3022. Rick Hagen (W/M)

Orvis Company, The (Fuzzy Leech Yarn, Scud Back, Bestco Eyes), Historic Route 7A, Manchester, VT 05254-0798. Phone 800-548-9548. Peter Brown. (O,T)

Orvis of Boston, 84 State Street, Boston, MA 02109. Phone 617-742-0288. Tom Keer. (O,C,T)

Partridge of Redditch (Sea Prince Hooks, SLF hanks and dubbing), Mount Pleasant, Redditch, Worcestershire, England B97 4JE. Phone 0527-541-380. Alan Bramley. (W/M)

Pennsylvania Outdoor Warehouse (eyes of all kinds), 1508 Memorial Avenue, Williamsport, PA 17701. Phone 800-441-7685 or 717-322-3589. (O, T)

Popovics, Bob, 125 9th Avenue, Seaside Park, NJ 08752. Phone 908-269-0777. (C)

Raymond C. Rumpf & Sons (Poly Flash Yarn, Bestco Eyes), P.O. Box 319, Sellersville, PA 18960. Phone 215-257-0141. (W/M)

Reed, Ellen, P.O. Box 1205, Islamorada, FL 33036. Phone 305-664-8050. (C)

Roman Moser (Plushille, Ghost Fiber), Kufferzeile 19 A-4810, Gmunden, Austria. Phone 07 61 25686. (O, T, W/M)

Saltwater Angler, The, 1218 Petronia Street, Key West, FL 33040. Phone 305-294-3248. Jeffrey Cardenas. (O, C, T)

Sanchez Custom Fly Tying, 5063 Fort Clark Drive, Austin, TX 78745. Phone 512-416-1384. Scott Sanchez. (C)

Spirit River (Dazl Eyes, Lite Brite, Polar Aire, Holographic Flash), 2405-68 N.E. Diamond Lake Boulevard, Roseburg, OR 97470. Phone 503-440-6916. Bill Black. (W/M)

Sponj-Lur (Sponj-Skin), 7551 Watson Industrial Park, St. Louis, MO 63126. Phone 314-968-2010. (W/M)

Stoddards, 50 Temple Place, Boston, MA 02111. Phone 617-426-4187. (O, C, T)

Stren (Lumiflex Skirts and Legs), 71 Southgate Boulevard, New Castle, DE 19720. Phone 302-993-8546. (T)

Tiemco Hooks (Umpqua Feather Merchants), Box 700, Glide, OR 97443. Phone 800-322-3218. Ken Menard. (W/M)

Umpqua Feather Merchants (Furry Foam, Salmo Web, Poly Flash, Bestco Eyes), P.O. Box 700, Glide, OR 97443. Phone 800-322-3218. Ken Menard. (W/M)

Universal (Glo-Brite Chenille), P.O. Box 626, 16 Union Avenue, Westfield, MA 01086. Phone 413-568-0964. (W)

Urban Angler, 118 E. 25th Street, 3rd Floor, New York, NY 10010. Phone 212-979-7600. (O, C, T)

Vetra, Phil (Dazzle Link), 4463 196A Street, Langley, B.C., Canada U3A-6A3. Phone 604-533-1410. (T)

Veverka, Bob, Cloverdale Drive, Underhill, VT 05489. Phone 802-899-2049. (C)

Wapsi Fly Co. (Sili Legs, Sili Tails), Route 5, Box 57 E, Mountain Home, AR 72653. Phone 501-425-9500. Karl Schmuecker. (W/M)

Wellesley Outdoors, 380 Washington Street, Route 16, Wellesley, MA 02181. Phone 508-653-9144. Bill Sullivan, Brad Wolfe, or Shane Bowles. (O, C, T)

World Class Outfitters, P.O. Box 1571, Islamorada, FL 33036. Phone 305-852-3177. Randy Towe. (O)

World Wide Sportsman, P.O. Box 787, Islamorada, FL 33036. Phone 800-327-2880. George Hommell. (O, T)

BIBLIOGRAPHY

◆ ◆ ◆

Angling and Fly Tying

Babson, Stanley M. *Bonefishing*. New York: Winchester Press, 1965.

Brooks, Joseph W. *Salt Water Game Fishing*. New York: Harper & Row, 1968.

Brown, Dick. *Fly Fishing for Bonefish*. New York: Lyons & Burford, 1993.

Camera, Phil. *Fly Tying with Synthetics: Patterns and Techniques*. Shrewsbury, England: Swan Press, 1992.

Harder, John R. *The Orvis Fly Pattern Index*. New York: Stephen Green Press, Pelham Books/Viking Penguin, 1990.

International Game Fish Association. *World Record Game Fishes*. Pompano Beach, Florida: IGFA, 1995.

Kaufmann, Randall. *Bonefishing With a Fly*. Portland, OR: Western Fisherman's Press, 1992.

Kreh, Bernard "Lefty." *Fly Fishing in Salt Water*. New York: Crown Publishers, 1974.

——— *Saltwater Fly Patterns*. New York: Lyons & Burford, 1995.

Leiser, Eric. *The Book of Fly Patterns*. New York: Alfred A. Knopf, 1987.

McClane, A.J. (Editor) *New Standard Fishing Encyclopedia*. New York: Henry Holt and Company, 1965.

Richards, Carl. *Prey*. New York: Lyons & Burford, 1995.

Roberts, George. *A Fly Fisher's Guide to Saltwater Naturals and Their Imitation*. Camden, Maine: Ragged Mountain Press, 1994.

Samson, Jack. *Saltwater Fly Fishing*. Harrisburg, PA: Stackpole, 1991.

Sosin, Mark, and Lefty Kreh. *Fishing the Flats*. New York: Lyons & Burford, 1983.

Stewart, Dick, and Farrow Allen. *Flies for Saltwater*. North Conway, N.H.: Mountain Pond Publishing, distributed by Lyons & Burford, 1992.

Talleur, Richard W. *Mastering the Art of Fly Tying*. Harrisburg, PA: Stackpole, 1979.

Waterman, Charles F. *Modern Fresh & Salt Water Fly Fishing*. New York: Winchester, 1972.

Wentink, Frank. *Saltwater Fly Tying*. New York: Lyons & Burford, 1991.

BONEFISH AND PREY

Bigelow, Henry B., and others. *Fishes of the Western North Atlantic.* New Haven: Yale University, 1963.

Bruger, Gerard E. "Age, Growth, Food Habits, and Reproduction of Bonefish, Albula vulpes, in South Florida Waters." *Florida Marine Research Publications* no. 3 (1974): 1–20.

Colton, Douglas E. "Patterns of Reproductive Maturation in the Bonefish (*Albula vulpes*) in Bahamian Waters." Photocopy of original from author. (n.d.), 1–9.

Colton, Douglas E., and William S. Alevizon. "Feeding Ecology of Bonefish in Bahamian Waters." *Transactions of the American Fisheries Society* 112 (1983): 178-184.

Colton, Douglas E., and William S. Alevizon. "Movement Patterns of Bonefish, *Albula vulpes*, in Bahamian Waters." *Fishery* Bulletin 81, no. 1 (1983): 148-154.

Crabtree, Roy E., Chris Harden, and Derke Snodgrass. "A preliminary report on age, growth, and reproduction of bonefish, *Albula vulpes*, from the waters of the Florida Keys." Paper submitted to the Florida Marine Fisheries commission. Photocopy from author, 1995, 1-26.

Erdman, Donald S. "Bonefish, *Albula vulpes* (Linnaeus), from Puerto Rico and the Virgin Islands: Habitat, Food, Spawning Season, and Leptocephali." Photocopy from author, 1975, 1-13.

———— "Notes on the Biology of the Bonefish and its Sports Fishery in Puerto Rico." Paper presented at the Fifth International Game Fish Conference, 1960, 1-11.

Fauchald, Kristian. *The Polychaete Worms: Definitions and Keys to the Orders, Families and Genera.* Los Angeles: Natural History Museum of Los Angeles County, 1977.

Feilding, Ann and Ed Robinson, *An Underwater Guide to Hawaii.* Honolulu: University of Hawaii Press, 1987.

Gosner, Kenneth L. *A Field Guide to the Atlantic Seashore.* The Peterson Field Guide Series. Boston: Houghton Mifflin Company, 1979.

Kaplan, Eugene H. *A Field Guide to Southeastern and Caribbean Seashores.* The Peterson Field Guide Series. Boston: Houghton Mifflin Company, 1988.

Manning, Raymond B. *Stomatopod Crustacea of the Western Atlantic.* Coral Gables: University of Miami Press, 1969.

McClane, A. J. "What the Bonefish Eats." *Fishing World,* March/April 1981, 60-71.

McClane, A.J., and Keith Gardner. *McClane's Game Fish of North America.* New York: Times Books, 1984.

McNulty, J. Kneeland and others. "Some Relationships Between the Infauna of the Level Bottom and the Sediment in South Florida." *Bulletin of Marine Science of the Gulf and Caribbean* 12, no. 3 (1962): 322-332.

Meinkoth, Norman A, *The Audubon Society Field Guide to North American Seashore Creatures.* New York: Alfred A. Knopf, 1981.

Miner, Roy Waldo. *Field Book of Seashore Life.* New York: G.P. Putnam's Sons, 1950.

Morris, Percy A. *A Field Guide to Shells of the Atlantic and Gulf Coasts and the West Indies.* The Peterson Field Guide Series. Boston: Houghton Mifflin Company, 1975.

Ricciuti, Edward R. *The Beachwalker's Guide: The Seashore from Maine to Florida.* Garden City, New York: Doubleday & Company, 1982.

Robins, C. Richard, and G. Carleton Ray. *A Field Guide to Atlantic Coast Fishes of North America.* The Peterson Field Guide Series. Boston: Houghton Mifflin Company, 1986.

Ruppert, Edward, and Richard Fox. *Seashore Animals of the Southeast.* Columbia, SC: University of South Carolina Press, 1988.

Ryan, Paddy. *The Snorkellor's Guide to the Coral Reef: From the Red Sea to the Pacific Ocean.* Honolulu: University of Hawaii Press, 1994.

Voss, Gilbert L. *Seashore Life of Florida and the Caribbean.* Miami: Banyan Books, 1976.

Warmke, Germaine L. *Caribbean Seashells: A Guide to the Mollusks of Puerto Rico and Other West Indian Islands, Bermuda and the Lower Florida Keys.* Narberth, PA: Livingston Publishing Company, 1961.

Warmke, Germaine L., and Donald S. Erdman. "Records of Marine Mollusks Eaten by Bonefish in Puerto Rican Waters." *The Nautilus* 76, no. 4 (1963): 115-120.

Williams, Austin B. *Shrimps, Lobsters, and Crabs of the Atlantic Coast of the Eastern United States, Maine to Florida.* Washington, D.C.: Smithsonian Institution Press, 1984.

Index